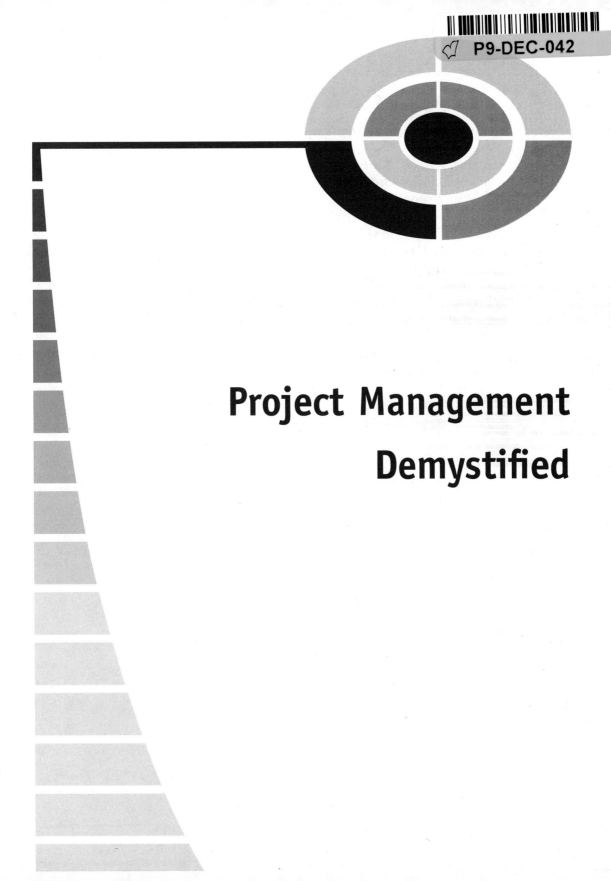

Project Management
Demystified

Demystified Series

Advanced Statistics Demystified
Algebra Demystified
Anatomy Demystified
Astronomy Demystified
Biology Demystified
Business Statistics Demystified
Calculus Demystified
Chemistry Demystified
College Algebra Demystified
Earth Science Demystified
Everyday Math Demystified
Geometry Demystified
Physics Demystified
Physiology Demystified
Pre-Algebra Demystified
Project Management Demystified
Statistics Demystified
Trigonometry Demystified

PROJECT MANAGEMENT DEMYSTIFIED

SID KEMP, PMP

McGRAW-HILL
New York   Chicago   San Francisco   Lisbon   London
Madrid   Mexico City   Milan   New Delhi   San Juan
Seoul   Singapore   Sydney   Toronto

The **McGraw·Hill** Companies

Cataloging-in-Publication Data is on file with the Library of Congress

To my mother, Edie Kemp, for sharing with me how to be practical and creative at the same time.

4 5 6 7 8 9 0 DOC/DOC 0 9 8 7

ISBN 0-07-144014-3

The sponsoring editor for this book was Judy Bass and the production supervisor was Pamela Pelton. The art director for the cover was Margaret Webster-Shapiro. It was set in Times Roman by Keyword Publishing Services Ltd.

Printed and bound by RR Donnelley.

McGraw-Hill books are available at special quantity discounts to use as premiums and sales promotions, or for use in corporate training programs. For more information, please write to the Director of Special Sales, McGraw-Hill Professional, Two Penn Plaza, New York, NY 10121-2298. Or contact your local bookstore.

CONTENTS

PREFACE

Welcome to an unusual way of looking at the world called *project management*. Project management is all about success. Successful projects deliver value on time and under budget. *Value* is anything that benefits the company—or the person—that receives it. The problem is that many projects do not succeed. Some fail altogether, costing time and money and delivering, well, absolutely nothing. Others come in very late or way over budget. Others solve the wrong problem, delivering a lot less value than expected.

Project management is the application of all the tools, techniques, and methods people have come up with to try to deliver success on unique, one-time efforts. These skills include managing time, money, and teams of people to deliver successful results, and a whole lot more.

There are a few reasons why project management (PM) is really interesting to me:

- I like to succeed.
- I like to do new and different things, that is, projects, rather than routine work.
- I do not like to reinvent the wheel. I like *best practices*. I have worked for ten years to find the best ways anyone has ever found for doing projects, and now I am sharing them with you. Some of these techniques are over 100 years old, some are less than five. But they are all tried and true. They work. We save time by learning from the best.
- When we learn PM we learn processes that work. This focus on process is why I say that PM is an unusual way of looking at the world. When we are in school we learn lots of things, but do we ever have a course that focuses on how to learn? Did you ever see a syllabus with topics like how to understand, how to think, how to write a paper? In the same way, in the world of business we are asked to succeed in many things. But how often does our boss sit down with us and say, "Here's how to succeed. Here's how to work together, do good work, and deliver what the company needs"?

Whether you are in a project management class in school or you are picking this book up to learn on your own, you are in for an exciting time, and an enriching one. If you are new to project management, then *Project Management Demystified* will take you from the very beginning through your first successful project.

If you are already an experienced project manager, then what has your experience been? If you have really consistent success, then you are ready to grow more, and take on bigger projects. If you have had hassles and challenges, if delivering high-quality results on time and under budget has not always been easy, if your customers are not happy with you, then *Project Management Demystified* can help. I aimed to make it the most practical book I could, with real-world tools and tips. Take a look at topics that might be new to you, or project knowledge areas that have been difficult to implement, and I am sure you will find some new tools, tips, and clarifications that will make it easier for you to succeed.

The *Project Management Institute (PMI)* offers a valuable professional qualification: certification as a *Project Management Professional (PMP)*. You can learn more about the PMI on the internet at *www.PMI.org*. If you join the PMI, you can download *A Guide to the Project Management Body of Knowledge*, usually called the PMBOK® 2000 guide. It contains much useful information. The PMI web site explains all the criteria for receiving and maintaining certification, including hours of training and hours of experience required. Local PMI chapters offer training classes.

How to Get the Most Out of This Book

I hope you will find this book to be an opportunity to learn, to think, to create your own solutions, to improve the way you work. Whether you are a novice project manager or a more experienced one, *Project Management Demystified* offers excellent tools to help you succeed.

FOR THE NOVICE READER

If you are taking an introductory course in project management, or you have managed three or fewer projects, I suggest you read this book in order through Parts One and Two, and learn the tools, Part Three, as you need them. Particularly, if you are doing a project—for class, or at work, or in your own time—use the tools and templates in this book to plan the project well and keep it on track.

FOR THE MORE EXPERIENCED PROJECT MANAGER

If you have managed a number of projects, read several books on PM, and perhaps already have your PMP certification, there is still a lot of value here for you in *Project Management Demystified*. I suggest that you review Parts One and Two. Pay particular attention to Chapters 2 and 3, and also the detailed tools in every chapter.

Then evaluate your own tools, and the areas where you find managing a project challenging. Pick the tools you need most from Part Three. If you have trouble keeping your boss posted on project status, then check out the Green, Yellow, Red status report technique. If you have trouble creating effective work plans and time estimates, then take a look at work breakdown structuring and time estimation. Pick one, two, or three next steps, and use the new tools on your next project.

FOR THOSE LEADING PROJECT TEAMS OR TEACHING PROJECT MANAGEMENT

If you want to put together a strong team for a high-profile project, you might do well to buy a copy of this book for each member of your team. No, that is not just a plug to sell more copies. Project management should not be a mystery to project team members—demystify it for them. Otherwise, they will think that they do all the work, and the manager just sits around pushing papers. Team members who understand project management can help a project succeed in these ways:

- *By being self-managed.* A team member who plans work and delivers high-quality results on time keeps the project moving. If every team member does that, the project succeeds.
- *By delivering accurate status reports.* A team member who evaluates how the work is going and states clearly what is done and what is not done every week without being asked reduces project management costs. If every team member does this, the weekly meetings can look ahead to improving quality or making the next steps easier.
- *By contributing to brainstorming sessions.* When all team members understand how to contribute to a brainstorming session, this builds a highly creative team that adds value to the project and creates an exciting work environment. People on projects like this often see them as peak experiences in their professional lives.

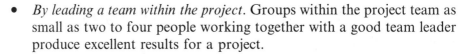

- *By leading a team within the project.* Groups within the project team as small as two to four people working together with a good team leader produce excellent results for a project.

If you teach project management in a classroom setting, then *Project Management Demystified* is likely to be an excellent primary or secondary text for a one-semester class. It can serve as the primary text if the class is focused on learning PM basics and completing projects successfully. For more advanced classes *Project Management Demystified* would be a practical supplement to a more theoretical primary text.

The Parts of *Project Management Demystified*

Project Management Demystified is divided into three parts for easy learning. Part One introduces the field of project management in four chapters. It is an in-depth introduction for the novice reader. The value of Part One for the experienced reader lies mostly in Chapters 2 and 3. In Chapter 2 the reader will find fundamental ideas that might be new. Application of these ideas to existing tools often has the effect of making them work. Chapter 3 evaluates why projects fail, and shows the six most important things a project manager should be able to do well to ensure success.

Chapter 4 introduces the optimal project and product life cycle, the System Development Life Cycle, laying out the stages or phases of a project. Part Two provides an in-depth, detailed chapter on the work and deliverable results of each stage. Most project management systems settle for four simple stages. In contrast, *Project Management Demystified* offers six stages. Adding a concept stage at the beginning of a project helps protect companies from losing lots of money by turning bad ideas into expensive project failures. Adding the transition to production stage allows the project team to prepare for and concentrate on the crucial moment of delivering the project to the customer. A lot of people call this the storm period on a project, and creating a storm in a customer's department does not make a project manager particularly popular. But if the customers know there will be challenges, and we lead them through those challenges to a better way of working, then we are very much appreciated. This chapter is key in helping project managers exceed customer expectations and deliver recognized success.

Part Three provides practical tools that take you step-by-step through the most essential project management processes, including estimation, work breakdown structuring, and managing a team to success.

Sidebars for Easy Learning

In *Project Management Demystified* we want to make it easy for you to learn and to find what you need to know. So we have created several different types of sidebars that will introduce key ideas. Here they are:

- *Terms*. Project management is full of jargon. The "Terms" sidebars give the meaning of a word the first time it is used. The same term can be found in the glossary at the end of the book.
- *Key Point*. These sidebars tell you the most important thing you need to know from a chapter or a section.
- *Quick Tips*. These give you the most basic way to complete a task. They are especially useful to the novice project manager and to the project manager who needs a quick reminder of the most efficient solution.
- *What This Means for You*. *Project Management Demystified* is full of stories of what can go wrong—or right. After many of the stories, in a "What this means for you" tip, we show you how to avoid the failure or succeed in the same way on your next project.
- *Something Extra*. Each of these sidebars gives the more experienced project manager a next step, a little tip that will make success that much easier.
- *Caution*. Once in a while, there are times not to use a certain tool or technique. These occasional cautions will keep you out of hot water.

Acknowledgments

My first thanks go to Scott Hoffheiser, my administrative assistant, who read and improved the whole manuscript and prepared the glossary. Malcolm Ryder read a previous version of the manuscript, and his insights are an invaluable part of this book. Many others provided all kinds of support, both professional and personal. On the professional side, Lee Krevat, of Sempra Energy, provided me the opportunity to teach this material to hundreds of project managers, and many other clients have used these materials, succeeded, and suggested improvements. On the personal side, I hope that I give my wife as much support in writing her book as she gave me on mine. Also, my brother, Steven M. Kemp, Ph.D., and my father, Bernie Kemp, were very supportive through the writing process.

ABOUT THE AUTHOR

Sid Kemp, PMP, is a certified Project Management Professional and a leading expert in project management for information technology, with over 15 years of experience. He assists Fortune 500 companies and major governmental agencies in the deployment of new technology and in developing and deploying custom project management methodologies. Sid has trained thousands of first-time managers and team leaders in PM—in public, corporate, and government seminars. He has over 10 years of experience as a trainer and author of training programs and manuals. Sid is the coauthor of *Budgeting for Managers* (McGraw-Hill Briefcase Book Series, 2003); *CDMA Capacity and Quality Optimization* (McGraw-Hill); and a number of instructional manuals and course texts.

Hello, Project Management

The four chapters in *Part One* introduce the big picture project management and give you everything you need to succeed on simple projects. In *Chapter 1: What is Project Management?* we define projects, management, and project management, and discuss why it is valuable to think of project management as an independent discipline like accounting or marketing, and why it pays to learn to manage projects well. In *Chapter 2,* you will learn *Tools to Use Over and Over,* fundamental concepts about the process of a project and ways to make projects succeed.

Success is also the focus of *Chapter 3: Six Keys to Project Success,* where we look at why most projects fail, run late, or blow their budgets, and what you can do to ensure that your project makes the top of the class by delivering real value on time and under budget.

Lastly, in *Chapter 4: The Project and Product Life Cycles,* we introduce the system development life cycle. We explain the value of breaking up a project into a series of major phases, or stages, and map out the stages a project goes through from beginning to end. We discuss the purpose of each stage, and the work requirements that ensure successful completion of each one. Each stage is like a step in a flight of stairs. You can't jump 12 feet. But climbing one step at a time, you can prepare yourself to reach the next step easily. Just so, each phase is designed to complete the planning and the work that will make the next stage easy.

By the end of *Part One,* you will be ready to plan and execute a small project, improve the project you are working on, and take the next step towards becoming a top-notch project manager. What is that next step? Reading *Part Two,* of course!

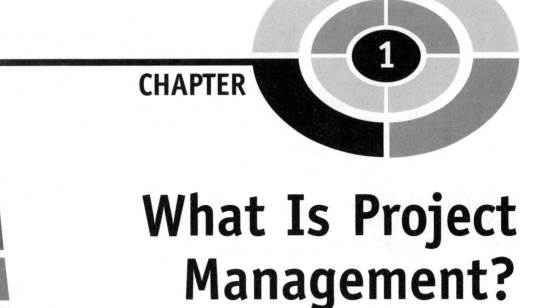

CHAPTER 1

What Is Project Management?

Leading to Success

Many people think that project management is a matter of creating schedules and budgets. Actually, that is the smallest part of the job. The biggest job is to bring people together to solve problems and take advantage of new opportunities. Yes, we manage information about value, quality, time, and cost. But we do that with a purpose. We do that so that we—and everyone on the project team, and also the customer—can make good decisions.

Then we write down those decisions, build an action plan, and help everyone follow the plan to success. And we change the plan when we need to.

Project management is not pushing papers. It is an exciting blend of working with people, clarifying ideas, and taking responsibility for actual results. And those results improve people's lives and build better companies.

Are you good at getting things done? Are you good at leading a team of people to get big things done well, on time, and under budget? On a scale of 1 to 5 how would you rate yourself at that? Whatever your rating, that is how good a project manager you are today. And, by the time you finish this book, you will be better. This chapter will get you off the ground by defining projects and management, showing why good project management is crucial to success, and giving you the big picture—the overview—of project management.

In This Chapter

Let us take a look at what is ahead:

- *Projects in everyday life* defines what a project is. Once you know, you will see projects everywhere: at work, at home, and at school.
- *Why management matters.* This section defines management and shows how good management practices ensure success, giving valuable results for time and money invested in a project.
- *Who's who on a project.* On a project there are many *roles*, many different jobs to do.
- *Choosing your project for learning.* Reading about project management is not the same as doing it. In this chapter you will pick a project to plan and implement as you read the book, so that you get hands-on experience.
- *Questions for learning.* Every chapter will end with questions for learning. This is partly a review, and partly a challenge to get you thinking like a real-world project manager.

Projects in Everyday Life

This may sound strange, but projects are all around us. We are doing projects all the time. As you will see, even reading this book might be a project. The PMI defines a *project* as a temporary endeavor undertaken to achieve a unique product, service, or result. A project is temporary because it has a definite start date, or project launch date, and a definite date of completion. The planned date of completion is when we think we will finish and deliver the results. The actual date of the end of the project is when we do deliver—or when we give up and call it quits. The other key element of a project is that it is unique. The result is not the same as anything else we will ever create. The work we do is not exactly the same as the work we do on other projects. Uniqueness is what distinguishes projects from routine, production work.

As Fig. 1-1 illustrates, work ranges from routine production activities at one extreme to varied, unique products at the other extreme. "Is this a project?" is not a yes/no question. Rather, the more unique the work is, the more project management thinking and tools are useful to help get the job done right.

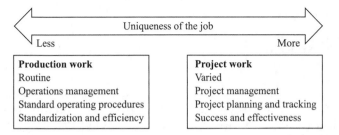

Fig. 1-1.   The uniqueness of the job distinguishes projects from production work.

Routine, repetitive work where deadlines are not crucial is production work, or operations. If you want to manage operations well, get steady people who like having a routine and develop written standard operating procedures. In production work, the goal is to produce the same results day after day. Management offers value by ensuring consistent results and increasing efficiency, that is, getting more work done at lower cost. Bookkeeping is a good example of operations work. If the work is cyclical, but each cycle has crucial deadlines and has some different work, then project tools become more useful. For example, I recommend that publishers and editors use project planning tools for magazine production, at least for the first several issues. Each issue of the magazine has unique content and the deadlines are crucial. As a result, project management tools are quite useful.

TERM

Production Regular, routine work that leads to the creation of products, services, or results.
Operations Another term for production work.
Effective The delivery of useful results. The more effective a process is, the more useful the results are.

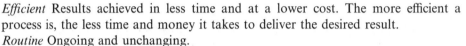
Efficient Results achieved in less time and at a lower cost. The more efficient a process is, the less time and money it takes to deliver the desired result.
Routine Ongoing and unchanging.
Cyclical Repeating in a similar pattern over time.
Unique Occurring just once, not routine or repeating.

Some jobs, such as building a custom house, are done just once. Project management is really useful here; in fact, project management methods have been used in the construction industry since the Empire State Building was built in less than a year, being finished in 1931.

WOWS AND WHOOPSES

Hot Construction
When girders arrived in New York City to be welded together to build the frame of the Empire State Building they were still warm from the steel forges in Pittsburgh where they had been forged, over 300 miles away. Why? Because fast production reduces cost. How? By using milestone charts, a technique you will learn more about in Chapters 4 and 7.

What projects demand the greatest project management skill and best tools? Those that use fast-changing technology like aerospace engineering and computer systems. In these fields, project managers often have to design their own tools, or change to new tools or newer computers in the middle of a project. Working in a constantly changing field demands the best project management methods, and many of these methods were developed by NASA during the Gemini and Apollo projects that got us into space and onto the moon. People who like this kind of work like change and new challenges, rather than steady routines.

Coming back to Earth, we find projects around us all the time. At home, preparing for a special event such as a birthday party can be a project. In fact, a number of people have come up to me in my project management classes and said, "I'm getting married this year, and now I know how to get everything ready for the wedding." Every wedding is unique, and so every wedding is a project. Staying married, on the other hand, is production work.

In school, preparing for a big exam or presentation is a project. So are bigger academic jobs, such as preparing for comprehensive exams or writing a PhD dissertation. At work, we can use project management for anything on a deadline, and for anything we have not done before.

Find the Projects in Your Life
Take a moment and write down all the projects in your life right now: at home, at school, in leisure or service activities, and at work. Just make a list of everything unique, everything with a deadline. We will come back to your list at the end of this chapter when we introduce the section "Choosing Your Project for Learning."

Why Management Matters

Many projects fail. In information technology—computer installation and software development—about half the projects fail, and over 80% run late or over budget. The failure of a large project can sink a small company. And the weight of many failed projects can drag down profits to the point where a big company is susceptible to acquisition by a competitor, losing its independence. If we add the human cost—the frustration and burnout—we see the situation is far worse. It is hard to stay with a company when a project you are on fails. And high staff turnover rates create out-of-control cost spirals that are one of the biggest problems in American business today. On the other hand, people want to stay with a company that is making progress, where they are on a creative team, working with a good manager, and succeeding. These experiences bring personal satisfaction and also a great deal of loyalty. People who are on successful project teams often say that they would not change jobs, even for considerably more money.

And we can make projects succeed. Outside NASA, it is not rocket science. Almost all projects fail because companies are not using even the most basic tools of project management well. And the basic tools—and more, the most valuable tools—are right here in this book.

Where Do Mistakes Come From?
W. Edwards Deming, the inventor of Total Quality Management, developed a process called *root cause analysis*. It is a way of finding out why things go wrong. It gets to the bottom—the root cause—of errors. Deming measured work in all kinds of environments, and found out that 94% of the time errors are due to people not following the right procedure for the job. It is not that people make mistakes, or make bad decisions. No, mistakes happen almost entirely because companies do not

organize and plan work well. As managers, we need to put the right processes in place and show people how to do them. That would eliminate 94% of all the mistakes we make. And that is the difference between failure and success.

WHAT IS MANAGEMENT?

QUICK TIP

Define, Measure, and Manage
If you want to manage something, you have to be able to measure it. And to measure it, you have to define it clearly, and define or choose your unit of measure. Sometimes, as with money and time, the unit of measure is already defined for us. We use dollars and cents to measure money, hours and days to measure time. But what is the unit of measure for quality? There is not any one unit, so we have to define it ourselves for each project.

We all talk about management, but we rarely stop and ask what management is. Management is the work we do to make sure the job—in our case, the project—gets done right. It includes these key steps:

- *Defining*. We define the work to be done. We define the requirements, what is needed; the specifications, what we are making; and the methods and units of measurement.
- *Planning*. We create a written plan describing what we will do.
- *Estimating*. We create a prediction of what it will take to do the job.
- *Communicating*. We work with others to create the plan, to make sure everyone understands and agrees, to improve the plan and the way we work, and to solve problems as they come up.
- *Tracking*. We compare what is actually happening to what we wrote in the plan.
- *Measuring*. We measure how well we are doing. We measure both the process of how the work is going and also the end product.
- *Reporting*. We report our *status*, where we are; our *progress*, how far we have come; and our *forecast*, when we think we will meet our goal.
- *Deciding*. We decide what to do, write down any changes in the plan, and make sure that people carry through with the work to be done.
- *Supporting*. We provide help and support, clearing the roadblocks so people can do their jobs well.

- *Coordinating*. We work out the details of bringing people and things together to make things work.

SOMETHING EXTRA

Processes and Results
When we calculate how much money we are spending, and compare it to the budget, or how much time we are spending, and compare it to the schedule, we are measuring aspects of the process of our work. In contrast, if we take the work results—say, a piece of software code, or a custom-built door for a house—and see if it works and satisfies the customer, we are measuring the results of our work. But there is a connection: Good work leads to good results; shoddy work leaves us with, well...

Managing also means taking responsibility. When we manage a project, we take responsibility for success. We may not always succeed, but we will do our best, work with others as best we can, and solve problems rather than complain about them.

CHANGING FOR SUCCESS

Now, ask yourself what you could do to make it right. If you had the time and money, what work would lead to a good result: a fixed computer, a better working relationship, better marketing materials? Answer that question, and you have done it! Done what? You have just had a bright idea that might be a good project.

Of course, it might be a bad idea when you look at it more closely. And even if it is a good idea, you will need to plan it well and manage it well for it to be a good project. By the end of Chapter 4 you will know how to do just that.

WHAT THIS MEANS FOR YOU

What Do You Manage on a Project?
The three most important things to manage on a project are quality, time, and cost. We seek to maximize the quality of the results while keeping costs down and delivering as soon as possible. But managing these three just scratches the surface. The Project Management Institute defines nine different areas we can manage to ensure project success, and each of them is very broad. We will introduce more as we go along.

We will come back to planning a project soon. First, let us take a look at what a project manager does, and what other people on a project do.

Who's Who on a Project

In this section we talk about the *roles* of the project manager and other people on a project. Please note that there is a difference between roles and people. One person can have several roles. For example, writing this book is a project, and I am the project manager. I am also the author—the person doing the writing. So I have two roles. Sometimes, a single role can be divided between two people. This only works if the people work together well. But there is an excellent "buddy" system of computer programming where two people write code together. While one is writing, the other is looking for errors or thinking of better ways to write the routine. They can also think through problems together. The buddy method, where two people share one role, reduces errors so much that it actually saves time compared to having just one programmer.

TERM

Role A defined set of responsibilities in relation to a project, work environment, or social situation.

So, knowing that one person may have several roles, or one role may be shared by several people, let us take a look at the roles on a project, starting with the project manager.

THE PROJECT MANAGER

The project manager has an exciting job. However, there is an ancient Chinese curse: "May you live in exciting times." In a well-run organization, project management is not cursed. The excitement comes from the challenge of doing new and unique work. In a poorly run organization, project managers may begin to feel cursed, especially on bad days. The key difference is that in a well-run organization, any worker, manager, or executive has a balance of responsibility and empowerment.

On one side of the equation, we have the results for which we are responsible: Defining the goal and delivering success. With that comes accountability for those results. In a well-run organization, we are empowered to achieve those objectives. We have the authority to make decisions. We have the financial resources and the team, or the ability to build the team, to get the job done. Our team has, or can acquire, the knowledge and skills needed to do good work. And we are allotted enough time to complete the job. Most importantly, though, we and our team treat one another with respect, and are respected within the organization.

Of course, that balance is an ideal, and almost all organizations fall short of it in one way or another. One of the biggest challenges of project management is to take responsibility and work to success under less than ideal conditions. As we do, we model good teamwork. If we do it skillfully, we lead our team to success.

The role of the project manager

If we look at it in the widest possible way, a project manager is responsible for:

- Defining the product or service being created, both its features and its specification, and assuring its value to the company.
- Defining the project plan, that is, how the project will be completed.
- Creating the project team, supporting and empowering team members, and leading the team to success.
- Keeping track of everything, catching problems early, and providing course correction when needed to keep on track.
- Managing the delivery process and ensuring customer satisfaction.

Another way of saying this is to say that the project manager defines the goal, defines the life cycle, which we discuss in Chapter 4, and ensures that all nine areas of project management are applied in each phase of the project.

However, that is an awfully big job. What matters most? Discussing that question with several expert project managers, we developed a list of six keys to success. As a project manager, if you take care of the *Six Keys to Success* we discuss in Chapter 3, then each project has a very high chance of success.

A good project manager commits to project success and does what it takes to get the job done. But a good project manager does not do this alone. We rely on our teams. For example, we rely on team members with technical expertise greater than our own. Our job is to bring these people and their

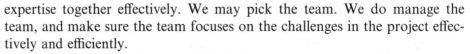

expertise together effectively. We may pick the team. We do manage the team, and make sure the team focuses on the challenges in the project effectively and efficiently.

Some of us may be junior in technical expertise, but, as project managers, we contribute essential work and skills to the project. Studies have shown that about half of the work on a project is not included in the specific tasks necessary to complete the project. That extra work has many elements, and most of them are key tasks of the project manager. Much of that work is involved with communications, with defining issues and resolving problems, and with keeping track of the work to ensure success. These are the day-to-day tasks a project manager must do to enable the project team to succeed.

Growing as a project manager

Many people choose technical careers, and then are promoted to management. Others may take a management track in school, then try to figure out how to apply the theory when they reach the world of work. People with a technical background (wizards and gurus though they may be) face particular issues in becoming managers, especially project managers. Young people, however well educated, face similar challenges.

- *From thing or data-oriented to people-oriented.* All jobs require some degree of work with things, data, and people. Most people make their first career choice because it is comfortable or exciting, but not too challenging to our personalities. If we like things, we head for the hardware, fixing computers or working with other kinds of equipment. If we like ideas, we turn to programming software or systems, or business management. If we like people, we might go into human resources, sales, or psychology for our first job. However, to be a successful project manager, we need to learn to work effectively with people even if that is not our natural propensity. The key difference is that things and data do what you tell them. People usually do not. We need to relax and enjoy unpredictability and diversity. Once we appreciate that people with different skills and different ways of thinking all cooperate on a project, and that the whole becomes more than the sum of its parts, people management becomes enjoyable instead of scary. Once we get over our allergy to listening, understanding, and sharing, working with people can actually be lots of fun.
- *From worker-bee to manager.* Many of us are used to getting things done by sitting down and doing them. We like to be dependable.

Management means less doing and more delegating. It means making a shift from dependable to reliable. A reliable person ensures that things do get done. We are independent, and we manage others. And our teams take on projects and deliver results.

- *From manager to leader.* A manager gets a team to get things done. Project management often requires an even higher level of work, called leadership. Leaders define what needs to be done (or create an environment where a group can come together and define it). They also provide initial inspiration and develop commitment among the stakeholders for a new idea. Project management, especially in the planning phases, in resolving team problems, and in turnarounds for projects in crisis, require leadership as well as management skills.

All of us grow in all three of these ways, and there is no limit to that growth, professionally and personally. Generally, though, we move through stages. First, it is most important to learn to work well with people, then to manage people in getting a job done, and then to defining the work to be done.

TERM

Lead To set overall direction and define goals.
Manage To take responsibility for reaching goals effectively and efficiently, and coordinate the team and resources to meet that goal successfully.
Independent Able to work alone and accomplish results without direct supervision.
Reliable Able to work consistently well with supervision.

The art of management is often called a soft skill because, unlike engineering, management is not supported by precise science and exact measurement. However, that does not mean that we are playing tennis with the net down. It would be more accurate to say that in hard-skill fields, such as engineering, the difficult work of defining goals, specifying targets, and establishing the units of measurement has already been done. In managing projects and people, more of this is left up to us.

The soft skills of management are perhaps more challenging than the hard skills of engineering exactly because we must define the standards, set the goals, and find ways to measure results. We cannot work in watts and millimeters. We must find ways of enabling people to succeed. Team management means bringing people together to accomplish more than each person could do alone. And project management means leading a team to deliver defined results on schedule, benefiting the organization for which we work.

However, we are not alone in doing this. Organizations such as the PMI, the Software Engineering Institute (SEI), which developed the Capability Maturity Model (CMM), and the ISO (the International Standards Organization, which offers its ISO-9000 and ISO-10000 series of quality engineering standards) have spent countless hours over the last few decades defining the work to be done and excellent methods for managing teams and projects.

OTHER ROLES ON A PROJECT

In a company, a project team can be organized in many different ways. Overall, there are three basic models at which we can look:

- *A project within a department.* When all the workers on a project are in the same department, they report to the same executive, and possibly work on many projects together. A good example would be an advertising campaign. Within the department, people with diverse skills—copy writers, graphic artists, media buyers, and others—work together to design and deliver the campaign.
- *A project in one department, with another department as customer.* Here, the work of the project is done by one group, say the computer systems development group, as a team with a project manager. But the results go to another group, say the accounting department, in the form of a new computer program that they will use. One department has the project team, the other department has the customers.
- *A project that pulls together many people from different areas.* Sometimes, a project is developed under leadership independent of any one department and brings together people and skills from all across the company. For example, when a car company designs a new model of car, the design team includes experts in customer design for the car, engineering design for car performance and safety, and assembly line design for efficient production. That is a cross-functional team. Similarly, if a book distribution company is opening a new warehouse, they might draw people from existing departments in warehouses all over the country and bring them in to the new location to set up the business, train people, and get things running.

Why does all this matter? In running a project, we need enough authority, empowerment, and resources to get the job done. We also need good communication within the team, and with our customers. Sometimes, creating that balance of empowerment and responsibility requires cutting across departmental lines. In that case, we need to make sure that everyone is free to work on the project and be rewarded for that work, even if they work for another department. And we need to make sure that we have executive commitment to the project from both the top leadership above the team, and also from the customer department.

The situation is even more complicated when more than one company is involved. When I manage a project for a client, the team may be entirely within my consulting company, or all team members (except me) may work for the customer. More often, my company's team works with some people employed by the client, and we pull together to create a team to meet the client's needs. And sometimes people from several different companies bring expertise to one project. This kind of variety of skills and business cultures keeps project management fascinating.

No matter where all the people come from, we can define several roles that exist on every project. The role is defined as a set of responsibilities. If the person—or people—in each role do their defined responsibilities, there will be no gaps. The project will be defined clearly. All the work will be done. And the project will succeed.

- *The project manager* takes responsibility for defining the purposes and goals of the project, building the team, defining the work to be done, tracking quality, time, cost, and other project elements, delivering success, and ensuring customer satisfaction. The project manager leads the team and tracks the work on a daily and weekly basis, making decisions to correct the course as needed.
- *The project sponsor* is the senior executive responsible for the project. The sponsor has authority over both the project team and the customer, and makes sure that all the resources necessary to succeed are available to the team. The sponsor kicks off the project at the initial meeting, promotes the project at the highest level of the organization, receives regular status reports, and intervenes when necessary to remove roadblocks for the project team or resolve conflicts between the project manager and the project sponsor.
- *The project lead* is the senior person in the customer department. The lead is responsible for defining all of the requirements or making sure that members of the customer team work with the project team to define them. The lead is also responsible for having the customer department learn and test the new service, product, or system that comes out of the project. The lead also helps define the value of the project's results; that is, the way the project will benefit the company,

and the dollar value of additional net revenue or cost savings expected and actually received from project results.

- *The project team*, led by the project manager, does the daily work of creating the detailed work plan, following the plan, and reaching the goal of the project. Team members will have different expertise and participate part-time or full-time in different parts of the project. Whenever possible, it is best if each team member plans and estimates the time for his or her own work, with help from the project manager as needed.

- *The customer* is not just one person. The customer is everyone in the central department receiving and using the results of the project. That can include data entry clerks, supervisors, managers, and executives. Each person needs to be able to use well the new or changed service or product coming from the project and see its value. And the executive needs to be able to define the value the project results have for the department. The customer, therefore, is central to defining the requirements at the beginning of the project, testing the project results, learning to use them, and benchmarking the benefits of the new system. In addition, because the customer usually receives the benefits of the project, the project cost is usually billed to the customer department.

- *Stakeholders*. A stakeholder is anyone who is affected by the project process or project results. In addition to the customers and the project team, anyone else who provides information to the project or receives some result from the project results is a stakeholder. Identifying all stakeholders early in the project process is an essential job for the project manager. The project manager then prepares a communications plan that defines the roles and responsibilities of the peripheral stakeholders, that is, the stakeholders other than the customer, the project team, and the sponsor.

- *Vendors and consultants* can contribute to the project in ways that add value, but are more limited than the work of the project team. They may deliver raw materials or components to meet project needs. Or they may provide expertise on a limited basis. When a consultant is involved in the project in depth for a length of time, we consider the consultant to be part of the team. When the vendor or consultant relationship is more distant or shorter term, it is managed through specifications, invoices, and contracts, as needed. The project manager takes responsibility for these documents and for ensuring that materials and services are delivered on time and to specification. In choosing vendors and consultants, the project manager should consult with their prior customers.

- *Other resources*, including the accounting department, internal and external audit, training services for the team or the customers, and many others may be of value. The project manager evaluates project needs to identify who can help and plans and manages communications with these people.

As the project moves forward, various project participants are doing more or less on the project. When a team in one department is building a product for a customer department, the customer is likely to be more involved in the beginning and the end, and less in the middle. When a major project is happening, the team may be very isolated from the rest of the company for months and years. In other cases, the team works alongside colleagues in the same department each day.

In any case, the project manager is on the job with the team every day. As project managers, we lead the team and we coordinate with all the other project stakeholders and participants. Our job is to make sure that everything done by all the participants comes together in the right way at the right time—or close enough—to ensure project success.

Choosing Your Project for Learning

There is an ancient Zen saying, "Talking about meditation is like scratching an itch on your foot—through your boot." The same could be said about learning project management. Reading about project management—or even taking a project management class—is not enough to make you a good project manager. You need experience. You need to manage a project. You will pick your project for learning right now.

Earlier in this chapter, I asked you to write down a list of projects in your life, at home, at work, and at school. Pull out that list now. One might just jump out at you. Also, take a look at the idea you came up with when I asked how you would solve an ongoing problem at work, for yourself or for a friend. That may be your project right there.

So, in this section, I will help you pick a project for learning. You can pick something you are already doing, or you can take on something new, or something you have been wanting to do for a long time. You can choose something in your personal life, at work, at school, or in a volunteer situation. But, as you choose, we want to be sure you pick something that will really help you learn to be a good project manager. So please carefully consider the following:

- *Keep it small.* Pick a project you can do yourself, or one you can do with just a little help. And make sure it is not going to take up all your time.
- *Pick something you know how to do.* If you have never picked up a hammer, do not plan to refurbish your kitchen for this project. You will spend your time learning how to do the work, and you will not be able to focus on the job as a project to be managed.
- *Give yourself time.* Do not pick something on a rush deadline. You will want time to plan, to track, to write everything down. You will probably do more planning than you really need to succeed on the project. Why? Because one of our goals is for you to learn to use the project planning tools. You will be planning just to learn. The success of the project will be a side effect.
- *Do not pile on the pressure.* We cannot learn when we are tense. So pick something that is not do-or-die.

QUICK TIP

If You Are Really Busy...
Earlier, I said that reading a book could be a project. Well, it is, if you set a deadline and set specific learning goals. If you have no extra time beyond what it takes to read this book, then reading this book is your project. When you finish Chapter 3 make a list of specific things you want to learn from reading the book. Make sure you pick tools and methods, not just ideas. In your project plan, write down what you will do differently after reading the book. Then your project is to read the book, learn the tools, and start using them.

Here are some good ideas for projects for learning that some of my students have used.

- Passing the Project Management Professional exam and becoming a certified PMP.
- Building a small web site for a non-profit organization.
- Cleaning out a closet, including putting in new hanging rods and shelves.

In Part Two we will come back to your project for learning in each chapter. We will also have a case study, a project I did last year, building a home theater system, to highlight key points of each project stage. So, what will your project for learning be?

Questions for Learning

These questions will do more than test your basic knowledge of project management. They will help you assess yourself as a project manager. Is project management right for you?

- Do you prefer routine predictable work? Or do you like situations where the work and the people are new?
- When you are asked to do something, but not given enough time or the right tools for the job, how do you feel? How do you address the imbalance between empowerment and responsibility?
- In your own words, explain the value of having a written plan for work to be done. Also mention any disadvantages that you see.
- Assess yourself. How good are you at creating and using to-do lists and checklists?
- Think of a project of which you were a part. Look at each person involved. Who was the project manager? The sponsor? The lead? The customer? Who was in other roles?
- On that project, were the roles defined and coordinated clearly? If yes, what happened? If not, then what happened?
- Review your project for learning. Is it the best project you can use to learn to be a good project manager? Do you want to pick another project? Do you want to make any changes to the project you are planning to use?

Tools to Use Over and Over

Over the last ten years I have examined business practices, trying to find the most effective tools for success. Believe me, there are a lot of different methods out there. But it seems that business is like chemistry. In chemistry, the millions of molecules that make up all the matter we know are built from about a hundred basic building blocks called atoms. More and more, I see that just about a dozen basic ideas, applied over and over at the right time and place, can build all the methods and techniques of project management.

Many of these basic elements are more of an attitude than a technique. Attitudes of understanding problems before we try to fix them, of following through, of being practical, of getting work done and delivering it, of working well together, and of doing good work are at the heart of project management.

If some of these ideas seem a bit vague now, do not worry. You will learn to apply them in future chapters. After you do, come back and re-read this chapter to review these basic elements. It is the same as in chemistry. At first, it is hard to believe that one atom, oxygen, can be part of air, and also of water, and also of rust. But when you understand how atoms make molecules, you see oxygen in all these places, and get to understand it better. Just so, after seeing how these basic building blocks are used throughout projects, you will understand these basic approaches for yourself, and invent new, effective ways of using them.

In This Chapter

I have organized these practical approaches into four categories: planning and communicating, organizing work over time, getting work done, and solving problems as a team.

- Planning and communicating
  - The 1:10:100 rule—the importance of planning
  - Planning in writing
  - Putting the job in front of your team
- Organizing work over time
  - Iteration: Repeating yourself over and over
  - Tasks and deliverables
- Being clear and coming to agreement
  - Inclusions and exclusions
  - Bending without breaking
- Getting work done
  - Prepare, do, follow through
  - Picture, plan, create, improve, test, fix, and deliver
- Solving problems as a team
  - The no-blame environment
  - Gap analysis
  - Gap reconciliation
- Questions for learning

Planning and Communicating

As people, we like to think that we understand one another, and that we remember things well. But all kinds of practical experience—backed by all kinds of psychological studies—show that two people coming out of a meeting where everyone thought they had agreed on everything are likely to have very different pictures of what was agreed on. This wastes a lot of time and money.

Just last week I was managing a small project where we were delivering eight specific improvements to a software program. Seven of them were specified clearly, and that work took about twelve hours. We did not have exact information about the other item, although it was on the list. That one item alone added four hours of work to the project. That is, it increased time and cost by 25%. We chose not to bill the client for the extra time, but the mistake left everyone feeling a fair bit less happy with the results of the project.

This small example shows the importance of planning in writing and communicating those plans clearly. But why does such a small mistake take so much time to fix? It is the result of the nature of project work, as explained in the 1:10:100 rule.

THE 1:10:100 RULE—THE IMPORTANCE OF PLANNING

Everything we make goes through three broad stages of development: conception and planning; building and testing; delivery and use. In the first stage, we are working with ideas, and our milestone is a written plan. In the second stage, we are building, and the result is the physical system, tested and working. In the third stage, the system is put into place, and then maintained for the length of its useful life.

There is a bottom-line fact about these stages. It is always least expensive to plan well, and resolve all problems in the conception and planning stage. It costs 10 times as much to resolve the same problem in the building and testing stage, and 100 times as much to resolve the problem when the system is in production. This is *the 1:10:100 rule*.

WOWS AND WHOOPSES

Measure Twice, Cut Once
An architect looked at a blueprint and realized he had made a mistake. He had placed a support pillar in the wrong location. He knew that he had to redraw the blueprint, which would take an hour. He could not decide whether to charge his client for the time it would take to fix his own mistake. At $500 per hour (back in the 1960s), this was not a small choice. He decided to find out what it would cost the client if he did not fix the mistake.

He called a building contractor and described the problem. He asked: "Suppose I hadn't found the mistake until the building was half-way finished. What would it take to fix it then?" The contractor replied that it would be a big mess. You cannot move a support pillar once the foundation had been laid. The architect would have to design a set of trusses and joists to support the roof, and it would take the construction team more than a day, about ten hours of work for the whole team, and $5,000 to fix the problem. This is the 1:10 ratio of the 1:10:100 rule. It takes ten times as much time and money to fix the building during construction as it would take to fix the blueprint before construction.

This got the architect more curious. What would happen if the problem was not discovered until the building was built? He called a maintenance engineer, who told him that the first symptom would be that the roof would sag and leak. To fix it, they would have to close the building for 100 hours (4 days). Between lost rents and repair costs, the total bill would be $50,000. So, one hour has become 100 hours, and for each dollar of expense in the planning stage, it will take $100 to fix the problem in the working building or production system.

The 1:10:100 rule is about the process of developing anything. It applies to every project in every industry, from construction to software development to advertising. So, we need to organize our work in a way that takes advantage of the 1:10:100 rule. The more good work we do early, the better.

The 1:10:100 rule is close to a universal law. It has been tested and found to be true across many industries. It even applies in software development, where we are building a computer program with software code, rather than creating a physical item such as a building. In *Software Inspection* Gilb and Graham devote an entire chapter to demonstrating the value of a software development method that focuses on extensive planning even before writing code. Over and over they demonstrate that a process that catches errors in the planning stage reduces project cost by a factor of ten. In addition, they have one case where a company wrote 80 software programs, 40 of them using traditional methods and 40 using software inspection. In production, the maintenance cost of the 40 programs written using project management best practices was 1/100 of the maintenance cost of the other 40 applications.

The 1:10:100 rule is also the way things work in nature. You hear it in the aphorisms "an ounce of prevention is worth a pound of cure" and "measure twice, cut once." These teach us to put planning and prevention ahead of action, making use of the 1:10:100 rule. Our goal in project management is to define what we are doing and then plan well so as to prevent problems. It may mean a slower, more costly start, but it ensures project success and lower total cost.

WHAT THIS MEANS FOR YOU

A Well-planned Project Takes Less Time

It is better to spend your money and time planning well up front. This can reduce project costs by up to a factor of ten, and reduce annual maintenance costs by a factor of a hundred. Every project should have at least three stages: Prepare a written plan; do the work and test the results; and deliver to ensure customer satisfaction. In Chapter 4 we have taken the three stages of the 1:10:100 rule—plan, build, and deliver—and divided them into smaller components, the stages of the *System Development Life Cycle*.

PLANNING IN WRITING

Although the planning process may happen inside your head or in a team brainstorming session, the results of planning need to be written down. In project management, a plan is always written. In fact, it is a very good idea for the document to contain both words and pictures. We can be sure different people share the same understanding if we look at words and diagrams together. This planning takes a lot of time. Using my example above, I could have obtained the right information about the eighth item, written it up, and sent it to the programmer in about 25 minutes of planning. Instead, we had four hours of extra work trying to figure out the problem and solve it.

Writing up plans and specifications is a lot easier than you think. Here are a number of techniques that can help you write better plans more easily.

- *Use a template*, either from this book or from somewhere else.
- *If you do not have a template, make one from an example.* Find an example of a past project plan, specification, or other item that your boss or team thought was a good one. Copy it and delete the information from the last project. Then fill in the information from this project.
- *Write badly, then rewrite.* The biggest barrier to good project writing is that people think they have to get it right the first time. The opposite is true. Get it wrong the first time. Be loose. Be sloppy. Unfinished sentences are okay, because it is the ideas that matter. Then, through rewriting and reviewing with others, improve what you have. It is said that no good book was ever written; quality comes out in the rewriting. The same is true of a project plan. By writing and rewriting,

we make use of two other tools from this chapter: iteration and the no-blame environment.

- *Interview people to write the plan.* Interview customers to get requirements. Interview team members to help them plan their work and estimate how long it will take. Then write their ideas into the plan. For a discussion of the best ways to do this, see the Prepare, Do, Follow Through section later in this chapter.
- *Brainstorm together, then write it up.* Two heads are better than one.

In planning, things start very loose and get locked down as we move along. Be sure to break your planning work into stages, including gathering information, taking notes, getting a template, creating an initial draft, and revising. As you work with other people, let them know what their role is: to provide initial information, to brainstorm and improve, or to review and approve, making changes only if they are necessary. We do a lot of planning early to get things as right as possible as early as possible. The later a change happens in a project, the more it costs, and the more likely it is to create other problems in other parts of the project or the schedule.

PUTTING THE JOB IN FRONT OF YOUR TEAM

Once we have a plan, we can show it to people. This does a lot more than just make sure everyone understands things the same way. Sharing a plan is a way to help people contribute and cooperate, to work together well instead of getting into conflicts. Figure 2-1 shows how this works.

The example shows the project manager working with the customer, but this works the same way with any project stakeholder or team member. When we put the problem in front of us and get on the same side, we start working together. When we face off across a table, we tend to go head to head, creating conflict. I mean this both figuratively and literally. I arrange meeting rooms so that everyone is on the same side of the table, looking at the problem. And I ask questions and introduce ideas to make it clear that we are defining issues, resolving difficulties, and facing challenges together, supporting one another as we do.

For example, say that I need a project team member to plan her work more carefully than she did before, coming up with more accurate time estimates. I prepare a template and a list of questions ahead of time. We sit together, and I respect her expertise about the best way to do her work. Through my questions, I get a picture of her tasks. I write them down and organize them. I show them to her and have her make changes or agree.

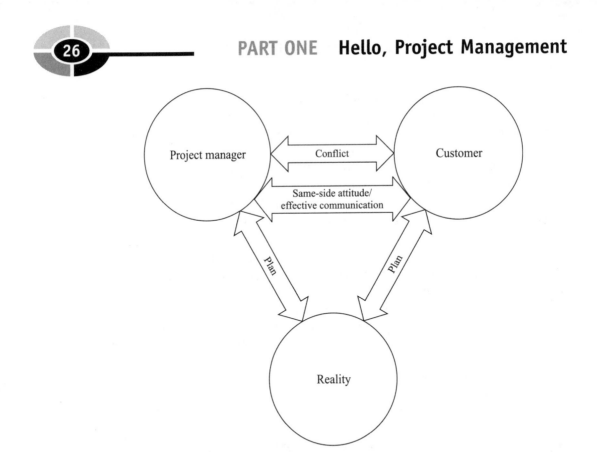

Fig. 2-1. Triangulation. Effective communications through the use of a plan to share a picture of reality.

When we have the task list done, we estimate the time together. The results include a good estimate, but also an appreciation of one another. I understand more of what she brings to the project, and she sees how my organizing and planning can leave her more appreciated by the entire team. This is certainly more effective than simply telling her that she has to plan her time better, without helping her do it. That would be going head-to-head, and would probably just leave her believing I do not think she does a good job.

Organizing Work Over Time

Scheduling, or planning project work over time, is a big job in project management. The key is to break it down into small, clearly defined steps. In building our schedules, we use several methods: iteration, definition of tasks and deliverables, and definition of larger stages and gates, also called phases and milestones.

TERM

Scheduling is the process of planning and coordinating work over time.

To iterate means to repeat over and over.

A task is a small job done by one person or a small team at one time delivering a specific result. *Action* and *step* are synonyms for task.

A deliverable is the result of a task. It can be given from one person to another, or handed off, and the next person can use the deliverable without needing to ask any questions of the first person.

A stage, also called a *phase*, is a large set of related tasks leading to the completion of a major deliverable, or milestone.

A milestone is the end result of a stage, a large part of the project completed and delivered.

A gate is another term for a milestone. This term emphasizes the fact that one does not just reach the milestone and then walk on. One comes to the gate, then has to open it to go through. Just the same, reaching a gate on a project is a process. We deliver, and the customer approves before we can go through the gate.

ITERATION: REPEATING YOURSELF OVER AND OVER

Much project management work—and also project work—can be thought of as small jobs we do over and over, making our work better and better as we move further along. The process of repeating a step over and over again, leading to a new result, is called iteration. Writing a plan can be seen as five steps, repeated over and over: Inquire, get information; think about it, write it down, read it. As we read it, we ask what is missing, what we are not sure of. That is another inquiry. Then we get more information, think about it, write it down, and read it again. As we do this over and over, bringing in other people to add information and ideas, to brainstorm, to come on board and agree, we build both the project plan and the project team by an iterative planning process.

Project work is also iterative. Team members do a task, check it, deliver the result, have the result reviewed by someone else, fix it, have it approved, and then do that for the next task and deliverable, and the next, and the next. Testing is an iterative cycle of test, find a problem, fix a problem, retest, and repeat until the product passes all tests.

Iteration also adds precision. This is most clear in estimation. When we make our first estimates of project cost, for instance, we do not have a lot of information, and our estimates are quite rough. Early on, we can only say that the cost will fall within a rather large range. As we learn more about the project, we narrow things down. Then we go back to the estimates, revising them and making them more and more precise.

WHAT THIS MEANS FOR YOU

Getting Unstuck with Iteration
Whenever you are stuck on how to do a job, ask yourself how you can break it up into small repeating pieces.

TASKS AND DELIVERABLES

KEY POINT

Passing the Baton
Think of each leg of a relay race as one task, and finishing the race as the project. As the lead runner, my task is to carry the baton the first mile, and my deliverable is the baton, which I hand to you.

Now, suppose I come to the end of my mile, exhausted and ready to drop. As you grab the baton, I say, "No, wait, it's not quite finished. I need to clean it, and check if it's cracked." As you try to run around the track, you are not just carrying the baton, you are dragging along a tired runner, the guy who did not quite get the job done, me.

That often happens when team members do not understand tasks and deliverables. If you can teach your team only one thing, teach them to understand tasks and deliverables.

Breaking a large amount of work down into small steps is a very important skill in project planning. Whenever possible, we help each project team member do this for his or her own work. The key rule is this: each step results in a deliverable. A deliverable can be handed off to someone else. If the person who did the work wins the lottery and leaves the project, never to return, someone else will be able to pick up the deliverable and do the next task. Projects should not depend on specific people. Rather, team members serve each other, and the project, by delivering work that others can use.

SOMETHING EXTRA

What Is Done Is Done

Here is a way to teach your team to understand deliverables. When a team member says something is ready, ask, "Is it done?"

If the person says yes, then ask, "Is there anything else you have to do?"

Often, they will say "yes, there is." Perhaps the team member will say, "It's done, but when Juanita gives me her piece, I'll add that." Or, "It's done, but I'll need to make whatever changes Robert requests." This means that the team member does not understand deliverables.

Reply, "If there's anything left for you to do, it isn't done." Then ask the team member to picture the deliverable in someone else's hands, and the recipient doing the next step without calling the team member who did the work.

Stages and gates, also called phases and milestones, are a larger version of tasks and deliverables. A stage or phase is a large set of related tasks, leading to a major deliverable, called a milestone. The milestone is evaluated by the customer at the gate. We will define stages and gates for projects in more detail in Chapter 4.

Being Clear and Coming to Agreement

Understanding and agreement are keys to project success. How do we get there? Including everyone is the most important step, and we will explore ways of doing this in several later chapters, including Chapter 5. As we include people, first we listen and then we incorporate their ideas. Next we get their commitment, and, lastly, their approval. We do this iteratively stage after stage.

Clarity, so that there is no ambiguity, no easy chance for misunderstandings, is crucial in keeping people committed. Our first topic, *inclusions and exclusions*, is a technique for writing a clear plan.

INCLUSIONS AND EXCLUSIONS

An *inclusion* is something that will be part of the project, and an *exclusion* is something we will be leaving out of the project. Here are some examples of inclusions and exclusion pairs:

- A list of customers who will use the service we create, and a list of other people who will not get the service at the end of the project, although they might get it later.
- A list of deliverables, such as products and specifications, that we will give to the customer, and a list of items that were requested, but are not part of the project deliverables.
- Instructions to a worker saying what work is to be done, and what work is to be left for others.

TERM

Inclusion Something that will be part of the project.
Exclusion Something that will be left out of the project.
Assumption Something thought, but not said, often leading to a misunderstanding. When written into the plan, an understood basis of the plan.
Specification A specific item, clearly defined in writing for an inclusion, or a document defining inclusions and exclusions in detail.
Expectation Something someone—most usually the customer—wants, which may not be clearly specified.

When we introduce inclusions and exclusions, we get people thinking and talking clearly about what will be done, and what will not. This helps us to bring out unspoken assumptions so that we can write them down, adding them to the specification. We then include a list of the exclusions—the things we will not do—in our project plan. Why write down the exclusions? Because people tend to ask for things, and then remember what they asked for, and assume they are going to get it, even if we said "no." Writing down exclusions helps us remind our customers of what we are—and are not—doing. Later, that will help us manage our customers' expectations. Some very experienced project managers have said that managing customer expectations is the hardest part of being a project manager.

SOMETHING EXTRA

Explain Your Exclusions

In a project plan, it is not a good idea to have an area labeled "Exclusions," with a heading that says, "Here is what we will not do." Instead, give your reasons. For example, you might say, "Here are ideas the customer considered. But, after reviewing the cost, the customer agreed not to implement them at this time."

For a web site design project, I put it this way: "The company came up with many good ideas for the corporate web site. However, web pages are hard to create the first time, and easy to add to later. In addition, Human Resources needed the initial web site running within three weeks, in time for the spring recruiting fair. Here are the other ideas we plan to add later." With all the ideas acknowledged and written down, and with everyone understanding the rush in Human Resources, everyone supported leaving off things they wanted until later.

BENDING WITHOUT BREAKING

Just because we have clarity about what we are and are not doing, that does not mean we should be rigid, or that we should never agree to change. We should listen to all change requests—no matter how unreasonable—and respond appropriately. Here are some general rules to consider when working on plans and when considering changes later:

- *Be flexible at the start.* At the beginning, during the stage when the plan is being prepared, you should be very open to change. We make every effort to listen to everyone and consider their ideas, including them when possible. We also explain that anything requested now is relatively easy; anything requested later will cost more and may be impossible.
- *Balance authority and responsibility.* When deciding whether to include something, it is always good to ask two questions: What is it worth? And, who will pay for it? The balance of authority and responsibility means that you should be given the resources needed to do the job. And I often find that as customers ask for features on a new software product they think of many things. By asking how much they are willing to pay for each feature, I can help them quickly prioritize their requirements, creating a list of reasonable size.
- *Remember: Late changes cost a lot.* Once the stage in which a planning document is written is finished, and it has moved through the gate and obtained approvals, it should, in general, not be changed. If we do this, then the item will cost ten times as much, due to the 1:10:100 rule. Make sure customers know this. Explain to them that any later change will have to be approved by everyone on the project all over again, creating extensive delays, and that errors are likely to creep into the project, causing problems that, perhaps, no one will catch.

When do we need to consider changes to a plan that is already approved, and which we are putting into action? Here are some guidelines:

- We should listen to every question and request, even if we think we are explaining things for the tenth time. Explaining things more than ten times is part of our job.
- We should see if there is any misunderstanding about the plan, or lack of clarity in the plan. If so, we should clarify it.
- Once the issue is clear, we need to decide what to do. There are very clear guidelines for adopting changes to project plans in Chapter 11.

SOMETHING EXTRA

Tell Your Customers About the 1:10:100 Rule
One of the nicest things about the 1:10:100 rule is its simplicity. Even busy executives can understand it. Explain it to them at the beginning of a project, and you will motivate them to give you information early. Remind them later, and they will understand why project change is costly and risky. Explain that it costs less to do a minor modification after the project is over than it costs to change the project plan midstream.

Getting Work Done

There are two basic tips for getting work done that the thousands of project managers I have worked with have found very helpful. They are actually two different versions of the same idea, a short one and a long one. It is valuable to do planning before even small tasks, and valuable to follow through to make sure you have the results you want.

PREPARE, DO, FOLLOW THROUGH

Even on the smallest jobs, work in three stages: Prepare, do, and follow through.

Prepare

When I teach project management, we do an exercise in class on planning work. During the exercise, people often say that the first step is to have a meeting. Every time we look at this more closely, it turns out not to be true. A meeting is never the first step. Before we can have a meeting, we need to plan the meeting. It helps to write down answers to these questions:

- Who should be at the meeting? What will each person contribute?
- What do we want to ask?
- What do we need to explain to the other person?
- What do we hope to have when we leave the meeting?

If we write down answers to these questions, we have an agenda, and our meeting is much more likely to get us what we want.

The same rule about preparation applies to small work tasks. When amateurs do minor home repair, they almost always have to leave the job site to go get some tool they did not know they would need. Professionals save a lot of time by knowing what they need, planning the job, and bringing everything they need for the job with them the first time. That can make the difference between a money-making business that satisfies customers and a money-losing one that leaves customers disappointed with delays. So, for every meeting and every small task, prepare before you do. And prepare with a written plan, even if it is just a short to-do list or a half-page agenda.

Do

If you have prepared well, then doing will come easily. We follow the agenda, work plan, or checklist. We have everything we need with us. We check off items as we go. We can focus on enjoying the work and doing it well.

Follow through

When we are finishing up, we check what we did against the agenda or to-do list. I always take a minute at the end of a meeting to make sure I have covered everything. At the same time, I ask myself if I can remember and use the answers I have obtained. I take any notes I need to be able to follow through.

Meeting notes contain two types of information: Decisions and action items:

- *Decisions*. Anything that people at the meeting agreed on is written down in plain, simple language. For example, if a delivery date is changed, we write it down. After the meeting, we modify the plan and make changes to the work schedule to meet the new deadline.

- *Action items.* During meetings, we decide to do things. However, often nothing happens. The first step in making sure that the right work gets done is to create an action item. An action item names who will do the work, has a delivery date, and describes what will be delivered. It can include any notes that will help get the job done.

Written decisions and action items allow us to follow through. Following through means taking effective action, leading to the results we want. All too often decisions are made, plans are changed, but people do not hear about the changes. Or we remember what was said in a meeting, but someone else remembers it differently, and then we do not have enough information to move forward.

To be effective means to have an effect. Follow-through for meetings means translating agreements and decisions into written plans that become effective actions. The ideas in the meeting result in a clear benefit: a better result than we would have had otherwise.

Follow-through is also important at the end of each job we do. As we finish a task, we follow through in these ways:

- *Check your checklist.* Review the checklist and make sure everything is done—and done well.
- *Expert extras.* Take a look at the job. Is there anything that will make it just a bit better?
- *Put away your toys.* Clean up after yourself. On a construction job, this can mean covering paint cans and cleaning brushes. For a bookkeeper, it means printing out a reconciliation, and putting copies of the invoices, marked paid, in the paper files. Why is it important? So that when you come back—whether for routine work or to track down a problem—the next job is quick and easy.
- *Ensure delivery.* It is not enough to know that you sent it. The customer has to know that they got it. On one occasion I sent off a book proposal. When I was done, I called the editor and made sure that he had got it and could open the document and read it. It is a bit of courtesy, and also prevents big headaches on those occasions where the package does not reach the customer. Care with this kind of detail is what makes customers remember you for providing great service.

PICTURE, PLAN, CREATE, IMPROVE, TEST, FIX, AND DELIVER

This is the longer version of plan, do, and follow through. This seven-step process works for larger jobs because it supports the creative side of project work. Projects call for individual creativity and team collaboration. The best projects redefine problems and come up with new solutions. So it makes sense to use the best tools for creativity and collaboration on our projects.

Picturing and planning

We add picturing to planning because we get better results when we have diagrams and pictures in front of us and in our minds, as well as words. When we are working alone, visualizing helps with creating the best solutions, and also helps us stay motivated. When we have a picture of what we are going to create, we really want to bring it into being. For example, each morning as I start to write this book, I look at a picture of the cover. I look at a list of what you will be able to do when you read this book. That keeps me focused on getting work done and on making sure that each chapter gives you what you need to be a better project manager. You can do the same by making a picture of what you are creating and putting it in front of yourself every day.

Adding pictures to our words also helps us as a team. Two people can look at the same plan and understand it differently. Two people can look at the same picture and agree, but not understand the details. But putting the two together makes a magical difference. When you have a picture and a thousand words, the team is on the same page and sees the same detail. That is the beginning of collaboration.

In collaboration, each person can suggest the best features and the best ways of doing things. These can be tested against the whole plan to make sure all the parts will work together. The result is a finished product that is better than the sum of its parts, a collaborative result that no one person could have created alone. That is the highest level of project success.

Creating and improving

In this longer version of doing, we create and improve. We work according to plan, and we check our work. But we also pay attention to how we are working and what we are making. Are there better ways of working, ways that will lead to a better result or get the work done faster? If so, we do them. Do we come up with ideas for improvements, ways of adding value to the project without adding much to the time or cost? If so, we suggest them to the project manager and the customer, and find out if they are worth doing. Caring about our jobs and the project is valuable to us, as well as to project results. It increases our sense of the value of what we do, our sense of participation, and our job satisfaction. As project managers, we do this ourselves and we also cultivate this attitude of attention, responsibility, and creativity with each person on our team.

Testing and fixing

Even on the smallest task we should take a minute to make sure we did the job right. And if we find a problem, we fix before we deliver. And fixing takes time. That seems simple and obvious. But I have seen dozens of project plans that have a test phase, and no time for fixing every problem the team finds. Either the project managers figured everything would go fine, or they just did not think about the time it takes to fix problems.

In reality, if we are testing we will be fixing, and we need to make time for fixing—and retesting after the fixes—in the project plan. Estimating the time the test cycle will take is difficult because we do not know how many problems we will find. We address this in Chapter 9.

TERM

Test cycle This is the time we take to check for problems, resolve them, and then retest to make sure we have really solved the problem, and not created any new problems, so that the product meets customer specifications.

When we picture, plan, create, improve, test, fix, and deliver, we create the best possible project results, and deliver on time and under budget. In Chapter 4 we will see how project managers have formalized this idea into a structure of stages and gates.

Solving Problems as a Team

The last set of tools we introduce in this chapter help create effective teams that work together to deliver results. These are the no-blame environment, gap analysis, and gap reconciliation.

THE NO-BLAME ENVIRONMENT

Our own attitude towards our work and our team creates the *no-blame environment*. If we focus on the reality of work and results, and not on personalities and blame, we take the first step. As shown in Table 2-1, we take the second step by making sure that each person has what is needed to do the job, so that responsibility and accountability are matched with authority, empowerment, ability, skills, knowledge, and resources. When the work environment has a

Table 2-1 Views of the work environment: Reality vs. personality.

Reality-based	Personality-based
Responsibility for actions and their consequences	Blame for failure
Accountability for results	Personal praise
Supported and balanced by:	Politics (in the negative sense of the term)
Clear job definition	Avoidance of responsibility
Authority	Micromanagement
Empowerment	Denial
Ability	Manipulation
Skills and tools	Anger
Knowledge, information, and methods	Criticism
Resources, including:	Excuses
People	
Money	
Information systems	
Information, including status and technical specifications	

balance of responsibility and empowerment, then each person's job is realistic, and we can focus on reality and success, not personality and blame.

When we create this balance, each person on the team takes on a job, and has what is needed to do that job. If we do this, then work gets done, and deadlines are met. If problems come up, we work together to resolve them. There is no need to ask who is to blame when something goes wrong.

It is not perfect. People make mistakes and misunderstand one another. We are part of those mistakes and misunderstandings. And we are also part of good work and success. And so is everyone else.

When we leave blame out of the picture, the team can focus on delivering the work. We can eliminate the negative aspects of dealing with personality. That allows the team to focus on the real gifts of personality, the unique qualities each team member brings to the job, improving the results.

Even in a no-blame environment, problems will come up. Instead of finger-pointing, we can address problems with two tools: gap analysis and gap reconciliation.

GAP ANALYSIS

We can view any problem as having two sides and a gap that needs to be closed. For example, if work is going slowly so that we will not meet a deadline, then there is a gap between how fast the work is going and the amount of work we need to get done. We can either speed up the work, or change the deadline. Either one closes the gap.

I recommend this kind of simple thinking focused on the present and the future: What is the gap? What choices do we have today to solve the problem and reach our goal tomorrow? Defining the gap and making decisions keeps the focus on moving from where we are now to our future goal. This turns the focus away from the past and away from blame.

In a way, an entire project can be thought of as a gap between where we are today and where we want to be when the project is over. And each job can be thought of in the same way. Is there a gap between resources, such as time and skill, needed for a job and the resources we have? If so, how will we close the gap?

In gap analysis, we draw a picture of where we are now, and where we want to be. We get a sense of the difference. Then we make a list of the specific issues. Often that gives us an obvious solution. Gap analysis and reconciliation are illustrated in Fig. 2-2.

If it does not, we try brainstorming. We focus on the gap, and ask how we can reconcile it.

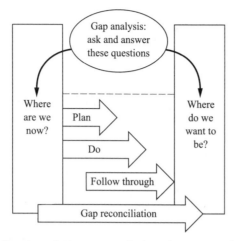

Fig. 2-2.   A project as gap analysis and gap reconciliation.

TERM

No-blame environment is a work environment that is focused on reality and success, rather than personality and blame.

Empower means to give the authority and ability to make decisions and take actions.

Gap analysis is a way of analyzing a problem that identifies two positions and defines the differences between them.

Gap reconciliation is a process, after gap analysis, of closing the gap in any appropriate way.

Brainstorming is a structured meeting or set of meetings used to bring a team or other group together to identify and solve problems or come up with creative results.

GAP RECONCILIATION

Gap reconciliation is a brainstorming process starting with the gap we found in gap analysis. We bring the team together, focus on the problem, give it enough time to work it out, and come up with the best solution we can. Often, we solve the problem entirely. If not, we know we have found the best option, and we know what the costs are. We may be giving up something we hoped to have. But we are getting the best result that we can. Once we understand that clearly, we can communicate our solution to the sponsor and the customers effectively and get agreement on the revised goals, delivery date, and plan.

Questions for Learning

Throughout this book we introduce specific tools for planning and communicating, organizing work over time, making clear agreements, getting work done, and solving problems as a team. You will get plenty of templates, tools, and checklists. But, before you do, think about what you already have.

- When do you use written plans now? When could you use them in ways you have not before?
- Write down the goals of your project for learning. Finish this sentence: When I finish this project, I will have _____. If there is more than one result, make a bulleted list.
- Now, write down the purpose of your project for learning. That is, what is the value you will receive when you finish? You can do this by finishing one of these sentences: When the project is over, I will be able to _____. When the project is over, I will be happy because _____. When the project is over, I will know how to _____.
- Do you use checklists? Do you keep a shopping list, and add to it whenever you think of something you need? How could you make better use of checklists?
- Do you ever have to interrupt yourself in the middle of a job to go get something you need? What could you change in the way you work so that this would not happen any more?
- How could you improve the way you plan for meetings?
- How could you improve the way you follow through after meetings?
- Can you think of a time where a meeting became confused, or even turned into a conflict? Can you imagine doing that meeting again in a different way by putting everything in front of the team at the meeting, and working on it together?
- Explain something you are doing in terms of inclusions and exclusions. What are you doing? What are you not doing? And why?
- Think of a time when having a picture as well as a written plan helped, or could help, you and a team focus on a job.
- Have you ever been stuck with a problem in testing, and no time to make a good fix and retest? What happened?
- The next time you have a problem, think of it as a gap. Where are you now? Where do you want to be? How will you close the gap?
- Would you say you work in a mostly no-blame environment, or in an environment with a lot of blame? How do you participate in that? Do you want to change the way you are doing that?

I hope this chapter has got you thinking in new ways. Let us turn your learning into practical experience. Pick any one, two, or three of the above questions, and write down what you will do differently from here forward. Those are your action items!

Now, we will turn our attention to the six most important things you can do to ensure project success.

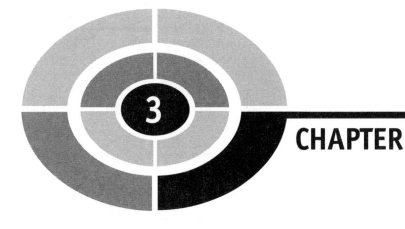

CHAPTER 3

Six Keys to Project Success

Now that you have seen the big picture of project management in Chapter 1 and learned some crucial tools to use over and over in Chapter 2 it is time to ask the question: What really matters? On one occasion, when I was teaching a project management course to computer professionals, one of them said to me, "Sid, this is a great course. But there's way too much here. What are the most important points?"

It was a great question. What do we have to do to ensure project success almost all the time? What few items should we learn first, and do well, to improve our track record? Once we do that, we can learn the details, extras, and enhancements later.

This chapter is the answer to that question. We present six keys to project success. Do these correctly and your project is almost certain to succeed. Other project management tools add value to a project, but they are not as important as these keys. In this chapter we highlight the most important aspects of these keys. Additional tools to help you with these key processes are covered in Part Two.

In This Chapter

- Why projects fail
- Key 1: Manage communication and teamwork
- Key 2: Define the project clearly
- Key 3: Create a detailed work plan
- Key 4: Ensure high quality
- Key 5: Use written change control
- Key 6: Follow through, deliver quality
- A project for learning
- Questions for learning

Why Projects Fail

If we want to understand why these six ways of working are, indeed, the most important keys to project success, then we must know why projects do not succeed, why they fail. A project is like a road trip. On a road trip, we start from where we are and try to reach a destination. How can a road trip fail? How can a project fail? Table 3-1 answers these questions.

Now we need to look deeper. We have seen the results we do not want. Now the questions are: Why do projects fail? What can we do differently so that they do not? The answers are in Table 3-2. In the first column, undesirable project outcome, you see the same list we saw on the right-hand side of Table 3-1. After that, we have the cause of that outcome. Then, in column three, key solution, we have the number of the key project method that prevents that mistake.

Now we know what actions lead to failure. We can avoid them by using the six keys to project success.

Key 1: Manage Communication and Teamwork

Communications is the process of listening to, and talking to, everyone on the project other than the core, full-time working team. *Teamwork* includes the processes of communication within the team and everything else that supports and leads the team to success.

Table 3-1   What is project failure? Comparison of a road trip with a project.

Road trip	Project
We end up driving to the wrong place.	We deliver something other than what the customer wants.
We get lost on the way.	We waste a lot of time and money without getting good work done.
We never get on the road.	We plan and plan, but never launch the project.
We forget something we wanted to bring.	We fail to define a key element of project success, so what we create does not work for the customer.
There is a change in plans, and we do not handle it well.	The customer requests a crucial change, and we do not follow through.
We forget someone we wanted to bring.	We fail to include a crucial customer or stakeholder in our planning, and the project result does not work as delivered.
We get to where we wanted to go, but it was so hard to get there that we are all exhausted and nobody has a good vacation.	We deliver project results, but they are not used well by the customer, and value is not realized.

COMMUNICATIONS

Each time I teach project management seminars, we review several projects. In every class I have ever taught, we have come to the same conclusion: The more communication, the sooner, the better. We define effective communication as two-way dialog with all concerned parties with feedback, leading to results. These are the essential steps to effective communication:

- Identify all stakeholders
- Prepare, listen, and learn
- Write down what you learn, show it to the other person, and get it confirmed

Table 3-2   Why projects fail: Causes and solutions.

Undesirable project outcome	Cause	Key solution
We deliver something other than what the customer wants.	We did not listen to the customer, but instead allowed ourselves or someone else to decide what the customer wanted.	Keys 1 and 2
We waste a lot of time and money without getting good work done.	We did not have a detailed work plan, or we did not pay attention to quality	Keys 3 and 4
We plan and plan, but never launch the project.	We did not write a clear definition of what we were doing, or we did not communicate and get commitment.	Keys 1 and 2
We fail to define a key element of project success, so what we create does not work for the customer.	We did not define the project clearly.	Keys 2 and 4
The customer requests a crucial change, and we do not follow through.	We did not follow through with written change control.	Key 5
We fail to include a crucial customer or stakeholder in our planning, and the project result does not work as delivered.	We did not include everyone, or someone got lost during the project	Keys 1 and 2
We deliver project results, but they are not used well by the customer, and value is not realized.	We did not plan and implement the overall project well, or we did not follow through	All keys, especially Key 6

- Keep everyone up to date
- Address problems when they arise
- Take action based on what you learn

A *project stakeholder* is anyone who is affected by a project or the resulting product or service. The customer is the primary stakeholder, but projects will fail if you only talk to the customer. You must talk to everyone involved. How do you find all the stakeholders? In brief, draw a picture of the system, show it to everyone you can think of, and ask each of them if they are a stakeholder, or if they know anyone else who might be. The picture is called a context diagram. The full process for creating a context diagram and identifying stakeholders is provided in Chapter 5.

Before each meeting it is good to prepare both a brief statement or presentation and also questions that will elicit information from the stakeholder. Depending on the stakeholder's role, you will need different questions. For the customers, you will need to learn what problem they want fixed, how the system will help them do their job, and how they work. For other stakeholders, you will need to find out how they will be affected by the changes that come with the new product or service, and what they have to contribute to the project to ensure its success. The basic process for interviewing stakeholders is covered in Chapter 6.

We really understand something when we take it in at least two different ways, and when we then express it in two different ways. We know something is real when we can touch it and feel it. We know a meal is good when it looks good and tastes good. In creating a project plan, therefore, we need to describe the project, and the product or service, in both words and pictures. We then walk the stakeholders through the words and pictures, and have them add their own ideas, and check our ideas. We capture all of this in writing, show it to everyone, and ask each of them to confirm that we have understood them correctly.

This may seem time consuming, but it is time well spent because of the 1:10:100 rule. If you get it right now, and make sure it is right now, then you will have measured twice and cut once, and your cut will be right on the money. In addition, you will be creating the written project plan during these meetings. An accurate written plan is essential for several reasons:

- When new people join the team, they can read the plan and get up to speed.
- The first written plan is the basis for all of the other plans, which will estimate time and cost, and manage quality, risk, and procurement.
- If the project is delayed, then it can be restarted from the written plan.

Although the most important project communications happen at the beginning of each project, communication should continue throughout the project. The communication within the full-time project team is part of teamwork, or project human resources management, but the communication with all other stakeholders falls into project communications management. Regular status reports should go out weekly, monthly, or as needed to each stakeholder. For peripheral stakeholders, you can ask them how often they want to be kept up to date. However, you cannot assume everyone reads routine status reports. Therefore, if the status is not right, it is essential to make an extra effort to be in touch with the appropriate stakeholders and ensure they have got the message. A good system for doing this, called Green-Yellow-Red is described in Chapter 12.

When someone tells you about a problem, or a possible problem, take action promptly. Check it out. Ensure everything is going well, if it is. If it's not, then the sooner you know, the less it will cost to stop the problem before it becomes serious. Serious problems create conflict on the team, reduce stakeholder commitment, cost time and money, and reduce quality. Prevent these consequences by being available, listening closely, being sure you understand, planning well, and taking prompt, effective action. Many managers do not like to talk about problems. They prefer to call them issues. I take the opposite view: A problem is a problem. Problems will happen. And we will prevent them when we can, and solve them promptly the rest of the time. The methods for doing this are discussed in Chapter 11.

SOMETHING EXTRA

The Project Communications Plan
If a project is complicated, or if there might be political conflict about it, prepare a communications plan. List each stakeholder, and write down how often you will talk to each one, what you will say, what you will ask, and what you will do with the information you get.

It is not enough just to listen to everyone and write down what they say. For communications to be effective, they must have effects. This is called *feedback:* communications which, when received, change our course of action. Throughout the project, the project manager should respond to all communications promptly. If what you hear or see causes you to take action, then take that action, ensure it is done correctly, and inform the stakeholders, particularly the ones who made the suggestion or request. If you decide to take no action, inform the stakeholders who made the request or suggestion, and explain your reasoning. Getting back to people and letting them know whether or not we took action is called closing the communications loop.

WHAT THIS MEANS FOR YOU

Take effective action based on the feedback you receive. Change your plan to meet the customer's needs or solve the problem, and then follow the new plan.

TEAMWORK

Creating, leading, and supporting a good team is essential to project success. There is a great deal of literature about teamwork for business. On projects, though, a good working team is not enough. The team must also be focused on the goal of the project.

The first step is to get a team of the right people. In the concept and analysis stages, we create a very clear picture of what we will be doing. This allows us to define the areas of expertise we need on the project. We get that technical, managerial, and customer expertise from people, whether those people are employees, consultants or vendors, or customer representatives.

As project managers it is our job to pull these diverse people into a coherent, cooperative team. It is essential that we teach and model good listening and respect. We also need to evaluate each team member with regard to his or her ability to listen, to express, and to participate on the team, doing high-quality work and delivering on time. As we work with our team members, we coach them so that they are able to motivate themselves to do their best, and to be respectful, helpful, and supportive to one another.

Working with our team, we divide the job into tasks, and estimate and assign the work. This is crucial to the motivation of every team member. People work best when they know what their job is, and they are given the resources they need to deliver the results for which they are responsible. As project managers, we ensure that each person has appropriate responsibilities, and the skills, resources, and authority to accomplish the task. We let each person work in his or her own way, as long as we receive clear status reports and deliverables are arriving on time with high quality.

Problems will come up. We address these using gap analysis and gap reconciliation to maintain a no-blame environment for the project, as discussed in Chapter 2. In addition, it is our job to help every team member see his or her role in the whole project, and to focus on making a successful product or service in every way he or she can. For example, if an individual needs more supervision, we offer it in a supportive way. We also need to explain each team member's role in providing status reports and assisting with project management. Sometimes, our team needs to brainstorm to get creative ideas or creative solutions to problems. Lastly, we must also be prepared to prevent and resolve conflicts within the team. Methods for team management are offered in Chapter 12.

When tasks are given to team members, we verify that they are ready to work through a method called stewardship delegation, which is the opposite of micromanagement. As tasks are completed, we verify that they are complete, and that they can be used by the team member(s) who receive that deliverable as input. These methods are described later in this chapter, in the section on ensuring high quality, and in Chapter 7.

When the final tasks are done, the product or service is delivered to the customer along with appropriate documentation and training, and the project is a success.

Key 2: Define the Project Clearly

It often happens that our projects are solutions to the wrong problem, or they create a product or service that nobody wants. Other times, the overall product is good, but we miss a key detail for the customer or a key stakeholder, and the system fails to sell or is rejected by the users. We can prevent this most cost effectively by performing a careful analysis at the beginning of the project, and creating a project overview that defines project scope, includes all requirements, justifies the project, and organizes the work of the project into a structured plan. In Chapter 6 we provide two templates, one for small projects and the other for large projects, explain all the fields in each form, and provide detailed instructions for interviewing stakeholders and preparing the project overview.

The customer is the focus of the analysis stage. Our goal is to listen to the customer, and all the other stakeholders, and create a written description of a solution, a product or service that solves their problems, and adds value to their life or work. That description is written to satisfy several audiences.

- In preparing the business case, we justify the product or service (and the project cost) financially to the customer(s), and to the company financing the project.
- In the project overview, we describe the product or service with its benefits and features for each group or class of users. We define what the product or service will include, and what will be excluded.

- In the technical specifications, we define the features in a way that can be understood both by the customer and also by the technical team who will build the system. Precision is important here. Any errors here will be replicated in other project documents, creating costly, time-consuming problems.

When analysis is complete, we know exactly what we are making, and our customer(s) know it is what they want, and the value it will have for them.

All of this work is part of project scope management. In the overview, we clearly define what the product or service will do, and what it will not do, who will use it, and who will not use it. This prevents scope creep, which is a project killer. *Scope creep* occurs when we allow additional features or customers to be included in the project in the middle. As we add more and more items and stakeholders, the project becomes more complex. Eventually, we are trying to do too much, and the project collapses under its own weight. To prevent this, we set limits early, and deliver what we can with the resources that are available. If new ideas come in, we say, "Yes, later. It's a great idea. We'll do it as soon as this project is done." The project overview functions as a project charter, stating our goal, and the limits of our goal, so that we are not required to try to do more than is possible with the resources we have been given.

To learn what the customer wants, we need to plan meetings with representative customers at all levels, including executives, managers, and users. We prepare and conduct interviews, listen to the customer representatives, write up and organize the results, and ask them to confirm and improve what we have written. We iterate this process, that is, we repeat it until we are sure that the resulting project description and product or service specification are clear, consistent, and of high quality. Then our plan truly represents what the customer wants.

WOWS AND WHOOPSES

A Project Overview Saves the Day
On one occasion I worked extensively with a client and his team over several months to develop a custom application that would support their extremely specialized work with rare documents. As we worked, we asked the executives who would fund the project if they were willing to read and review the project overview. They said they did not have the time.

As we presented our plan and asked for funding, we began to encounter challenges. Some of them came from lack of understanding, and others were politically motivated. Most of them came to me by e-mail. I promptly and politely responded to each request with a short paragraph addressing the executive's concern. The key manager on the customer side did the same. Eventually, we won over the doubters and the project moved ahead again.

Someone asked how I was able to prepare such clear, concise responses to the questions and challenges I received, and do it so quickly. I replied that I had not done it quickly at all. The customer manager and I had anticipated these issues and answered them in the project overview. Whenever I received an e-mail, I went to the overview, clipped out the paragraph that answered the question, and sent the reply.

The time spent early on was well spent. The well-written, thorough overview that the executives would not read got the project through a crisis, preventing conflict, increasing executive commitment, and saving a great deal of time.

Key 3: Create a Detailed Work Plan

Once we know what we are going to make, we can plan how we are going to make it. The project overview defines our starting point and our goal, and our next step is to make a detailed work plan. The detailed work plan, called a *work breakdown structure* (WBS), is essential because every other project planning document is based on it. From the WBS, we will generate our schedule, our budget, our quality plan, our risk plan, and our procurement plan. Therefore, we need to create the WBS very carefully, and ensure that we have not missed any steps. This is not as difficult as it sounds. In Chapter 7 we provide a seven-step plan to creating and validating a WBS.

Each line in the WBS will be a single task that will produce a deliverable. The deliverable, or output, of each task becomes the input for another task or tasks. In creating the WBS, we use several different methods to ensure that we define each task and deliverable precisely. In this way, the WBS becomes a linked series of steps. Each task, like a stepping stone, gets us one step closer to the other shore. When we finish each step, our feet are planted solidly, and we can take the next step. When a set of tasks are completed, we have a set of deliverables that make up a milestone. The tasks and deliverables and intermediate milestones are organized into the phases of the system development life cycle, and each phase ends with a major milestone.

One of the keys to a successful work breakdown structuring process is to make it a team effort. Each person defines how he or she will do his or her own work. You ask questions and guide the worker in picturing the work and ensuring that all the steps are included. Methods for encouraging the team to join you in this effort, guiding them in the process, and writing down and verifying the steps are all given in Chapter 7. Later, when the team member is doing the work, you both share an understanding of what is to be done. That makes it easy for the team member to provide status reports, and for you to track the work as it moves along, and make adjustments to keep the project moving along smoothly.

If the WBS is not done well, problems are almost sure to happen. If steps are missing, then there are necessary tasks that do not appear on your list. As a result, they are not included in the estimation process for the project schedule and budget. The project is likely to run late and require additional funding. In addition, we need a thorough WBS to write the quality plan and the risk plan. Without these, we may build a product that does not work, or we may run into unexpected events and not be prepared to deal with them.

On the positive side, if you create a good WBS with your team, and everyone understands it, then the budget, schedule, risk, and quality plans are easy to prepare and are accurate. Also, the team has an excellent understanding of what they are doing, and why. They can see how each thing they do affects the rest of the team, and how it makes a difference to the customer. When a team participates in creating the plan together, it produces synergy. The team is more than its individual members. People come up with creative solutions to problems, find ways to speed up work, reduce costs, and add value to the product. The result is a highly successful project.

Key 4: Ensure High Quality

Quality management is one of the most difficult aspects of project management. Time and cost are predefined by society and have units of measure, but we must define quality individually for each project. Quality is that which adds value. Each beneficial feature of a product is an element of quality that we need to define, measure, and test. By beneficial features, we mean more than just the features that the user will see. We also mean technical features that ensure reliability or reduce support costs. We can look at a typical cellular phone as an example. Engineering for long battery life and good sound quality provide features that benefit the customer directly. Making a strong unit that will survive being dropped down a flight of concrete stairs reduces maintenance costs. Also, properly programmed electronics that allow phone activation, resetting of key features, and repair over the air interface reduce support costs. As you can see, many different aspects of quality should be defined in analysis and design.

There are five steps to quality management: defining, planning for, controlling, assuring, and delivering quality.

In addition to ensuring the quality of the product, we also have to ensure the quality of the project. Good work leads to good results. How do we ensure that the work our team does is good as we go along, so that we find and fix problems before final testing? The five steps of quality are fully explained in Chapter 13.

Key 5: Use Written Change Control

The first four keys to success cover creating a plan and working according to it. But that is not enough: Change is inevitable. In almost every project, there are some changes. Good analysis can reduce the number of changes, but it cannot eliminate them. Therefore, we need a method of managing changes to the plan during the project. The method is called change control, and it is discussed in Chapter 8. In Chapter 11 tools for the change control process are provided.

The most basic rule of change control is that all changes must be in writing. Otherwise, some team members will know about the change, and others will not. The result is a product with the front end of a horse, and the back end of a donkey. And you will end up looking just as foolish.

If the changes are written down, then you can keep everyone, team members and stakeholders, on the same page.

WOWS AND WHOOPSES

One Lost Change Spells Disaster

I never get away from project management. I was flying out to deliver a PM training course, and it transpired that the person sitting next to me on the airplane was a project manager for a manufacturing company. His cautionary tale is the best way I know of teaching the importance of change control.

He was the project manager for the development of a new assembly line component that promised to be a big hit for his company. His company builds equipment for cardboard box manufacturers. He gathered a group of customers, company executives, and engineers to discuss a bright idea, and it grew into a very good idea. At the end of the think tank sessions, they had a detailed specification for a new component that almost all the customers would want to buy.

The think tank did their job so well that only one change was suggested during the entire length of the project. It was a simple suggestion: In order for the device to attach to the assembly lines used by half of their customers, a certain piece inside the machine would need a hole cut into it.

The project manager verified the change was essential, and spoke to everyone about it. Everyone knew.

But, somehow, no one did it. The change was never written down, the piece was never changed in manufacturing, and this error was missed in prototyping and testing.

The company produced over 1,000 machines to fill initial orders, and sent them to their customers. Over 500 machines were returned because they could not be installed. The cost of taking the machine apart, removing the one component, punching a hole in it, and replacing it was so great that they lost money on the project, instead of it being one of their biggest successes ever. And the losses were so great that the company was threatened with perhaps needing to close.

The lesson: Change control only works if it is written down and everyone is told about the changes. Be sure to learn and use the change control tool in Chapter 11.

Key 6: Follow Through, Deliver Quality

Many projects have created excellent products or services, and still been failures in the end. Why? Because no product or service adds value unless it is used. In use, it fulfills its function. Success depends upon user acceptance, value added through productive use, and that value being greater than the cost of support for the life of the product, including the cost of obsolescence and decommissioning.

Just as a batter or golfer learns that follow-through, focusing on the part of the swing that happens after we connect with the ball, is crucial to a good hit, so we must follow-through beyond delivery, and ensure project success through a thorough transition to production stage where we ensure that we have done all we can to create customer satisfaction and reduce production support costs. This includes:

- Delivering the product or service, installed and working.
- Ensuring effective use of the product through delivery of appropriate documentation and training, including support for future training.
- Ensuring responsive ongoing customer service.
- Ensuring low-cost, effective product or service support.
- Performing a project review.

All of these points are covered in detail in Part Two, especially in Chapters 9 and 10.

Review: Cover All the Bases With These Six Keys

At the beginning of the chapter, we listed seven different ways we can fail. We can really boil these down to just four. Projects fail when we:

- Leave key people out of the project
- Make the wrong product or solve the wrong problem
- Forget the 1:10:100 rule
- Do not finish what we start

Following the six keys discussed in this chapter ensures that we do not make these four mistakes. Without these mistakes, we create a product or service everyone wants, we create it efficiently, and we deliver it successfully and ensure customer satisfaction. Let us take a look at the six keys once more by applying them to your project for learning.

Your Project for Learning

Remember the project for learning you chose in Chapter 1? It is time to dust it off. Think about your project in terms of each of the six keys. On this project, think about how you will:

- Manage communication and teamwork
- Define the project clearly
- Create a detailed work plan
- Ensure high quality
- Use written change control
- Follow through, deliver quality

Think about this, and write down your answers. Then ask yourself the following questions: Which of these six keys could I apply right now? Which ones do I need to learn more about? For which keys do I need a template I do not have, or detailed instructions? For which ones do I feel comfortable that I can manage the project well enough to ensure success? Write down those answers. Then, as you read the next seven chapters, you will do the project using the tools in this book. Be sure to focus on the tools you most need to learn.

Questions for Learning

Use the six keys to success as your own means of becoming a successful project manager. When you understand their value and know how to use the tools to do the work of the six keys, you will be able to ensure success on your projects. Do this exercise to start making the keys work for you.

EXERCISE

Create Your Own Guide to the Six Keys

Get out six pieces of paper, or create a word processing document with six separate pages. At the top of each page, write down one of the six keys. Then, on each page, write down the questions below, and answer them.

Write your answers to these first three questions as if you are explaining them to your boss so that you can justify the time it takes to plan and manage a project well.

- If you use this key, what will it do to help the project succeed?
- If you use this key, what problems will you avoid?
- Without blame, describe a past project at work that failed because this key was not used, or was not implemented well.

Write the answers to these questions for yourself, and for a team leader or colleague who wants to learn the keys:

- What tools do we need to make this key work?
- What are the instructions for using each tool? (Write your own, or refer to a page in this book.)
- On a scale of one to five, one meaning the tool is new to you and five meaning you know it well, rate how well you can use this tool now.
- If your rating is three or lower, write down what you will do to learn the tool better. And put a date on it, so it is an action item.

One of the best ways to learn something is to teach it. If you were asked to give a five-minute presentation to a project team explaining why and how to use this key, what would you say?

CHAPTER 4

The Project and Product Life Cycles

Over billions of years natural systems have grown and changed, incorporating new species while maintaining the balance of nature. As project managers, we find that nature is the best model for successful growth and change. When we grow our systems in the way that plants and animals grow, when we change our businesses following the evolutionary model by which ecosystems grow, we succeed. Over the last 40 years this natural model has been adapted and adopted for the development of information technology systems and for project management.

Of course, theoreticians and consultants are always proposing new ways of organizing our work and managing our projects. The term System Development Life Cycle (SDLC) itself has become a political football and just one more misunderstood concept. But if we review 50 years of project failures and successes, we will find that those projects that followed nature's model have largely succeeded, while those that tried to take shortcuts or skip steps ran into big trouble. In the words of Nobel-prize-winning physicist Richard P. Feynman, in his Minority Report to the Space Shuttle

Challenger Inquiry, "For a successful technology, reality must take precedence...for nature cannot be fooled."

In this chapter we will explore and define the essential components of a successful life cycle, and then introduce the life cycle we recommend for projects. Part Two provides a detailed chapter on each stage of the life cycle.

In This Chapter

- Stages and gates
- Learning from nature: the system development life cycle
- Learning from evolution
- A closer look at the life cycle
- A project for learning
- Questions for learning

Stages and Gates

In Chapter 1 we introduced the idea of tasks, the individual steps of a job, and deliverables, the results of each step that can be passed on to another person who can take the next step. Now, we want to expand this idea. A large set of related tasks is a stage, and a review of a large set of related deliverables is a gate.

I used to use the terms phases and milestones, and now I use stages and gates. Both terms are commonly used in project management. I switched because the idea of reaching a milestone implied completion and success. But the reality is more like reaching a gate or a checkpoint. We deliver a major deliverable to the customer, just as we open our suitcases when we get to customs at an international airport. The customers then inspect what we offer, and decide if they like it. If they do, they let us through the gate. So the word gate, unlike the term milestone, tells us that we have to satisfy the customer to pass through. And that will take some time, which we should include in our plan.

Milestones have been around for about 2,000 years. They were used on the Roman roads that ran from Egypt to England. These stone markers told you how much progress you had made on the way to your destination. The modern equivalent are the green highway signs that say, "New York

City 100 miles." Project managers have adopted the term for a point in a project where we can clearly say, "We have come this far, and we have this far to go."

It is important to say that a milestone is a set of clearly defined deliverables. "Fifty percent done" is not a milestone, because we cannot be sure that the second half will go as easily as the first. When we are halfway through a task, we do not really know where we are. And it would probably be difficult for someone else to take over and finish the job. So, a milestone must be composed of completed, tested, useful items. In the early stages, our milestones are likely to be written documents such as plans and specifications, but they are deliverable in the sense that they have been read and approved. Once they are accepted, the customers, the stakeholders, and the project team commit to follow the plans and use the designs. In later stages, tested components and working systems with some features operational are our milestones. The final milestone is the end of the project: a working product or service, fully tested and operational, adding value to the company and a smile to the customer's face.

Each phase ends with a milestone. However, we can also have smaller milestones within each phase to mark our progress. If we compare a project to a seven-day road trip, each phase is one day, and the motel we reach that night is our milestone. But the places we stop for lunch and take rest stops each day are shorter breaks, milestones that let us know we are on the way to a successfully completed journey. So, we will break our project up into phases, and end each phase with a milestone.

The type of work we do in each phase or stage is guided by the planning: growing:using 1:10:100 rule from Chapter 2. In the first three stages, concept, analysis, and design, we are working on paper, planning the project and designing what we will make. We do more planning than you might expect because it reduces project cost, time, and risk. Staying in the "1" of the 1:10:100 process until the plans are excellent—not perfect, but excellent—gives us the best results at the lowest cost. The development stage is the growing, or "10," process of the 1:10:100 rule. This is when we actually do the work, make what we are making, and test it. When we are ready to deliver, we move into the last two project stages, transition to production and project close. These two stages are in the using, or "100," process of the 1:10:100 rule. Any earlier errors we find here will be costly to fix. Even when everything from the project is done well, the transition to production stage is challenging. Some companies call it the *storm period* because it is a challenging time for the project team and the customer as the new product or service is integrated into the customer department, and the customer has to learn to work in new ways.

Learning From Nature: The System Development Life Cycle

Every mammal goes through a series of stages in its life, completing an entire cycle. The biological terms for the stages are conception, implantation, gestation, development, maturity, old age, and death. Each stage has its gate, illustrated in Table 4-1.

Based on the biological life cycle, project managers and systems developers have created a system development life cycle, or SDLC. There are many versions and variations, but for now we will focus on the basics, the life cycle we will use in *Project Management Demystified*, shown in Table 4-2.

As you can see, the SDLC closely follows the biological life cycle. The key stages are at the beginning, where we can still fix problems at low cost because we are still in the "1" factor of the 1:10:100 rule. This table also differentiates the project life cycle from the product life cycle. A project is a process that creates a product. Therefore, the first five stages are the project life cycle stages. At that point, the project is over, and the product or service is in production. Operations and maintenance supports the relatively stable, mature production stage. Products and services have a stage beyond maturity, where they are bringing in less value or revenue. This is more of a concern for marketing than it is for project management. Therefore, we will focus our attention on the project stages.

However, we will address the entire life cycle, even though the project ends with transition to production and project close. There is real value in this. If we do not think about and understand production and maintenance, then we will design products and services that do not work. There were a number of project management systems that focused exclusively on analysis, design, and development, or even just on design and development. They produced systems that were unsupportable, and gave project management a very bad name.

In some ways, project managers are like parents. As parents, we try to give our children a happy childhood, which prepares them for adulthood. As project managers, we try to create a happy, energetic team. But that team, and our project, has a focus. And that focus is the mature productive stage of the product life cycle. Good analysis and design, followed by good development, leads to products and services that have high value and low cost of support. This is the production value of the product or service, and the ultimate value of the project.

Table 4-1   Stages and gates in mammalian life.

Stage of life	Process	Gate
Conception	The combining of genetic information from two different sources	Fertilization
Implantation	The biochemical matching of the fertilized egg with the genetic and biochemical makeup of the mother's womb	Implantation of healthy fertilized eggs, resulting in nourishment. Abandonment of unhealthy eggs, preserving resources
Gestation	Growth and development in a protected environment. Systems grow without having to function: Lungs grow without breathing; legs grow before walking	Birth
Development	Interaction between the organism and the environment. Learning	Achieving independence and adulthood. Able to function independently and contribute to the society and ecosystem
Adolescence	Final testing and proving of the skills of adulthood	Full, successful functioning as an adult. In human society, high school and college graduation and first job
Maturity	A long period of adding value to the ecosystem	Decline of ability to function
Old age	A period of reduced ability to function independently and increasing vulnerability	Death
Death	A process of life ending, learning and memory being lost, and the disposition of the components of the living system	The component parts return to the ecosystem to be incorporated into new beings. The purpose and value of the organism is fulfilled by a newly born replacement

Table 4-2   The system development life cycle (SDLC).

1:10:100 cost ratio	Stage	Process	Milestone
1	Concept	Combining ideas from customers with ideas from technology to produce new opportunities and solutions to problems	A written description of the concept and an initial plan for development
1	Analysis	Defining the purpose and goal of the project. Identifying all stakeholders and creating a complete list of functions and features	A project overview and related documents describing the value and functions of the system
1	Design	Complete planning of the technical specifications of the product or service and all project-related plans (time, cost, quality, risk, procurement)	A complete, approved product or service and project plan, approved funding, and a team ready to go
10	Development	Buying, building, integrating, customizing, configuring, testing, and improving the product or service. Creating documentation	A working product or service ready for use, with documentation
100	Transition to production	Final testing and product or service changes, customer testing, completion of documentation, training, and deployment	A working product or service in use, people trained, system in production

Table 4-2 The system development life cycle (SDLC) (*Continued*).

100	Project close	Post-project review. Measurement of value to customer. Final customer review and project report. Financial and legal closure and reassignment of team	Project completion with lessons learned
Project ends, product or service is in production			
100	Production and maintenance	A long period of adding value to the organization with the system in use. Its net value is its value minus the cost of support	Decline of ability to function as system becomes outmoded
100	Obsolescence	A period of reduced ability to function independently and increasing vulnerability	System failure or decommissioning
100	Decommissioning	The value of the system being separated from the system so that it can be replaced. Information being properly and securely transferred to the new system, appropriate disposal of components	The component parts discarded or recycled. Information transferred to the replacement system. The replacement system, built in its own life cycle, fulfilling the function formerly fulfilled by this system

Our projects, products, and services will follow this cycle. It is an inevitable natural process. If we want to succeed in project management, we should follow nature's lead. We should not skip any steps. We should plan for, and manage, each stage in a natural progression.

This is not to say that the process is completely rigid or locked down. Early implementations of the SDLC for computer systems in the 1960s tried this inflexible approach. It worked well for very large projects because it kept them from going out of control. But this approach proved to be excessively expensive, over-organized, and unrealistic for smaller projects and for projects where the project team was buying and assembling components, rather than building everything from scratch. As a result, we will be flexible in our approach. We will introduce this flexibility in Chapter 6 through the technique called the double waterfall.

Learning From Evolution

It is important to understand that nothing lives forever. When an animal or a person is mature and adding value to society, we tend to forget that the value that that animal or person offers is separate from the organism. There is a simple reason for this: in our society, we do not like to think about old age and death. But the fact is, we will all grow old and die, and the products and services we build will all become outmoded and break down. When they do, they leave a void. That void is the value the system used to have, that is, the need it used to fulfill.

That value and need is an element of the larger system: the business, society, or ecosystem to which the system contributed. In ecology, it is called the niche of the organism. In project management, defining that niche, that crucial set of functions the business needs, is the key to designing a new product or service to replace or improve upon the old system.

In nature, evolution fills this role. If the ecosystem has not changed, then evolutionary pressure will tend towards stability, and the children will be much like the parents. Nature will replace each organism with a similar organism in the next generation.

But if the ecosystem is changing, or if there is a missing part, evolutionary pressure causes adaptation through the preference for new variation. For example, on the Galapagos Islands, where Charles Darwin first studied, very few species of finches arrived by chance from the mainland. The finches differentiated widely, fulfilling many different roles usually held by many other birds and mammals with their evolution producing appropriate tools, such as specialized beaks, to allow them to function in their niches.

Nature: The Master Engineer

The living space of our whole planet is the ecosphere, the ball of water and air supported by earth and lighted by the sun, where life can flourish. It is a system, and the measures of quality in the system are: biomass, the total weight of life on earth; biodiversity, the number of different species; and ecosystem stability, slow and cyclical fluctuations in environmental factors.

When a problem arises, nature does not just fix the problem; it improves the whole system. Let us take a look at a case study.

About two billion years ago, the ecosphere had a major problem. Plants had been producing a waste product called oxygen for about two billion years, and it had increased to toxic levels. Too much oxygen kills plants. It also causes spontaneous fires around the entire planet, which create rapid fluctuations in temperature. To bring the ecosphere back into balance, it was necessary to develop a better way of getting rid of that toxic waste product: oxygen.

The primary component of the niche that needed to be filled could be stated as, "A new organism is needed to use up oxygen." But that one feature was not a full specification. What was the best thing to do with the oxygen? How about if it was combined with carbon, to create carbon dioxide? Plants like carbon dioxide. But where will these new creatures get the carbon? Well, they could eat plants. But, to eat enough plants, they will need to be able to run around. And if they eat plants, they will get nitrogen as well as carbon. What can they do with the nitrogen? Mix it with other chemicals and dump it out the back.

And so, a specification was born. Breathe in oxygen, exhale carbon dioxide. Run around and eat plants. And dump fertilizer out the back. Animals evolved. (Congratulations, you were part of the solution.) The solution worked. With animals around, the excess oxygen was used up steadily, and massive fires became rare.

But this solution did much more than solve the basic problem of eliminating excess oxygen. It had a lot of what executives like to call added value. According to the three key measures of value in the ecosphere:

- Biomass increased many thousand-fold. The fertilizer dumped by the animals became soil, nourishing the growth of both plants and animals.
- Biodiversity increased rapidly. Plants evolved ways of avoiding being eaten, and ways of taking advantage of parts being eaten (such as pollination of flowers and spreading of seeds through edible fruit). Animals diversified as they adapted to the changes in plants.
- Stability increased. The excess accumulated oxygen decreased, and the new stable level of oxygen was optimized for both plants and animals. The biosphere also got a new, higher level of atmospheric carbon dioxide and a more stable global temperature.

Designing and Delivering Products and Services That Add Maximum Value

What can we learn from nature's example? In planning a system, define the niche. Look at all the inputs and outputs, and define functions that will add value to the business as a whole in important ways. It is not enough just to solve one problem.

Likewise, we must design and build our products and services to fit in with the whole organization (or our customers) and provide many benefits, many kinds of value.

A Closer Look at the Life Cycle

The project life cycle is important enough that we have devoted Part Two of *Project Management Demystified* to it with one chapter for each stage. Here, we take a closer look at the stages and gates of the project and product life cycles.

STAGES OF THE LIFE CYCLE

Here are the stages of the SDLC that we will explore more thoroughly in Part Two.

- *The concept stage.* Not every bright idea is a good idea. The concept stage is our chance to evaluate every bright idea. When we do, we can discard the ones that will not work early, saving time and money. We create a context diagram, which illustrates the role of the new product or service in our company. We can create a basic plan for the good ideas, and use that plan to explain our ideas, build support for the project, and secure funding. The gate at the end of the concept stage is used to stop bad ideas from becoming projects that waste money. We want and expect many ideas to be cancelled at the end of the concept stage, and only projects with real value to move forward.
- *The analysis stage.* This stage is all about the customer and the stakeholders. We seek to define what they want at all levels. We document the purpose and value of the system, the goals of the system, and a detailed description of functions and features. We add details to the context diagram. We review the project plans with all stakeholders,

defining what the product or service will or will not do. We complete
the stage by getting a commitment to funding and support for the
project.

- *The design stage.* We design the product or service, and also the project, the process that will create the product or service. We create a plan
that addresses all nine areas of project management knowledge to our
project and specifies how we will manage each of them throughout the
project. When the design stage is complete, we have approval to go
ahead, and we begin to build the system.
- *The development stage.* We create the product or service. This involves
building, buying, integrating, customizing, and configuring components. We write the documentation. We test each component and the
whole system, and fix problems as we find them. The key job of the
project manager is tracking the project to the plan, ensuring that all
work is being done on time and on budget. This includes adjusting
the product and project plans with change control, as needed, and
managing unexpected events through risk management.
- *The transition to production stage.* Every system, no matter how well
designed, built, and tested, encounters surprises when it hits the real
world. The transition to production stage is similar to our first job
after high school or college. When we graduated, we thought we were
ready for the real world. But our first job teaches us what we really
need to know. The same is true with the products and services we
create. The pilot test and the user's first encounter with the system is
sometimes called the storm period. So, in the transition to production
stage, we get ready for the storm. We finish all testing and documentation. The storm starts when we deliver the product or service. We
provide training and deploy the system. As project managers, we
track everything daily and have teams ready to solve problems as
soon as they appear.
- *Project close.* At this point, the project is over, and the productive
period of the life of the product or service we created begins. As project
managers, we finalize the details. We evaluate project results and processes, and prepare a lessons learned document. We ensure financial
and legal closure. The project team may stay together for a new
project, or may be reassigned. Either way, we make sure to take care
of our people.
- *The production and maintenance stage.* At this point, the project is over,
and the ongoing production life of the product or service continues for
a number of years. The product or service is adding value—making
money, helping the organization succeed, or making a customer happy.

And it is being maintained and supported. If we did our job well designing the system and delivering on the project, the value is high, and the time and cost for maintenance is low. Standard operating procedures (SOP) are in place for maintenance and support, and we also occasionally enhance or upgrade the system to meet new needs or to adjust to changes in the production environment.

- *The obsolescence stage.* At some point, the annual net value of the system drops. This will happen sooner if maintenance is poor. When it happens, we are faced with a choice: we can perform a major upgrade, hoping to enhance value and performance; we can discard the system and replace it; we can live with the reduced revenue or benefit; or we can get out of the business of providing this product or service altogether. Some companies make a living supporting legacy systems. For example, there is still at least one company that sells vacuum tubes for old televisions and stereo systems. Why? Because there is still a market, and there is no competition. The challenge of this stage is to keep maintenance costs low, and to find a graceful way to migrate from the old system to its eventual replacement.

- *The decommissioning stage.* Too often, we just let old systems die. This is costly and risky. The first cost is the opportunity cost: How much money could we have made if we had created a new system in time to provide continuity of service? Another cost is in the loss of customers and reputation. Another lies in the loss of the value of the knowledge contained within the old system. Risk lies in the potential theft of valuable information from improperly decommissioned systems. Proper decommissioning prevents all of these costs and risks. We identify the date by which the old system will fail, and we launch a new project to deliver a new product or service before that date. We plan for the transfer of information from the old system to the new one. We define safe, appropriate, and perhaps profitable ways of decommissioning the old equipment. We test the new system in parallel with the old one, to ensure that the new system produces results as good as, or better than, the old one before the changeover. After the changeover, we implement the decommissioning plan, properly and securely disposing of the parts of the old system.

These stages compose a complete cycle, from nothing, through a valuable life, and back to nothing. Planning and executing well the stages through project close is the job of a project manager. Succeeding means adding significant value to our company and our society in many ways through the products and services we create.

THE GATES

Each stage ends with a gate. The gate is a process of evaluation that will end with approval if all goes well. However, it is not a rubber stamp. The project team, the customer, other stakeholders, and perhaps outside experts should perform a genuine evaluation of the results to date. At a gate, there are three possible outcomes:

- If the results are good, then we move ahead to the next stage.
- If there are minor problems, the project team fixes them, and we move ahead to the next stage.
- If there are major questions or doubts, then the project stakeholders, led by the project sponsor, re-evaluate the project. It may need a major overhaul, or it may need to be cancelled.

KEY POINT

Evaluate One Stage Before Starting the Next
As we approach a gate, we focus on working with the customer to get through the gate well. We should have the team do little or no work on the next stage until we are through the gate, until the prior stage is approved. Otherwise, we risk violating the 1:10:100 rule; we risk designing or developing the wrong product, or a product with major flaws.

In going through a gate it is important to keep a same-side focus with all project stakeholders. Their critique of the correctness of the project work to date, and their re-evaluation of project value, is not a criticism of you, your work, or your team. Rather, it is a supportive process that ensures that the team and the customer are still on the same page. Sometimes, needs change, and project changes are required in response. Sometimes, misunderstandings are discovered. Leave your ego at the door, and be ready to learn from and work with your customers.

Going through a gate is a process that takes time. Table 4-3 shows the deliverables and steps for each gate.

As we mentioned above, it is thoroughly appropriate to cancel a project at the gate at the end of the concept stage. We hope that any project that makes it through the concept stage will succeed. However, if we see that a project will never deliver value greater than cost, we should stop before too much money is wasted. Therefore it can be appropriate to end a project at any gate.

Table 4-3　Deliverables and steps for each gate.

Stage of which the gate is the end	Deliverable	Evaluation steps
Concept	Brief plan	Is there support for the concept? Does the plan offer enough value? Does the approach fit the company?
	Initial cost estimate	Are costs in line with value and with available resources?
	Initial time estimate	Are the delivery date and staff allocations useful to the company?
	Risk assessment	Is the overall level of risk acceptable?
Analysis	Project overview	Is there support for the project? Does value exceed cost? Is the schedule acceptable?
	Product or service specification	Does this meet the customer's needs? Is it what they want?
	Context diagram	Will the new product or service fit into the company?
	List of stakeholders and roles	Is everyone included? Will everyone sign on?
	Risk plan	Have all major risks been identified? Are stakeholders confident risk can be managed and the team can succeed?
Design	Detailed work plan and schedule	Is the schedule acceptable? Are resources available to do the work?
	Detail budget	Is cost acceptable?
	Detailed risk plan	Have all risks been identified? Are risks, mitigation plans, and contingency plans acceptable?
	Quality plan	Is quality plan acceptable?

Table 4-3   Deliverables and steps for each gate (*Continued*).

Development	The product or service, tested and ready to use	Does the product or service meet all specifications? Are customers confident of value and success?
	Technical and user documentation	Are documents complete and correct? Do they meet customer needs?
	Delivery or installation plan	Is the plan for delivery or installation (during the transition stage) acceptable to the customer?
Transition	A fully operational, documented, supported product or service	Is everything working to the customer's satisfaction? Are all problems resolved, or accepted for resolution under customer management?
Close	Legal and financial closure	Are all contracts completed and documented? Are all invoices paid?
	Project lessons learned	Has everyone learned all they need to learn to do a better job next time?

SOMETHING EXTRA

The Checkpoint

There is a kind of marathon for horses called an endurance ride. Horses and riders go day and night for five days to cover hundreds of miles. There are frequent checkpoints. At every checkpoint, a veterinarian checks your horse. If the horse is overstrained, you are out. Why? Because winning is not everything. Staying healthy and winning means a lot.

Just the same, when your project comes to a gate, and the customer is evaluating your deliverables, you should evaluate your team. How are they holding up? Do they need anything from simple praise to new tools to a new team member with special expertise? And let the team do a check up on you and the project. Is there anything you could do to do a better job? How are they feeling about the project?

In doing this, you take care of the team, the project, and also yourself.

Your Project for Learning

Review your project for learning. Make a rough sketch of the stages of your project. Answer these questions:

- What work will you do during each stage of the project?
- Exactly what will you deliver at the end of each stage?
- Who will approve each stage? Do not forget to include yourself.
- What do you hope to learn at each stage?
- What do you hope to have at the end of the project? Can you picture it clearly now?

If you need to know more about the stages in order to answer these questions, go ahead and read Part Two.

Questions for Learning

In your own words:

- I believe that the stages of human and animal life are a good model for projects. Do you agree or disagree? Why?
- Think of a project that failed or ran into trouble. Can you identify a step that was missed, or not done well?
- Think of a project that went well. Can you describe the work done in each stage?
- Explain why customer review is essential at each gate.
- You are talking to your team. They are anxious about an upcoming gate. No one is sure the project is acceptable to the customer. Explain to your team why the review is good, even if it means the project may have major changes, or may be cancelled altogether.

PART TWO

A Project, Start to Finish

Processes and Tools for the Project Life Cycle

In Part Two we give you everything you need to succeed in each stage of the project life cycle. We introduced the cycle and explained its value in Chapter 4. Now, let us look at the beginning and end of each stage.

- *The concept stage* begins with a bright idea. If the idea is a good one, we define project goals and move on to the analysis stage. If the project is not worth doing, the gate at the end of the concept stage is our chance to abandon the project before we waste time and money.
- *The analysis stage* begins with a general outline of project goals and scope. We fully develop the definition of the output of the project: the

detailed requirements for the product, service, system, or changes to a system that we will deliver when the project ends. The analysis stage ends with a full definition of project value and goals.

- *The design stage* can start when we know all the requirements for what we are making. Then we plan how to make it, that is, we create the project management plan. And the team defines exactly what we are making, that is, the product or service specification. The design stage ends when all plans, including the design specification, the project schedule, the budget, the teamwork and communications, the quality, and the risk plans are all in place. If they are approved, we go through the gate into the development stage.

- *The development stage* is the first part of the life cycle where we are doing, rather than planning. As a result, we are in the "10" of the 1:10:100 rule. All of our earlier planning pays off now. The team does the work necessary to create the product or services. We, as project managers, track the work against the schedule, budget, quality plan, and risk plan. We prevent problems and keep things on track. At the end of the development stage, we have a high-quality product or service, tested and ready for the customer.

- *The transition to production stage* is the time when we deliver the product or service to the customer. At the beginning, the product or service is ready, and so is the customer. Or at least we hope so. At the end, the customer is using the product or service, it is adding value, and it is time to close the project.

- *Project close* is the final stage where we take care of legal and financial closure, ensure that the team is properly reassigned, and evaluate the project and its results. Project close is counted as a separate phase because it can continue after the product or service is delivered to the customer. However, it has been included in Chapter 9, as the processes are quite short.

The project moves ahead as each stage feeds into the next. However, it is important to realize that gates serve a genuine function. We cannot assume a project should go ahead. If our initial evaluation was wrong, or if the situation changes, then the project may be of no value, or of less value than the cost, to the customer. In that case, it is best to cancel the project. Of course, the sooner the project is cancelled, the better, because it means less wasted time and money. That is why there are three gates during the planning stage.

Project cancellation does not mean failure for the manager or the team. Failure in business comes from wasting time or money. If the situation changes and the project is not needed, it is better to stop sooner, so that we do not waste further money. This can be hard to do if the team, the customer, and others are invested in the project. Gates help. Each gate is a chance to ask: What is best for the company right now?

But let us turn our attention to success. In Chapter 2 we said that a process can succeed if we have the right resources and tools. The following chapters define everything we need to succeed in each stage of the project. Each stage is thought of as a process with a beginning, a middle, and an end. And, for each stage, we provide:

- *Key points,* where we discuss the most important issues for each stage.
- *Resources,* where we discuss what you need to complete the stage.
- *Roles,* where we define who does what.
- *Input,* where we describe the information and things that we have at the start of the stage. From the second stage on, the inputs of each stage are the outputs of the prior stage, plus the approval given at the gate.
- *Process,* the work the project manager and the team do during the stage.
- *Output,* the end results of the stage that go through the gate.
- *Key tools* for the stage, including forms, templates, and processes.
- *Key concepts* for the stage, a review of what matters most for you, your team, and your customer.
- *Our case study,* building a home theater system, illustrates important ideas and tools from each stage.
- *Your project for learning,* where you apply the tools to your project, learn the tools, and move your project towards success.
- *Questions for learning.*

CHAPTER 5

Concept: A Good Idea Can Be a Bad Project

A project begins with an idea. Before we go any further, we should make sure that it is a good idea.

People feel positive about bright ideas. However, there are a lot of bright ideas that are not good ideas, or are not right for a particular company at a given time. So the first stage of a project is a winnowing process. In the concept stage, we work as a team to take bright ideas and make them into really good ideas. And then we separate the good ideas from the bright ideas that are really not worth pursuing.

As people come up with bright ideas and hear about things that work at other companies, determining what projects are really worth doing can be a challenge. If you work with computers, you may hear that everyone else is going wireless, but that does not mean that right now is the best time to make expensive changes to your computer network. The best approach would be to ask: In what locations are the cost savings greatest? At those locations, are there any capacity, security, reliability, or other issues that would be reasons not to go ahead? What is the most beneficial place to install our first wireless network, and how quickly can we grow? Evaluating the actual net benefit of ideas before we launch projects is what the concept stage is all about.

The concept stage is not just about ideas; it is also about people. We work to ensure that everyone who should know about the idea hears it, evaluates it, and improves it. That way, there are many people who can point out flaws in an idea and stop us from spending time and money on a project that will not work. Even more importantly, if the idea is a good one, it will be well defined and have a lot of support from many sponsors and champions by the end of the concept stage.

In This Chapter

- Key points for the concept stage
- Resources for the concept stage
- Roles in the concept stage
- Inputs for the concept stage
- The process of the concept stage
- Outputs of the concept stage
- Key tools for the concept stage
- Key concepts for the concept stage
- Our case study: Is it time for home theater?
- Your project for learning
- Questions for learning

Key Points for the Concept Stage

The key points we want to look at for the concept stage are:

- Project work vs. project management
- Brainstorming to improve ideas as a team
- Winnowing to select the best ideas
- Evaluation by stakeholders
- Defining project scope

PROJECT WORK VS. PROJECT MANAGEMENT

In project management, we are planning and managing the work of the project. What exactly are we managing? Stage by stage, what work is done on a project, excluding project management? Table 5-1 answers that question. Table 5-1 illustrates several key points about requirements gathering and project management:

- The deliverable of each step is the starting point for the next step. Therefore, if each step is done well, the next step can succeed.
- Good work on a later step cannot always find and fix problems due to poor work on an earlier step. For example, it is possible to design a system exactly to the customer requirements without ever discovering that the customer requirements are wrong to begin with. Then we build and test the design. When we deliver, we have got a working system that does not do what the customer wants and needs. In fact, this happens all too often.

Table 5-1   The work of the project, by stage, with deliverables.

Stage	Task (job to be done)	Deliverable (document or result)
Concept	Get an idea of what the customer wants and why	Goal and purpose
Analysis	Learn exactly what the customer wants	Requirements specification
Design	Make a picture of a solution that will give the customers what they want	Design specification
Development	Make the product or service the customer wants and test it	Product or service
Transition to production	Give the product to the customer and make sure it works	Working supported product or service
Project close	Formal close of financial and legal issues, reassignment of team	Project lessons learned
The project ends here		
Production	A product or service providing value greater than its cost operating in the production environment	Value each year of operation

- When the work is done well, there is a logical progression. The customers define value in general, and then tell us what features will be valuable. We design a product or service with those features. We build the product or service, and test it to make sure the features work. We give it to the customers and make sure it works as planned. The customers use it, and receive the value they asked for in the first place.
- Although there is a logical progression, each step is a creative response to the inputs, and is not directly derived from them. A custom-designed house for a family of four does not have four rooms. It has the rooms necessary to give the owners of the house what they want, whether that is six rooms, or ten, or more. On every project, the design must provide all of the functions the user has specified, and also meet other requirements, but the design is its own creative product as well.
- Project management guides this entire process, ensures quality, manages time and cost, and clears the way by reducing risk. Within project management specific areas of knowledge have specific functions. Each one applies in every stage.

  - Scope management defines the big picture, creating the space in which this detailed specification can be created and, if necessary, modified through change control.
  - Quality management ensures that the specification is accurate, and then ensures that the system meets or exceeds the specification.
  - Communications management helps ensure that the specification is complete and accurate, and also keeps customer and stakeholder expectations in line with specifications.
  - Human resources management supports the team in doing the work.
  - Procurement management helps with cost control, reduces risk, and extends the team outside the borders of the company.
  - Project integration management ties all of this together by ensuring that we do all the work of project management appropriately, so that the project will succeed.

In the concept stage, it can be hard to separate project work from project management. As we define the goal and value, we are both defining the product or service itself, and also defining project scope. In analysis, there is some division of the work of the project, requirements specification, from the work of project management, communications and scope specification.

However, once we reach the design stage, then there is a clear separation of the work to be done, design specification, and the job of managing that work, project management. The project management aspect of the design stage is planning the work of the rest of the project. In development and transition to production, project management is quite distinct from project work. We track and guide the work according to the project plan we created during design.

The System Development Life Cycle (SDLC) is sometimes called the waterfall because, as we move down through one gate to the next stage, it is like going over a waterfall—we cannot go back up. As our team carries the work downstream, finishing one stage and starting the next, we chart the course ahead and make sure the boat does not get swamped and sink, or go off course and down the wrong river.

BRAINSTORMING AND WINNOWING

The most important work of the concept stage is to define the project goal and to make sure it is worth pursuing. A concept stage that results in the rejection of an idea and the cancellation of a project is a success. Far too many projects that are not feasible or cannot show a return greater than cost are started, and then money is spent on a project with no real value. Other projects start without a clear definition, and what is ultimately delivered does not work. A well-run concept stage prevents these errors using two processes: brainstorming and winnowing.

We use *brainstorming* to get everyone involved to improve the bright idea and make it better. But then we need to also spend time *winnowing*, eliminating the dirt while leaving the gold dust behind. In winnowing, we may find *project killers,* facts that clearly and obviously show that a project will not work or will not be worth doing.

Brainstorming to improve ideas as a team

Brainstorming is important because each person brings a different perspective, a different set of issues, and different knowledge to a project. Maybe I have a great idea, but think that one part of it is too expensive. Meanwhile, you did not know the idea was worth doing at our company, but you know an easy, inexpensive way of getting what we need. Separately, we would never think of doing the project. Together, we realize that we can do it, and that it will make a real difference for our company's success.

Brainstorming has other values as well:

- When people take enough time to talk things through, we really get onto the same page. There is much less chance of launching a project based on a misunderstanding of what we are making.
- We can enhance the value of what we are making by bringing in more good ideas in the details.
- Several people may think something is a good idea, but one person may know why it will not work. By including everyone early, we discover project-killers early.

For a good brainstorming process, it is essential to include everyone, though not necessarily all in one meeting. We do this through a process called *stakeholder identification*, where we find everyone who might care about a project or the product we are thinking of making. Once we find the stakeholders, we make sure to include them in the brainstorming and winnowing processes.

Winnowing to select the best ideas

CAUTION

Brainstorm Before Winnowing
It is essential to brainstorm about an idea before putting it through the winnowing process. Otherwise, a good idea may be thrown out because it looks like it will not work. But actually, if we had thought it through a bit more, we would see that the idea could be implemented.

Once we have identified all stakeholders for a potential project and made an idea as good as we can by brainstorming, it is time for winnowing. To put it simply, the idea is as good as it can be. Now, is it good enough to assign the resources and launch a project to make it real? In winnowing, a project moves out of the concept stage and forward into the analysis stage if:

- We are as sure as we can be that there are no project-killers.
- All stakeholders are committed to supporting the project.
- The projected value exceeds projected cost.
- This project is a better use of our resources than any other activity we could do with the time and money it will take.

The first three points can be resolved by looking at the project all by itself. To address the last point we may have to compare several projects that are under consideration, because we may be able to do one or two of them, but not all of them. Also, we have to consider the possibility of doing no projects at all, and continuing with production work as it is now. We evaluate all of these choices and decide what projects to start, if any.

SOMETHING EXTRA

Iteration of Brainstorming and Winnowing
We can apply the principle of iteration to brainstorming and winnowing. For example, we can brainstorm ways to increase marketing and come up with several projects. Then we pull stakeholders together to look for project-killers, winnowing out the worst ideas. Then we brainstorm again, improving the remaining ideas. Then we winnow again, deciding which one or two ideas are best for the company's mission, available resources, and current situation.

EVALUATION BY STAKEHOLDERS

Who should evaluate a bright idea? This is a key question for the concept stage. Using a tool called the *context diagram* we will identify all stakeholders for the project. A stakeholder is anyone who is affected by the project process or by the resulting product or service. Stakeholders are the natural people to evaluate an idea that might become a project. Each stakeholder will evaluate the benefit, cost, and feasibility of the project from his or her own perspective, relating to the idea from the view of the system he or she maintains that will be changed by the new product or service, or by the work of the project itself.

A key stakeholder is a stakeholder who has a central role in the project. The product or service that he or she supports or uses will be affected by the project and its new product or service. The customer is always a key stakeholder, and there are others as well. The context diagram, which we will introduce in this chapter, is an excellent tool for identifying stakeholders. Stakeholders who have only a relatively small connection to the project are called peripheral stakeholders. For a full description of the process of identifying stakeholders and working with them, see Chapter 12.

Sometimes, we cannot actually work directly with primary stakeholders. In that case, we identify one or more customer representatives. A customer representative is a person who is able and willing to represent the customer accurately. The customer representative may end up working full time on a medium-sized project, and a large project may have several customer representatives. If the customers are internal to your company, then the customer representatives might be one person, perhaps a business analyst, from each group that will use the new system. If the customers are external businesses or consumers, then they may be represented by your company's marketing division.

EXERCISE

Third Generation Cell Phones

The third generation (3G) cellular telephone networks that started coming out in 2002 are able to support transport of visual images. How could this be turned into new services for customers?

An innovative cellular telephone company in Japan thought of including a digital camera in the cellular telephone. People could take photos and instantly send them to others. Before the expensive steps of designing and manufacturing these phones began, marketing experts, acting as customer representatives, evaluated the idea. They probably conducted surveys and ran focus groups, which are marketing techniques for turning customers into customer representatives.

The idea is working well in Japan, where the nation's second-largest cellular telephone company had a rapid growth spurt and was gaining market share in the summer of 2002.

Suppose someone said to you: Would this work in the USA? Should we try to sell cell phones with digital cameras here?

How would you go about answering that question? Who would represent the customers?

DEFINING PROJECT SCOPE

The last key point in the concept stage is scope definition. We often speak of scoping out a job, or the scope of a project, but we rarely define the term precisely. The *scope* of a project is a high-level description of what is included and excluded in the resulting product or system, and in the process of completing the project. Defining the scope requires identifying all key stakeholders and getting their input. The key tools we use for scoping out a project are the idea of inclusions and exclusions, the scope definition statement, the context diagram, and the project overview document. You will learn to use all of these in this chapter.

Resources for the Concept Stage

The time and money spent on the concept stage of a project should be relatively small compared to the potential project cost. The effort could be as little as one business analyst or project manager, working part or full time, for several weeks, and meeting with stakeholders when they are available. However, for a project that might cost $10 million or more, spending up to a few hundred thousand dollars on the concept stage is quite reasonable. If an idea shows itself to be unworkable early in the stage, we can save time and money by shelving the idea before it is fully developed. If the idea looks promising, then all the effort put into the concept stage is worth it. It will pay off due to the 1:10:100 rule. Projects with a clearly defined goal and early stakeholder agreement have a much higher chance of success.

QUICK TIP

Does Every Project Need a Concept Stage?
Some projects have to happen. For example, an audit is a project, but an audit department may be legally required to perform a particular audit. If the project has to happen, is there any need for a concept stage? Well, yes and no. It is certainly the case that the project will happen, that it will not be cancelled. Nonetheless, it is still a good idea to get key stakeholders on board early and make sure that they all understand what the project is doing and why it is happening. In this type of situation, the concept stage can be rolled into the analysis stage. But it might be better to have a formal sign-on at the end of the concept stage where each stakeholder identifies the resources the project will need and commits to making them available as the project progresses.

Roles in the Concept Stage

As the project begins, it is important to create the team and gather supporters rapidly in the concept stage. It is especially important to contact those who are potentially opposed and those who are doubtful. If we reach them early on and let them know that we want their involvement and input, then we can work more effectively with their resistance later on. There is one exception to this. If there is someone who is habitually opposed, who is going to reject the new idea without consideration, then do not bring that person in until the idea is clarified and you have created a communications approach that is likely to work.

Here are the roles people may have during the concept stage:

- *Project manager.* This is you, the primary person in the concept stage. For small and even medium-sized projects, you will possibly be the only person putting in a substantial amount of time. Everyone else may be involved only through meetings and communication with you. Whatever your job title might be, your role on the project is project manager. For small to medium-sized projects, a business analyst who knows customer needs and appropriate technology can do an excellent job managing the concept stage. For larger projects, a skilled technology person might be more appropriate.

- *Project sponsor.* A project sponsor is an executive who is willing to back the project, secure funding, ensure staffing, and promote the idea. No project can succeed without one. Some ideas have support from the beginning, or may even come from, or through, a sponsor. Otherwise, you will need to find a sponsor during the concept stage, or decide not to launch the project. The sponsor should have the commitment and resources to provide support for the project, as described in Chapter 12.

- *The customer(s).* The customers, whether internal or external, are our primary stakeholders. We need to make sure that our idea will really benefit them when it becomes a product or service, and maximize that benefit. We need to address the customer at multiple levels. In business, we address the executive, managerial, and production levels. For consumers, we address perceived value, real value, and resistance. We may need to distinguish the buyer from the user, and engage in marketing studies. When we are creating a new or modified product or service for consumers or to sell to many businesses, we will need to use customer representatives. Someone in our company's marketing department can act as a customer representative or provide representatives through focus groups.

- *Key stakeholders and the more important peripheral stakeholders.* We do not need to find all of the stakeholders during the concept stage, but we do need to find all of the important stakeholders. Which ones are important? Anyone who might be able to tell us about a project-killer, and anyone who can improve the idea significantly or add to our understanding of its value significantly. When we finish the concept stage, we should be able to say that the idea is basically sound and does not need major changes, that the project will work, and that everyone who will be heavily involved in the project supports it. Other stakeholders, the peripheral stakeholders who will have very little involvement with the project, can be brought in during the analysis phase.

- *Vendor sales representatives and pre-sales technical staff.* Often, the idea we are evaluating comes from a vendor, and consists of bringing that vendor's product or service into our company, with or without customization. In that case, the vendor's sales representative and pre-sales technical staff are key participants in the concept stage. Their knowledge of the product or service is crucial. But remember, they cannot know if the product or service is a good fit for our company, which is the question we must answer.
- *Technical experts.* A variety of technical experts, internal and external, should be consulted during the concept stage. Often, these consultations are brief and cost nothing, but it can also be appropriate to hire an expert to evaluate or improve an idea. External experts include the vendor's pre-sales technical staff and also independent experts.
- *Prior customers or users.* If you are considering buying a vendor's product or service, ensure that prior customers are satisfied with both the product or service and the vendor. If you are planning to implement a new technology yourself, try to find other companies in your industry that have already implemented the technology for the purpose you intend. Also look for companies that have already launched projects and are ahead of you in the implementation process. If you can learn from their mistakes, then your chance of success is higher.

Later in this chapter we introduce the context diagram, an excellent tool for identifying stakeholders.

SOMETHING EXTRA

Defining Roles and Reporting Structure

If your project team and its customer are all in one department, then the sponsor is likely to be your boss, or your boss's boss. But if you work in one department, say, information technology, and are delivering a new product, say, a computer network, for use by another department, then the sponsor may be on the customer side. In your communications plan, you will need to identify three separate sets of relationships among project stakeholders: The corporate reporting structure that will be in place before, during, and after the project; the project status reporting structure during the project; and the project communications network, which is not about reporting results, but rather about providing information so that everyone has what they need to get the job done.

Inputs for the Concept Stage

The inputs of the concept stage include:

- *The bright idea.* A written statement, anywhere from a paragraph to a few pages, defining the idea to be evaluated.
- *The person or people offering the idea.* It is important to know where the idea came from. Ideas will be evaluated differently depending on the expertise of their source. Is the source of the idea a customer, a marketing person, or someone on the technical side? Did the idea arise in consultation among people from different groups? Does the source of the idea know and understand your company? Or is the idea being promoted by a vendor? Might the source of the idea have a bias about its value or self-interested reasons for promoting it?
- *Information about similar past projects or proposals.* If work has been done to evaluate or create this product or service in the past, at your company or elsewhere, you will want to know about it.
- *A knowledge of your customer and market.* The idea must bring value, either by being profitable or by reducing costs. Therefore, the concept stage team must have access to expertise, reports, and research capability that can define what will really benefit the customer.
- *A knowledge of your own organization.* Part of the evaluation in the concept stage is the determination of whether the idea is appropriate to your organization. There are many bright ideas that are not right for your company, or not right for it right now. Therefore, you need access to value, vision, and mission statements, as well as development programs, initiatives, and goals. It is also good to have a working knowledge of what kinds of projects have succeeded and faltered in your company in the past, and why.

In some organizations, the mission, vision, and values of the whole company and the division are articulated and defined in writing. If that is the case, and if those written statements accurately reflect the goals and activities of the company, then seeing if the new idea fits with the goals of the company is relatively easy. If an organization does not have such written statements, then it will be necessary to interview influential executives to determine if the idea has merit, and if the project can succeed in the corporate environment. If the organizational mission, vision, and value statements are not adhered to, then it will be necessary to respond to the realities of the corporation more than to the written statements.

The Process of the Concept Stage

The work to be done in the concept stage can be broken down into these steps:

1. Write down the idea.
2. Create a context diagram.
3. Identify stakeholders and modify the context diagram (iterative).
4. Hold brainstorming sessions to refine or redefine the idea and modify the context diagram (iterative).
5. Revise the context diagram and draft the scope statement and project overview.
6. Hold brainstorming and decision meetings to evaluate the idea (iterative).
7. Prepare the end-of-stage scope statement, project overview, and context diagram.
8. Prepare the end-of-stage proposal. If the proposal is for continuing the project, prepare a budget for the analysis and design stages.
9. The gate at the end of the concept stage: Hold formal meetings to decide if the project should be dropped, or should move ahead into the analysis stage.

Any step marked iterative may be repeated more than once in a cyclical fashion. Let us look at each of these steps in greater detail.

WRITE DOWN THE IDEA

It has been said that any idea that will sell can be explained on a cocktail napkin. Another way of thinking of this is that, if you want to sell an idea, you had better be able to explain it on a cocktail napkin and make it exciting. Entrepreneurial executives and investors want to know what it is, and why it will make a difference. The focus should be on customers and value.

If the initial idea is technical, it will take a good deal of work to define the business value of the idea. If the initial idea is from the business or marketing side, it may take quite a bit of work to determine technical feasibility. In either case, the project overview will help a great deal in this process, and the brainstorming processes will have everyone helping you improve the idea before it is evaluated.

We can create shorter documents, including a one-page executive summary, from the project overview. The project overview is the core of all the other documents, such as task lists, budgets, schedules, and risk plans, that we will create if the project goes ahead.

CREATE A CONTEXT DIAGRAM

The context diagram, described below, is the most important tool of the concept stage. It shows how this idea fits into your company and into the systems used by your customers. In creating the first draft of the context diagram, your own best idea is good enough. That picture will identify potential stakeholders. You can contact them, and have them correct the diagram and help you identify other stakeholders. The context diagram will also begin to define the inclusions and exclusions for the product or service you are proposing.

IDENTIFY STAKEHOLDERS AND MODIFY THE CONTEXT DIAGRAM (ITERATIVE)

The context diagram will contain the names of customers, systems, and organizations that will use or be affected by the new product or service. Looking at those customers, systems, and organizations, ask who is responsible for them and who knows most about them. Explain to each of them the idea on which you are working. Ask if they are the right person. If they are, then have them help you refine and improve the idea. Whether the person you are speaking to is the right person or not, ask who else you should talk to. Find and talk to all the right people. As you do this, revise the context diagram and build a list of stakeholders.

HOLD BRAINSTORMING SESSIONS TO REFINE OR REDEFINE THE IDEA AND MODIFY THE CONTEXT DIAGRAM (ITERATIVE)

As you talk to people, you may find that the idea is good and workable, or that it does not seem to be. Or you may find that it is not clearly defined yet. In any case, prepare and hold a brainstorming session. During the session, the idea may change, perhaps almost beyond recognition, or give birth to other ideas. That is exactly what should happen. In brainstorming, the goal is not to accept or reject the idea, but to improve or transform the idea, so that the best idea the team can come up with can be defined and evaluated in the following steps.

REVISE THE CONTEXT DIAGRAM AND DRAFT THE SCOPE STATEMENT AND PROJECT OVERVIEW

I hope you took good notes during the brainstorming session. Now is the time to incorporate all of those notes into a revised and more detailed context diagram. You will also draft a scope statement and begin creating the project overview. All of these tools are described below.

HOLD BRAINSTORMING AND DECISION MEETINGS TO EVALUATE THE IDEA (ITERATIVE)

At the next set of meetings, you will present the ideas for improvement, but also for evaluation. Early in the session(s), get feedback as to whether people think the ideas are as good as they can be. When they are, begin to address the question of whether the idea is valuable enough to develop into a full-blown project. Methods for early cost and time estimation are given in Chapter 10.

PREPARE THE END-OF-STAGE SCOPE STATEMENT, PROJECT OVERVIEW, AND CONCEPT DIAGRAM

Write up the results of the set of meetings you just finished. If you are going to propose that the project move ahead, then take the time to do this carefully. Every hour of good work now goes a long way to preventing project disaster later. On the other hand, if you are going to propose shelving the project for later or canceling it, then a clear write-up without excessive detail is sufficient. It is important that your write-up be clear because this idea may be reconsidered or a similar idea may be proposed in the future, and you will want people to be able to draw on your work when performing future evaluations.

If a vendor's product, system, or service is part of your proposal, include their materials in your package. However, keep the focus on the value to your company and your customers.

PREPARE THE END-OF-STAGE PROPOSAL. IF THE PROPOSAL IS FOR CONTINUING THE PROJECT, PREPARE A BUDGET FOR THE ANALYSIS AND DESIGN STAGES

At this point, as project manager, you are ready to present your company with one of the following four recommendations:

- Go ahead with the project, approving a schedule and budget for the analysis stage, and perhaps also the design stage and the entire project.
- Continue further research in the concept stage.
- Shelve the project until a future date, or until a particular future event, when it should be re-evaluated. (For example, you might recommend waiting until another project is complete, and specialists on your staff have more time, and have the company re-evaluate it at that time.)
- Cancel the project, either because it will not work, because it will not add value to the company, or because it cannot be completed within a reasonable time and cost.

If you are proposing that the project move ahead, then it is best to prepare all the documentation necessary for an effective project launch. A thorough scope statement and initial project overview, accompanied by a clear context diagram, are invaluable.

You will probably also need to prepare a presentation including a brief statement of goal and purpose (small enough to fit on a cocktail napkin), and a business case demonstrating the financial value of the project. Discussions of tools for demonstrating financial value, such as Return on Investment (ROI), can be found in Chapter 10.

THE GATE AT THE END OF THE CONCEPT STAGE: HOLD FORMAL MEETINGS TO DECIDE IF THE PROJECT SHOULD BE DROPPED, OR SHOULD MOVE AHEAD INTO THE ANALYSIS PHASE

During the process of defining the stakeholders, you probably have identified all of the key players essential to project success. For the project to move ahead, you will need clear commitment from a project sponsor at the executive level who has the authority and financial resources to back the team and promote the project. In addition, you will need sign-on from all of the key stakeholders.

These meetings should not be pro-forma. We use the term sign-on, rather than sign-off, for a very important reason. If you ask someone to sign off on an agreement, they think that, if they sign, they are letting you do all the work. That is too easy. If you ask someone to sign on, you are asking them to commit time and money to the effort. It sounds like they are joining the navy. And that is exactly what you want. You want each stakeholder to understand that they are on board this project, and that its success or failure is success or failure for everyone on board. You want them to ask how long the tour of duty is, and if the trip is hazardous duty. The sooner that each stakeholder identifies risks, the easier it is to manage and mitigate those risks. (Chapter 11 contains tools for identifying and managing risks.)

KEY POINT

The Blob

Have you ever seen the classic sci-fi movie *The Blob*? Have you ever tried watching it twice? The second time anyone sees the movie, we come to the scene where the blob is sitting in the laboratory going "bloop-bloop," and it is smaller than a basketball. We all start yelling at the actors: "Kill it now, before it takes over the high school!"

Have you ever been on a project that felt like a re-run of *The Blob*? You know the project should have been ended long ago, but it goes on, with more and more money being wasted.

Why does this happen? There are two reasons. Money has already been spent, and it needs to be justified. Or, an executive promised to deliver the product or service. In both cases, canceling the project and delivering nothing causes embarrassment. A brief, objective evaluation in the concept stage can prevent projects that should never get started by canceling them before much money is spent and before public promises are made.

If the management of your company is not convinced that you need a concept stage, ask them if they have ever found themselves in the middle of a big job they wished they had never started. Then tell them about killing the blob.

Outputs of the Concept Stage

If the concept stage takes over one month, you should prepare monthly and quarterly status reports. These should include up-to-date time and expense reports, a projected budget for completing the concept stage, and a status report defining work done and the next steps to be taken. For a full description of how to work with status reports, see Chapter 12.

When the concept stage is complete, the list of final outputs depends on whether the project is approved, cancelled, or shelved for future consideration. If the project is shelved, then the outputs are:

- A description of the time or event that should trigger reconsideration of the project.
- The statement of value.
- The project overview, as much of it as was completed.
- The context diagram.
- A file of working notes.

If the project is cancelled altogether, the first item should be replaced with a reason why the project was cancelled. In a large organization, this can prevent someone else from launching a project that has already been researched, evaluated, and turned down.

WOWS AND WHOOPSES

We Already Know It Will Not Work Yet
A project manager at a Fortune 500 energy utility was asked to evaluate the costs and benefits of installing a new telephone system using voice-over-IP technology. At the beginning of the concept stage, she asked around, and discovered that five other project managers in different groups had already been asked the same question. Each of them had done a lot of work, and ended up shelving the project until the technology was less expensive. She was able to come to the same conclusion with a lot less work: She just told her boss what the other managers had already discovered, and added updated notes about when the price of the technology might change.

Create a central location for all ideas, so that future project managers can see what everyone has already thought of and tried out. This will shorten your concept stage and reduce costs.

If the project is approved to move into the analysis stage, then the following items should be delivered at the end of the concept stage:

- A business case, including the statement of value and scope statement.
- A project overview with a defined purpose, a goal statement with inclusions and exclusions, a list of stakeholders, and as much other information as is already available.

- A schedule and budget for the analysis stage, and perhaps for the design stage as well.
- An initial plan describing the life cycle of the project—including whether it will be developed in one project or multiple projects, and including the deliverables of each stage.
- The context diagram, possibly with some details moving towards a set of data flow diagrams, and other technical specifications.
- A well-organized file of working notes.

Key Tools for the Concept Stage

The most important tools for the concept stage are the *scope statement*, the context diagram, and the project overview. In this section, we introduce these tools and teach you how to use them. Completed examples are included with the case study later in this chapter.

THE SCOPE STATEMENT

Scope statements will look somewhat different for different kinds of projects. Let us look at a list of issues we must always address, in any scope statement.

- *Business value.* From the business perspective, why are we creating this system? What is the value? What is the return on investment?
- *Crucial issues and needs.* What is driving this project? And what are the critical, absolute features, deadlines, or cost limitations that we already know, if any?
- *Business or consumer functions.* What work will the system do? What will it not do? What kind of work will people do on the system? What business functions will be enhanced by the system, and what groups will benefit? If the produce or service is for consumers, why will they use it? How will they use it? What will it do for them? What will be the value that customers perceive?
- *Scope of change.* The project will change or replace an existing product or service. Are we creating an upgrade, that is, significant changes to a current model, or are we creating a whole new product or service? What will be replaced by the results of our project? In a business, what tool or system will they stop using when they start using this

one? For consumers, what products or services (ours, or competitors')
will they stop using if they buy our new product or service?

Let us look at the different forms a scope statement might take, and the
different additional items, by looking at three very different projects: the
design of a new advertising campaign, the creation of a new or upgraded
computer system, and an audit of a business division.

For the advertising campaign, we would identify:

- The products or services being advertised.
- The expected increase in sales from the campaign, compared to its cost.
- Whether we are creating the campaign for new products or services, or
  for existing ones.
- Whether we plan to create new names and terms for products, or
  reorganize product lines.
- The media we plan to use (television, web sites, e-mail, radio, and so
  forth).
- The target audience.
- The length of the campaign.
- A sense of what will be done in-house, and what will be done by
  vendors, and which vendors, if we know.

For a computer system, we begin with the general list of items you saw above,
and we can add:

- *Details of the scope of change.* It is important to identify whether the
  project is an entirely new system, fulfilling a new function, the replacement for a manual system, the replacement for a legacy system, or the
  upgrade of an entire existing system. Even a new product or service has
  competition. For a new product or service, the question to ask is: How
  did the customer do this job up until now?
- *Data systems.* What platforms, including telephone networks, computer hardware, operating systems, database engines, networks, and other
  tools will the system work on? What systems will it not work on? What
  systems will receive data from the new system? What systems will send
  data to the new system? What wireless technologies and equipment are
  part of the system, and what wireless technologies and equipment will
  the system interface with?
- *Data.* What data will be in the system? What data will be excluded?
- *Users.* Who will input data? Who will manipulate the data? Who will
  receive reports? Who will not be affected directly by the system, but be

affected indirectly? Who will have to change the way they work? Define users by organization and department, and also by name.

- *Support personnel.* Who will maintain the system? Who will help or train users?
- *Security.* How will organizational security be affected by the new system, and by its installation? If there are customer security concerns (perceived or real), what are they? How will they be addressed?
- *Other people and organizations.* Audit groups, peripheral organizations, vendors, and customers may be affected by this project. All of these should be identified.

However, the scope statement for an audit looks very different. The overall structure of an audit is very similar from one to the next. The purpose is either mandated by law or justified by a clear business need. So the audit scope statement focuses more on the details.

- *The customer to be audited.* It could be a company, a division, a department, or a project.
- *The audit trigger.* We name the law or regulation that requires the audit, or the executive justification for the audit request.
- *The list of auditable items.* This is a detailed list of what will be examined by the auditors.
- *Relevant regulations or statutes.* An audit compares reality against the rules. Which rules? This list may actually be routine, or it may be developed later, in the analysis stage.
- *Past audits of this customer.* If this entity has been audited before, then a copy of prior audit results.
- *The audit report recipient.* Who will receive the completed audit? Usually, the executive director, or the board of directors.

As you can see, a scope statement varies with different types of projects. You can build your own scope statement for the projects on which you work. Simply make sure you are answering all the important questions about the project for all the key stakeholders.

We can combine these aspects of scope with the concept of inclusions and exclusions in order to define our scope precisely. The *scope definition matrix* for a wireless communications system in Table 5-2 illustrates this tool.

Working alone, we cannot define the scope of a new project. Indeed, project scope is driven by the business and by the customers of the project. Therefore, to define the scope, we must identify the stakeholders and meet with them. The context diagram will help us identify stakeholders.

Table 5-2   Scope definition matrix with inclusions and exclusions.

Scope area	Inclusions	Exclusions
Business value	Ways in which the system will help the business or its customers.	Value some users might expect which is not realized by implementation of this system.
Business operations or consumer functions	Business functions that users will perform on the system, or consumer use of the system. Functionality for the customer.	Activities that the system will not support. Define what system (computerized or manual) will be used to perform those functions.
Scope of change	Is this a new system or an upgrade, or an addition of a component or an enhancement? What old systems are being upgraded? Is any new hardware being acquired? Are any components or licenses being upgraded?	What related systems are not being changed?
Telephony, data, and wireless systems and equipment	What telephony, data, and wireless systems and equipment, including platforms, operating systems, data bases and data management tools, and networks, are being affected or replaced?	What systems are in place among the customers, but will not support the new application?
Data	What data will the system work with? What system(s) currently hold this data? How frequently is the data updated, backed up, or archived?	What related data is not on this system? What system(s) hold that data?
Users	Who will use the system? Identify both business units or departments, and also specific users.	What users will not have access to the system? Pay particular attention to users who might want access but who will not have it.
Support personnel	Who will support the system? Who will support the users? What documentation and training will the project need to deliver to these people so they can do their job? What do these people know that could improve the quality of the project?	Who will have no changes in responsibility in relation to support of the new system?

Table 5-2   Scope definition matrix with inclusions and exclusions (*Continued*).

Security	What security systems will the new application change? What security systems will the new application interface with? What issues of security affect installation of the system? What security procedures will change? Customer security issues (including perceived issues), and how they will be addressed	What security systems are mentioned but are not affected by the new system?
Other people and organizations	Identify anyone else who uses the application or information from it. Identify regulatory organizations and others who may contribute to system requirements.	Identify people who might think they will work with the new application who actually will not.

THE CONTEXT DIAGRAM

The *context diagram* is a picture of the product or service as it will appear in its environment when the project is over. We use it as a visual aid for the scope statement. It shows how our new product or service will fit into the company, department, or the household that will use it.

Generic context diagrams

The generic context diagram for a product or service (Fig. 5-1) includes the product or service we are creating in the large circle. The surrounding boxes are external systems or components with which our product or service is likely to interface. In a systems model such as a context diagram, people or groups of people are considered to be systems. Where appropriate, we identify communication between external systems. The curved lines between the system we are creating and each external system or component represent the data flows that will move between our system and each particular external system or component. If we fully define these data flows and their transmission requirements, we have specified all of the interface standards that our system must support in order to function properly.

If your product or service has different customer groups, you create a box for each one, as they will have different inputs and outputs. There can also be many peripheral stakeholders, and many linked products or services. For example, as illustrated in Fig. 5-2, a computer program that we develop

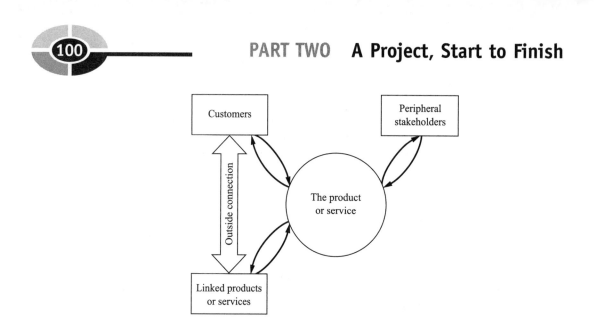

Fig. 5-1. Generic context diagram.

for a company might have employees in one or more departments as the customers. Peripheral stakeholders would include people who got reports from the computer program, but did not actually use it, and also support personnel. And the linked products or services would be any computers running the program and any other programs that exchange data with the program we are making.

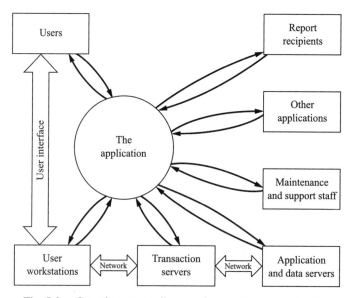

Fig. 5-2. Generic context diagram for a software application.

Create Your Own Template for a Context Diagram

For context diagramming to make sense, you have to try it out. And each industry would have a different basic context diagram. So, whatever kinds of projects you do, make your own basic context diagram. See if you can build a template that will get you started on the context diagram for any project. Or, if you do more than one different type of project, do one diagram for each. For example, if you are in marketing, and sometimes you design whole marketing campaigns, and other times you design individual advertisements, create a context diagram for a campaign, and another one for a single advertisement. Once you have created the diagram, try it out. As you use the template, you can improve it.

Creating a context diagram for a new product or service

It is not important that your first draft context diagram be correct, and it almost certainly will not be complete. Developing the context diagram is an iterative process, and we do it by meeting with stakeholders, showing them the picture, and making improvements. The goal is to put down what you know, and identify what you do not know. The diagram may be full of question marks. (Here is a practical recommendation: In any document or diagram, put a double question mark "??" wherever information is uncertain. You can then use "??" as a search string to find all unfinished points when revising documents.)

Your draft context diagram will identify a few systems, components, and people who will interface with the new product or service. For each system, identify the person responsible for that system or component, or someone who knows a lot about it. If you are not sure if someone will be a stakeholder, meet with that person and ask. Make a list of all the people, and get in touch with them. Meet them, show them the context diagram and your scope statement, and get them to help you improve it.

In preparing agendas for those meetings, it is good to consider the following:

- You can make contact by e-mail, but a meeting by phone or in person is better because it is easier to ensure mutual understanding, especially when trying to build a picture of products and services that do not yet exist.

- Send your agenda with questions and diagrams in advance. Walk through the materials with the person during the meeting.
- Take clear and extensive notes. For a meeting with several people, assign a note-taker.
- Here are some of the questions you should be sure to ask:

  - Are you responsible for this system or group of users? If not, who is?
  - Is there anyone else you can think of who might use this service or product?
  - Is there anyone, or any other system, that is not in the context diagram, who might be affected?
  - Can you give me the official name and common terms used for any of the elements on the context diagram?
  - Can you give me any available system documentation for each component on the context diagram? If not, who might have it? Do you think it exists?
  - What do you see as the value of this product or service?
  - Do you see any problems connecting the new product or service with your system?
  - Do you think the users you know about would want this product or service? Would they be able to learn it and use it? What would make it more valuable? What would make it easier to accept?
  - Do you think this idea is a good one? Can you think of ways to make it better? Can you think of a better idea altogether?
  - Do you already know about another product or system anywhere that works like this one?
  - I do not want to waste the company's time and money on a bad idea, or on something that just will not work or will not be accepted. What do you really think of the idea? What are the barriers to success?

- Ask open-ended questions first. The most important thing is to get people thinking and talking.
- You will need precise technical information, but if you miss it in the first meeting, you can always request that they send it later.
- You may end up having more than one meeting with each person, or you may organize some individual meetings and some group meetings.

As we build the context diagram, it is very important to realize that there may be multiple classes of users. Each *user class* will use the product or service in a different way, and will have a different set of requirements for the interface.

When this happens, our box called "users" on the context diagram may become several boxes, each naming a different user group. A user class is defined by how the people in the group use the system, and not by whether the people are all in the same place. In a systems model, a person or group of people can be viewed as a system and a component of a larger system. From this perspective, a user class is a subsystem, composed of people that use the system in a particular way for a particular purpose or set of purposes.

THE PROJECT OVERVIEW

It is important to create one single document that provides a coherent summary of the purpose, goal, and status of the project, and keep it up to date throughout the project. If this one document is clear, consistent, and coherent, then it links all of the other work of the project. We can call this document the *project overview* or the project charter. If we include and focus on financial justification, it can be called the business case. It is longer than the one-page executive summary, but shorter than the detailed documents that support the overview and provide full details on each aspect of the project.

Table 5-3 presents the project overview, a five-page form. Table 5-3 is a project overview form with field definitions. We discuss the fields that are filled out in the concept stage and the ideas behind them below. You can download a blank copy of the project overview for copying—and also other tools from this book—by going to *www.qualitytechnology.com* and clicking on *Project Management*, or going directly to *www.qualitytechnology.com/books/pmd.htm.*

Key concepts in the project overview

In this section, we define key terms in the project overview, and identify best practices for gathering this information for those items that need to be complete in the concept stage.

Purpose
The purpose of a project is the reason why the organization should invest money and resources in the project and commit to it. *Hard dollar value* refers to a value that can be calculated as a change to net revenue, that is, either an increase in revenue, or a decrease in costs. Other *Hard value*, especially for not-for-profit and governmental organizations, includes the ability to continue operations and fulfill key mission objectives.

Table 5-3 Project overview with field definitions.

Project name A short descriptive name recognizable to all stakeholders.		

Project sponsor (customer, executive level) The highest executive involved on the customer side.	**Project lead (customer, managerial level)** The manager of the customer group primarily responsible for the project.

Project manager The person who manages the project team on a daily basis.	**Date created** For this document.	**Date revised** Most recent change.

Short purpose
The primary financial and other benefit to the organization, in 80 characters or less.

Purpose
The hard-dollar value and a description of all the types of hard-dollar values on this project.
A description of the soft-dollar benefits of this project.

Goal and inclusions
A high-level description of what the system will be, who will use it, and what they will accomplish.
A description, either conceptual or brand name, of any architectural, platform, and programming language decisions.
A list of features and functions.
A list of user classes, and what each user class will do.
Any other information regarding scope inclusions is added as it is determined.
Where appropriate, split stages of delivery, and describe what will be included in each stage.

Key exclusions
In each area where there are inclusions, also list exclusions, items that will not be included in the project. Defining these out-of-scope items clearly defines the context boundary very clearly. Add any items requested by users that are out of scope.

Table 5-3 Project overview with field definitions (*Continued*).

	page 2
Project name:	

Initial environment
Problem to be solved. What problem exists now which will be solved by implementing the new system? What work cannot be done, or cannot be done well, until the new system is in place?
Business processes. All current business systems that will be changed or replaced by the new system. The current form (manual or electronic, and in what formats) of information that the new system will hold.
Customer description. If the customer is a separate company or companies, or a set of consumers, write a description of the customer as user, and buyer/decision-maker, and a description of any relevant elements of their business environment or life situation.
Computer systems and other equipment or facilities. All systems that will be replaced by, or interact with, the new system. Include hardware platforms, operating systems, and data management systems. Also include user interfaces and systems that will receive or send data through import/export functions. If the existing systems are documented, a reference to those documents should be included here.
Risk evaluation. What elements of the initial environment are undocumented or unknown? What things might we find that would create problems for the project?

Desired delivery date (imposed) From the customer.	**Desired budget maximum (imposed)** $ from the customer.
Required delivery date (imposed) From the customer, and a fixed requirement.	**Required budget maximum (imposed)** $ from the customer, and a fixed requirement.
Estimated delivery date Calculated for this project.	**Estimated budget maximum** $ calculated for this project.

Assigned account code(s) or other accounting approval information
Any information you need in order to be able to assign time, money, and purchase requisitions to the project.

Other constraints (operational limitations which cannot be changed by the PM)
Any "rules of the game" for the project, such as accounting and purchasing rules, or external regulatory requirements, or safety requirements, or management procedures, which must be followed during the project.

Key assumptions (operating procedures set by the PM, which the PM could change, but which team members should follow unless the PM changes them)
Any decisions made by the project manager that will guide the work of the team. This might include choice of project life cycle, status report methods, weekly and other meetings, choice of tools, and documentation standards.

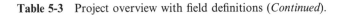
Table 5-3   Project overview with field definitions (*Continued*).

		page 3
Project name:		
Initial team members		

Name	Role	Definite/possible
Include the name and title, role, or specialty of anyone being considered for the project. If they are definitely on board (they and their boss agree) then list D in the third column, otherwise list P. This list is of team members only. A similar list for stakeholders appears on page 5.		

Options being considered
Any unresolved issues of architecture, scope, or the inclusion of specific features are listed here. Identify the options and which stakeholders prefer which options. Attach decision matrices where appropriate. As a decision is made regarding each option, move it from here to the Goal and Inclusions section. Decisions may be made during concept, analysis, or design stages, but should be complete by the end of design.

Notes towards a support plan
Any information you receive from stakeholders regarding documentation and training for operations support staff or the help desk should go here. Identify new tools they might need to learn and new applications with which they might need to work.

Notes towards a test plan
Any information prioritizing tests as most crucial or most likely to run into trouble.
Any issue regarding user tests, end-to-end testing, or technical test plans, so that it can be included in the test and quality plans.

Table 5-3   Project overview with field definitions (*Continued*).

	page 4
Project name:	
Initial list of milestones	

Phase	Milestone(s)
Concept	For each project stage, a complete list of deliverables, and a list of who will approve those deliverables.
Analysis	
Design	
Development	
Transition to production	
Production	A description of the benefits of production steady state and routine maintenance operations.
Decommissioning	An estimation of the minimum life of the project in production, in years. A list of any events, such as changes in business operations or changes in IT platform, which would require an evaluation of this system to see if it needs a maintenance release, upgrade, or enhancement to keep functioning, or if it needs to be replaced.

Table 5-3   Project overview with field definitions (*Continued*).

	page 5

Project name:

Stakeholder identification (include this information for each stakeholder defined below)

Name

Employer (including site if multi-site firm)

Client (if different from employer)

Supervisor (if also listed as stakeholder)

Contact information (*at least* e-mail and city, state, country)

Contact restrictions (when *not* to contact this person, about what issues not to contact this person, constraints such as "do not contact without getting ok from supervisor," etc.)

Stakeholders and their concerns

Use this section to document any concerns raised by any stakeholder which need to be resolved for stage approval. Also use it to identify any concerns you have regarding the ability and willingness of stakeholders to contribute to the project.

Executive

Managerial

End-user

External

Notes

Risk
Any possible future events that could reduce quality of the results, create a delay, or cause the project to go over budget.

Procurement
Any notes regarding items or services to be purchased.

Any other issues

Soft value, including *soft dollar value*, refers to any benefits that cannot be quantified exactly. Soft value benefits assist the organization, but either cannot be quantified at all, or are too unpredictable to quantify reasonably at this time.

There are seven different changes to an organization that can benefit the organization while it is in normal operating and production mode. (Other benefits exist for organizations that are starting, being sold, closing, or making major changes to operations.) Each of these changes can provide hard dollar benefit, soft benefit, or both. For a list of these changes, a method for identifying and defining value for a project, and tools to assist in the process, see Chapter 10. It is a good idea to learn the methods of defining value before running the brainstorming meetings of the concept stage.

Goal

Describe the goal as it will exist when it is complete. That is, describe the product or service working in the production environment. For example, you might say, "The quality team for Widget Model #3 will use the Wireless Production Tracking system at all times while the assembly line is in operation. Wireless nodes mounted on assembly line equipment will deliver real-time measurement of production variables such as temperature and pressure that affect the quality of all plastic components of Widget Model #3. These data will be automatically monitored and displayed at the Control Center, and quality engineers will be able to view the information on their wireless PDAs from anywhere in the assembly plant." Be sure to describe the result, not the process or the system. Be sure to describe the users using the system in a way that benefits the organization.

In the inclusions section, you can add information about system features and functions.

Initial Situation

The initial situation should explain how the functions to be performed by the new system are performed today, and what the limitations or problems of the current systems are. In addition, it should describe the existing environment with which the new system will have to interoperate. Investigating the initial situation well and describing it accurately are crucial steps in identifying risks. There is a saying in the world of computer project management: "Before you can drain the swamp, you have to find the alligators." The problem is that the only way to find the alligators is by draining the swamp! And draining a swamp takes a lot longer (and is a bit more risky) when there are alligators in it. So a careful alligator hunt at the start is a good idea. It is similar on any project. For example:

- On a project to modify computer software, if the existing program code is poorly documented, the project takes much longer.
- On a building reconstruction project, the project is much more costly if there are flaws in the foundation or leaks in the roof.

To put it simply, what we do not know is dangerous to the project. So, to be sure there are no project-killers, we should investigate and report on the following five items in the concept stage:

- Problem to be solved
- Business processes
- Customer description
- Computer systems and other equipment or facilities
- Risk evaluation

If we cannot complete our evaluation in the concept stage, we can seek to find the major risks first, and leave notes for detailed research in the analysis stage.

Imposed vs. Estimated Time and Budget

An imposed delivery date or budget comes from the customer. It is not based on an estimate, and no one is saying that the project can be completed by that date for that much money. The customer is saying that the business requires or desires that the project team meet this date, and deliver for this much money. The imposed time and cost items can take one of two forms. Either they are absolute requirements, or they are desired goals. For example, if the space shuttle is launching on a certain date, and you are managing a project to develop experimental equipment for that shuttle flight, your delivery date is imposed. One day late, and your equipment will not be on the shuttle when it takes off. On the other hand, if a company hopes to have a new financial system in place by May 1 so that they can make sure it is running by the new fiscal year, that is an imposed deadline, but not a strict one. The company will still accept the project if it runs late. The same distinction applies to money: An imposed budget requirement is an absolute dollar limit. An imposed budget that is desired is a limit the customers want, but they might be willing to pay more.

TERM

Imposed Set by the customer, whether or not it is possible in the project.

Estimated Arising from within the project, as a result of evaluation of project resource requirements.

Required Established as an absolute limit.

Desired A preference, but there is some flexibility. Exceeding the desired time or budget is not, in itself, a project-killer.

For most projects, accurate estimation cannot occur in the concept stage. If you are familiar with the customer group and the type of project, and it is not very large, you may be able to give an estimated range. But do not let yourself be locked into a budget until the requirements are gathered and evaluated in the analysis stage. Methods of cost estimation are discussed in Chapter 10.

Constraints and Assumptions: The Rules of the Game

These two boxes, taken together, define the rules or guidelines that the project will follow. *Constraints* are imposed on the project by the organization or from outside the organization. *Assumptions* are decisions made by the project manager. As an analogy, think of the project manager as a football coach. The rules of football are constraints that the project manager cannot change, and they limit the options for ways to cross the goal line. The team rules are set by the coach, and should be followed. However, if you think the coach should change the rules, talk to him or her. The same applies on projects. Constraints, organizational or regulatory requirements such as contracts with vendors and sole source justification documents may slow down a project, but they are unavoidable. Assumptions, decisions the project manager makes need to be adhered to by the whole team for the system to work well. But the decision could change, and if a team member has an idea that might be better, or a good reason for an exception to the assumptions, the team member should suggest it.

Here are several effective ways to use written constraints and assumptions during a project.

- Go over the constraints and assumptions when you first create your team. Make sure that everyone knows the rules of the game, and that everyone also knows that they can make suggestions and propose new ideas that might change the assumptions.

- Review these lists when creating a risk plan. Each item will help you identify things that could go wrong.
- Have this information available for any new team member who joins the project. It will help bring him or her up to speed quickly.

Options Being Considered: Conflict Management

This section allows you to identify decisions that need to be made which have not yet been made. If all the facts are collected and everyone agrees, you will go ahead and make the decision. So, a decision still to be made indicates either a lack of sufficient information, or a potential conflict.

In the case of a lack of sufficient information, identify the decision criteria. For example, you might say, "If the price quote from Vendor X is below $10,000, we will use its services. Otherwise, we will seek an alternative vendor." For another example, you might say, "We have placed a request for information with three vendors. Each one will present their product, and we will review ability to conform to requirements, customer service quality, and cost in making our decision. See the attached document for our decision matrix." Once the information is gathered, make the decision, and adjust the goal and inclusions to reflect the decision.

In the case of conflict, note the options, the stakeholder(s) who prefer each option, and their reasons. You can attach a decision matrix that you will use to resolve the conflict.

Writing down disagreements prevents arguments and bad feelings. It allows you to focus on the project itself, and ask the question: "I see what you want, and I know what I want, but what is best for the project?" These methods of triangulation and depersonalization are discussed in detail in Chapter 12.

This completes our discussion of the project overview form as we use it in the concept stage. We complete the project overview during analysis, so we will return to the form in the next chapter. It is important to remember that the project overview is a living document throughout the concept and analysis phases. During this time, it should be constantly changing as it is updated based on meetings and phone calls and reviewed by various stakeholders.

Key Concepts for the Concept Stage

Project communications management and scope management are the two most important areas of project management knowledge to apply during the concept stage. This makes sense, because we are trying to talk to everyone who cares about what we are doing and define what it is that we are creating on the project. In addition, risk, time, and cost management may play important roles.

COMMUNICATIONS MANAGEMENT

Within communications, the key issue is finding everyone who is responsible for systems that will be changed by the work of the project, presenting the idea, and listening to them. It is very important that the exchange be two-way, and that the results of the conversation be written down into the project overview and other documents. Discussions that are not written down do not lead to change; therefore, they are not effective.

SCOPE MANAGEMENT

In scope management, it is important to understand the different concerns that different stakeholders have regarding the project. Executives want to understand value, sales staff want to understand the product and its functionality, support staff want to be assured that the new product will be easy to maintain, and so forth. Each of these concerns should change the original idea, increasing its value while reducing its production cost and maintenance cost. An effective concept stage can take a marginal idea and make it worth pursuing.

WOWS AND WHOOPSES

The Team Approach to Projects

There is a project management technique called *Concurrent Project Management* that illustrates the benefits of brainstorming and teamwork at the beginning of a project. In the mid-1990s an American automobile manufacturer decided to try it. They took a sleek concept car and gave it to a project team.

In the past, cars had developed in a five-year process. The design team would pass the car to the engineering team, who would pass it to the assembly line team. Any major problem forced a restart of the entire process. For example, if an assembly line could not be built inexpensively for the required wheelbase (size of car), then the whole process would start again from the beginning.

Concurrent project management brings an expert from each area into the initial team. In this case, the team that designs assembly lines looked at the plans up front, and said, "You know, we have some empty assembly lines with a wheelbase two inches longer than your concept design. Could you make the wheelbase 104 inches? That would lower startup costs by millions." The designers did it on the spot.

This team approach led to a much more rapid exchange of information than there was in the old way of doing things. The result was that the first car rolled off the assembly lines after only 18 months rather than 60 months. And the Dodge/Plymouth Neon is a pretty nice car.

Since that time, all of the major automobile manufacturers have adopted concurrent project management, which was pioneered by Hewlett-Packard for the manufacture of printers.

WHAT THIS MEANS FOR YOU

Rapid, clear communication can take an idea, or even an entire industry, and move it from being a losing proposition to being a success.

CONCLUSION

Total quality management pioneer Dr. Joseph M. Juran once defined a project as "A problem scheduled for solution." We would respectfully expand on this idea. A project has a purpose, and that purpose may be to solve a problem. But that purpose may also be to take advantage of a new opportunity.

Even more important, a project starts with a good idea: a good solution or a good innovative concept. A bad idea scheduled for implementation is not a project: it is a recipe for disaster and a waste of time and money.

In the concept stage, we are both working on the project and also managing the project. Defining the product or service and its value, and documenting all the ideas, is the work of the project. Ensuring that we speak to all key stakeholders and include their ideas, validating the idea or deciding to cancel the project, and building commitment for project success are the major focal points of our work of managing the project. In doing this, we increase the business value of the project process and the resulting product or service.

The concept stage will have different functions in different corporate cultures. In companies that resist innovation, the concept stage can be used to stimulate excitement about and energy to develop new ideas. In disorganized companies, the concept stage can be used to ensure refinement and validation of ideas before money is spent on something that just will not work, or will not work as planned. In either case, this stage provides essential functions for the corporation and for the project. It protects corporate assets by focusing them on projects that are likely to bring about good returns, and it protects projects in several ways:

- The concept stage assures that projects are well defined.
- It supports early inclusion of ideas that enhance project value. (Due to the 1:10:100 rule, the earlier a good idea is included, the less it costs.)
- It provides an opportunity for the project manager to find possible project-killers and either resolve them or cancel the project early.
- It provides an opportunity to built support and enthusiasm for the project among key stakeholders, and to identify resistance and potential problem areas.

Our Case Study: Is it Time for Home Theater?

Life should not be all work and no play. So our case study—if it works—will enhance our free time. We want to move beyond having a television and a pretty good stereo. With movies like *Lord of the Rings* being made it is time to watch DVDs on wide screens with surround sound. Or is it?

For a mere $25,000 I could get a full home theater system professionally installed, if it would fit in my living room. But what can I do for $2,000? That is all the money I want to spend.

My wife and I came up with this idea recently. As we talked about it, wondering if we really wanted to do it, we entered the concept stage. Our process included brainstorming, winnowing, a prototype test, and holding a final decision meeting.

Our first brainstorming session focused on the question: What would we really get out of this? Our results were:

- We would really enjoy movies more if we played DVDs, which have higher quality than tapes, if we saw them on a larger screen, and if we had high-quality stereo or surround-sound.
- It would be great to get better sound when playing music CDs.
- We do not need to upgrade our cable; the focus is mostly on movie rentals.

Then we asked what it was worth to us. And we decided $2,000. But is that possible? It was time for a bit of winnowing. A quick review of technology told us that, in our price range, flat-screen televisions and the new wide-screen format were not possible. On the bright side, we could keep our CD player, tape cassette player, and record player. But could we get a good television, surround-sound receiver, DVD player, and speakers for $2,000? More reading and more searching around the home electronics store led to a discovery: There is a big price jump in the cost of a television at a certain size. The size grows every year, but, in 2003, it was 26 inches. A 28-inch television cost well over $1,000, but a 26-inch television was well under.

Was a 26-inch television big enough to meet our needs? Time to test a prototype. We went to a video store and looked at the televisions. Ignoring the price tags, what was the smallest size that was comfortable. How close did we have to be? The good news was that we liked a 26-inch television. The bad news is that it would need to sit in the middle of our living room, not against the far wall.

Brainstorming gave us a solution. We would put the television on a rolling cart. We could keep it against the wall, and roll it out when we needed it. Not your classic home theater installation, but neither was it $25,000.

We wrote up our goals and a quick list of the items we would need to buy, with approximate costs. We added a large margin for sales tax and unexpected expenses. And we went back to the basic questions: Is this what we really want to do? Of all the things we could do with $2,000 and the time it will take to plan, buy, and set up this home theater, would we rather do this than something else?

And the answer was yes. And that was the end of the concept stage.

Your Project for Learning

Now is the time for you to begin, work on, and complete the concept stage of your project for learning. Create a scope statement, a context diagram, and a project overview. If anyone other than yourself is involved, have a brainstorming session.

When you evaluate the idea, it needs to pass two different sets of criteria. First, is the project itself worthwhile? Second, is it suitable to be your project for learning? Will you have enough time to try out all of the different forms and templates in this book on your project.

Of course, not every project needs every form and template. If you picked a small project for learning it may well be the most over-documented project in history. But that is the point. You are using all the forms, templates, and methods to learn them, not simply because they are needed on the project.

Make sure your evaluation is genuine. Maybe, from what you have learned in this chapter, you now see that your original project for learning is too small, too large, or too complicated. Or maybe some external situation has changed and you cannot do that project. Perhaps you were going to paint your house, and you decided to buy a new one instead. That is no problem, it is just another learning opportunity. Write up a concept stage recommending that you cancel or delay the project, or not use it as your project for learning. Then take a new project for learning through the concept stage.

Questions for Learning

Try some of these exercises to prepare yourself for managing a concept stage.

- You have been asked to evaluate a technology that a company is very excited about. You do, and you find a project-killer: The only vendor who can supply and support a key component is in financial trouble, and may not be around for long. How do you present your case for canceling a popular project?
- You have performed a concept stage evaluation and found that the project cannot be created reliably yet. It will rely on MMS cellular telephone technology, which has not been fully specified or deployed. You recommend putting it on hold. What are the key events to watch for that indicate it is time to do the project?
- You are in the concept stage for selecting a vendor to provide laptop computers to a sales staff in the USA, Canada, Mexico, and Europe. Make a list of service features that you would present for a brainstorming session with sales executives and vendors.
- You are buying a new computer for your home. You plan to keep the same printer and internet service. If you have a home network, you are also keeping that. Create a context diagram for the new computer. Do not forget to include users and software programs.

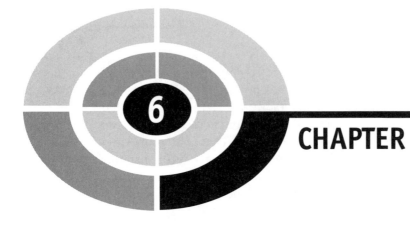

CHAPTER

6

Analysis: What Does the Customer Want?

In the analysis stage, our focus should be on the customer and the other stakeholders. We found the most important stakeholders in the concept stage. Now it is time to find all of them, listen to all of them, and create a specification that is the best it can be for every stakeholder. To listen well, we guide people by asking the right questions. The ideas, templates, and tools in this chapter will help you prepare the right questions and document them in a way that makes the next step, the design stage, easy.

High-quality work in the analysis stage is extremely important. The earlier errors creep into a project, the more likely the project is to be delayed, exceed cost projections, or fail altogether. Table 6-1 shows common errors in the analysis stage and their consequences. The rest of the chapter shows how not to make those mistakes.

The primary job of the concept, analysis, and design stages is planning, and the results are usually written documents. So how do we tell them apart? The concept stage is a quick process, improving and validating (or rejecting) the idea of the project. It uses only a small percentage of the total time and money spent on the project. The analysis and design stages are much longer.

Table 6-1   Errors in the analysis stage and their consequences.

Error	Result
No written plan, or vague plan	Project delivers a product that no one wants
Plan without a clear purpose	Product does not benefit the company
Product with a clear purpose, but no defined goal	Product delivered with the wrong features, of little or no value. Endless change requests delay the project
Project with no clear rules for change control	Many changes requested, leads either to conflict or to a project that grows beyond manageable proportions
Project plan does not include assumptions	Major components are not included in product, or do not work correctly. Project runs over budget or fails due to unexpected problems
Project plan does not define environment	Product does not work correctly, or conflict arises about what is and is not part of the project
Project plan is too detailed	All the time is spent planning, and the project never gets off the ground
The project plan is written and then not referred to	Teamwork never really develops. People talk, but do not understand one another. Costs and delays go out of control

Indeed, by the end of design, a project may be 60% complete in terms of total duration or total effort. In rare cases, the figure is even higher. So what is the difference between analysis and design?

- *The analysis stage* focuses on the customer and asks the questions, What are we trying to make? What is the product or service the customer wants, in detail? We create a set of requirements and an overall project plan.
- *The design stage* comes next. It focuses on the technical team. We ask the questions, How are we going to make the product or service? What are its specifications? What will it cost? How long will it

take? We create a technical specification that, when built, will provide all of the features of the design specification. And we create a detailed project plan with work schedules. From the detailed project plan, we complete the budget, the schedule, and the risk, quality, and procurement plans.

An excellent way to succeed on technical projects is to perform the analysis stage from the top down, and the design stage from the bottom up. The concept stage gives us an overall picture of the project. During analysis, we start with this big picture and we drill down, creating detailed set of requirements. In the design stage, we turn this around, and go from the bottom up. We define each feature of each component or module. Then we build a plan to create each module. Putting it all together, we build upwards from the details to a complete, accurate budget, schedule, and project plan.

Strategically, top-down concept and analysis stages of work ensure that we are solving the right problem and creating the product or service with the highest value possible. Bottom-up design work ensures that what we are making will work. The engineers who know the details start with the details

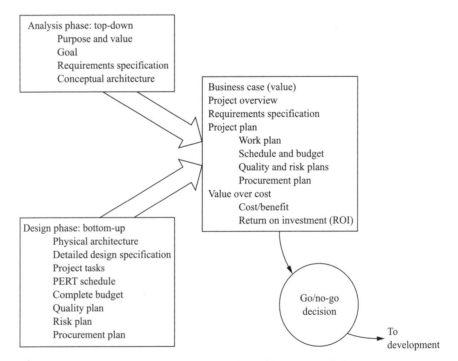

Fig. 6-1. Top-down analysis and bottom-up design.

and build a plan for a working system designed to the specification of the users who understand the big picture.

Figure 6-1 illustrates how the combination of top-down analysis and bottom-up design come together to create a complete, high-quality project plan that has a high chance of success.

In This Chapter

- Key points of the analysis stage
- Resources assigned to the analysis stage
- Roles in the analysis stage
- Inputs of the analysis stage
- Process of the analysis stage
- Outputs of the analysis stage
- Key tools for the analysis stage
- Key concepts for the analysis stage
- Case study: The historic battle of the cellular base station
- Conclusion
- Our case study: High-tech home theater
- Your project for learning
- Questions for learning

Key Points of the Analysis Stage

There are ten key points to keep in mind for a successful analysis stage:

- *Customer focus.* The customers will tell us what they want. We will often have to guide them, both in terms of questions, and also in seeing the vision of the project, so that we can get them talking, listen to them, and really understand what they want and need.
- *The project vs. the product or service.* In the analysis stage, we are creating two separate plans. One is the project plan. This is outlined in the project overview. It is about the team, and how the team is going to do the work. The second plan is for the product or service. This is often called the requirements specification. We describe what the product or service must do for the customer; that is, we define all

of the interfaces of the product or service, all the features it has for the customer, and what makes it work with other parts of the business or customer environment.

- *Project sponsorship.* We need to ensure executive commitment and sponsorship that will guarantee funding and staffing, and also protect us from interference.
- *The business case: value and cost.* During the analysis stage, we need to complete our full definition of the value of the project. We also need to improve our time estimate and cost estimate. If cost exceeds value, we must either make changes to the plan, or cancel the project.
- *Communications methods.* Because of the need for communication with people of different backgrounds (technical and non-technical), we need to focus on creating shared understanding, building cooperative teamwork, and managing and preventing conflict.
- *Architecture: buy, configure, customize, build, or integrate?* There are many ways of creating the product or service that is the goal of the project. Some projects are completed simply through the purchase and installation of a vendor's product. Others require extensive custom design and creation of a new, unique product or service. Others are a blend of purchasing, configuring, and customization. During the analysis stage, we must choose the most appropriate, most cost-effective way of creating the product or service.
- *Scope definition, requirements gathering, requirements specification, and quality definition.* These are four different terms for the same job: finding out and writing down what the customer really wants. We will discuss this further below.
- *Gap analysis: imposed vs. estimated budgets and schedules.* What do we do when the project will cost more, or take longer, than the customer wants to pay or wait?
- *Change control rules.* How do we manage changes to the plan? This is discussed in Chapter 3. The tools are available in Chapter 11.
- *Risk management.* How do we prepare for what might go wrong?

When we deliver the product or service at the end of the project, we will need to explain or demonstrate products and services to customers who may be enthusiastic or resistant. Even when we know that the project is of value, people resist change, they resist having to work in new ways. Enthusiastic customers are a project risk: If their expectations exceed what we can offer, they will be disappointed and may not use the product or service. Customers who are resistant to new technology are also a project risk: They may be unwilling to learn, use, and get the best use out of the new system. As project managers, we need to do more than explain our project to our customers; we need to help them be comfortable with it and the change it will bring.

Four of these topics deserve more extensive treatment here.

SCOPE DEFINITION, REQUIREMENTS GATHERING, REQUIREMENTS SPECIFICATION, AND QUALITY DEFINITION

These four very different-sounding ideas are actually talking about the same thing: Finding out what the customer wants and writing it down. We began this process at a high level in the concept stage, and now we need to complete the details.

Whatever we call the process, it has one purpose: Understanding what the user wants, and translating that into a technical document so the project can succeed. If we do this, we will have a clear definition of the scope, and we will not suffer from scope creep, where we keep adding more until the project becomes too big and fails. We will have clear requirements and be able to create a clear design specification for the engineers. And we will be able to define quality at the beginning, so that, when we deliver quality at the end, the customer says, "This is exactly what I wanted, and more." Quality is meeting and exceeding customer specifications and expectations. But to do that, we need to define the specifications, and manage the expectations. Scope and quality management will help us do the former, and communications management will help us manage expectations.

GAP ANALYSIS: IMPOSED VS. ESTIMATED BUDGETS AND SCHEDULES

Honest time and cost management must distinguish between what the customer requires or wants, and what is possible. Customer requirements for time and cost are called the *required schedule* and *required budget*. In ordinary language, "I have to have it by October 31, and it had better not cost more than $10,000." These are imposed limits. Or, the customer might be more flexible. "I hope it's working by October 31, and I'd like to spend about $10,000." That is a *desired schedule* and *desired budget*; it has a bit more flexibility, but it is still imposed by the customer. During concept or analysis, we get these figures from the customer, along with any account codes or other budgetary information, and we put it into the project overview in the appropriate fields. We can think of this information as the customer's *time and cost specification.*

Then we forget about the customer's imposed requirements or desires for a while. Why forget about it? Because any thought about what the customer wants interferes with good estimation. Trying to meet a target is not estimation, it is wishful thinking. *Estimation* is the engineering art of developing our best guess as to what the cost and delivery date will be, independent of what anyone wants. The questions: "How long will it take?" and "How much will it cost?" are good focusing tools. But questions like, "Can we get it done by this date?" "Can we do it for only this much money?" add bias, reducing the quality of the process.

Early in the project, the customer will probably want a precise cost estimate. Unfortunately, we will not be able to provide a truly precise estimate until the end of the design stage. This gap between the time the customer wants an estimate and the time we can give an accurate estimate is real, and it cannot be avoided. But it can be managed. We can manage customer expectations by educating customers about the realities of estimation. We can even involve them in the estimation process. And, throughout, we can present our best estimates with a clear sense of the limitations of those estimates while respecting the customer's need to control and manage costs and get results in the time frame useful to their purposes.

When we do have estimates ready (whether they are broad ranges, or later more precise figures), we may face another gap. What if the projected cost exceeds the customer's budget, or the projected schedule results in delivery that is too late? These are gaps between the customer's imposed requirements and the estimation of what the project needs to succeed. We need to perform gap analysis, and then close the gap.

Again, what we must not do is avoid the problem. If we do, reality will catch us later.

We should understand that the root cause of the problem is conflicting requirements. The customer's time and cost specification is not aligned with our current understanding of the customer's functional requirements specification. We can make decisions about the product or service we are creating that are time–cost–quality trade-offs. We find the best result we can give the customers for the time and money they have, or they want to commit. If we communicate this poorly, we will sound like we are saying, "You can't have what you want." But if we communicate it well, they will understand: "If we don't address this now, then the project will go well over budget. Why don't we work together and come up with the best solution we can now?"

EXPLAINING CHANGE CONTROL RULES AND MANAGING CUSTOMER EXPECTATIONS

If we could follow the system development life cycle perfectly, completing each stage without errors before starting the next, change control rules would not be needed. But that is impossible. Projects are made of people, and that means misunderstandings and errors we do not catch, assumptions that will catch us up later, and occasional poor work. As a result, we need a process for correcting course as the project moves forward. Without a doubt, due to the 1:10:100 rule, the fewer errors that pass from one stage to the next, the better. But we also need a way to correct the errors that do get through. That is *change control*.

Change control is a progressive process. In the concept stage, the big picture of the scope of the project is very fluid. But, at the close of the concept stage, large changes to scope should be very restricted. If we change the scope, we are really starting a whole new, different project, and we should start again.

In the analysis stage, all of the details of the customer's requirements are flexible. The customers are learning about the technology, and we are learning about the customers' wants and needs. But once we agree on what we are doing, we write it down in the project overview, in the requirements specification, and in support documents. From the end of analysis forward, all changes to the requirements specification should be in writing, following the procedures of written change control. It is essential to lock down these documents, as they are the input for the work of the design stage. Any change in the description of the purpose and function of the system we are making will force a restart to the design process, where we define the product or service that will achieve that purpose. These restarts mean that much work done up to that point was wasted, and we begin to see the losses resulting from inadequate early planning.

In the design stage, the technical specification is very open, and can be changed. But, at the end of the design stage, the technical specification is locked down, and the project plan is in place. The design documents are the input for development work. Changes during development require a restart on the development work, with much of the earlier work being wasted. To avoid the costs and risks of these changes, at the end of design, all future changes require written change control.

And the project manager must approve all future changes. If your sponsor supports this, then he or she is giving you the authority you need to make the project succeed.

Clearly, this one issue of customer expectation and change control brings together many project management tools. We provide these tools in other chapters, as follows:

- The authority/responsibility matrix is explained in Chapter 2.
- The change control process is given in Chapter 11.
- A variety of techniques for managing expectations and creating team efforts to resolve gaps are available in Chapters 2 and 12.
- The double waterfall method, which can close the gap between time and cost limits and system requirements, and also help customers accept written change control, is discussed later in this chapter.

Some experienced project managers would say that the change control rules proposed here are too strict, that there are better methods. And I agree. Those methods involve alternative life cycles. However, I would suggest that these alternative, more flexible approaches require a level of project management expertise that is rare, and, even more importantly, they require a level of customer commitment and involvement that is even rarer.

WOWS AND WHOOPSES

What It Takes to Accelerate a Project

An IT project was moving along well. One of the reasons it was going well was that there were weekly meetings with the sponsor, the customer representatives, and the project team. At these meetings, the group worked out all problems together.

The sponsor came to the project manager and said, "This is good, but we want to deliver sooner. I've heard about a new method called JAD, joint application development. I hear it speeds things up. Can we use it?"

The project manager said, "I know JAD. It would work for this project. But we'd have to meet three times a week."

The executive answered, "I don't have time for that, and neither do the customer representatives. You meet three times a week and speed it up, okay?"

If the team meets without the customer, then that development is not very "joint." And without the customer validating the team's work, the team cannot get work done any faster.

The lesson: Accelerated projects require more customer commitment and involvement.

Resources Assigned to the Analysis Stage

The budget and schedule for the analysis stage are prepared and approved at the end of the concept stage. The project sponsor should support you by allocating necessary funds and encouraging participation. Although it is not possible to create a detailed work plan for the entire project as early as the concept stage, you can create a detailed plan just for the analysis stage. For instructions on creating a work plan, starting with a Work Breakdown Structure (WBS), see Chapter 10.

Due to the customer focus of the analysis stage, the customer managers, user representatives, and working staff will need to commit significant time to working with you. Your job is to elicit requirements from them and create a requirements specification.

The amount of time needed from technical experts and technical team members will vary. If the project is working with existing technology that you understand and explain to the customers, then the demand on their time will be relatively light. But if you need to learn more about the technology, then you will rely on them more. And if you are creating a prototype—physical, or computer-based, quick working models of the final product—then they will be working to build the prototype, present it to the customers, get feedback, and improve the prototype.

The project team has some other important jobs, even if they are not yet signed on full time. Each team member should be asked to define his or her own work breakdown structure with your help. In addition, the team should become familiar with the project overview and assist with quality planning and risk planning.

Working With a Busy Engineer
Time estimates are more accurate if the person who will do the work creates them at a detailed level. But suppose you approach Joe, the engineer or a programmer who will be working with you, and he says, "I'm sorry. I'm not due to start design for another two months. And I just don't have the time right now." How do you convince him to take a few hours now to prevent problems later?

First of all, make it as easy as possible. Offer either to work with him, or to provide him with templates with clear instructions. (Some people prefer one; others prefer the other.) Secondly, engage in a conversation about his own past experience. For example, ask, "What did you like least about working on projects in the past?"

Joe might say, "Being given two weeks for a job that I know takes four."

You reply, "Joe, this is your chance to prevent that from happening this time. If I make the estimate, I'll probably get it wrong. But if you take just a couple of hours right now to clue me in, then you'll estimate the time yourself. Tell me now that it's going to take three weeks, and I'll get you the three weeks you need."

Make a strong effort to do this whenever you can. It will give you more accurate estimates and a better understanding of the project. More importantly, it will give each team member control over his or her own work. People are much more productive when they are in charge of the design of their own tasks and estimate and define their own work schedule.

As project manager, you will be coordinating all of this communication and building the project plan and requirements specification. On large projects, you will focus on the plan, and assign the specification work to your team.

Roles in the Analysis Stage

People in several different roles come together to make the analysis stage a success.

- *The project manager* coordinates all activities; manages communication and builds the project overview. On a small project, the manager also creates the design specification, completes the business case, and prepares other support documents. On a large project, the manager builds the team and assigns and coordinates these tasks, assuring completion of all documentation and deliverables.
- *The project sponsor* approves funds and assigns staff. He or she also promotes the project at the executive level, building interest, enthusiasm, and commitment. The sponsor is available to resolve conflicts and to provide resources and ideas for solving problems that cannot be solved at lower levels.
- *Customer representatives and business analysts.* Knowledge of the customer is essential to success in the analysis stage. If the project is destined to support a single department or division, we can create a role called the customer lead. The lead is at a managerial level, and works for the sponsor, who is at the executive level. If the product is to be sold to customers, then marketing represents the customers, and should also be prepared to do research and coordinate focus groups. If a project affects several internal divisions, we will probably be calling upon business analysts. Business analysts sometimes work for the

customer department, and sometimes work for the computer division group. In either case, they understand the customer's business process, and they can define that process for the project team. They become the voice of the customer. We must address the customer's concerns on all levels: executive, managerial, and worker. For a discussion of the levels of a customer group, see Chapter 12.

- *Customer service and support staff.* When the project is over, we will turn the product or service over to the customer service help desk and the technical support staff for production maintenance. They are our customers. Their knowledge of the current system (the one we are changing or replacing), and their knowledge of how the customers work and the problems they have, are essential to good requirements specification. If we listen to them during analysis, we can create a better product or service (one that is more valuable to the customer) and reduce long-term operations, administration, and maintenance (OA&M) costs.

- *The users of the product or service.* We cannot avoid them. We cannot only deal with them through representatives. In some small or large way, we must communicate directly with the people who will use the product or service we are creating. Otherwise, we run the risk of business failure by creating a product that our customers do not want or need.

- *Other stakeholders.* During analysis, there is a diverse group of people we need to make contact with, although briefly. If a system is primarily to be used by one department, it still delivers reports and perhaps receives input from other departments. As we complete the details of the context diagram, we identify these people. We then meet with them, and ask them to specify the component or report that they care about or are responsible for. We arrange to meet with them again during development so that they can test this item.

- *Project workers and experts, including technical and engineering staff.* This is our project team. Depending on how the work is organized, some will be involved full time, and others part time. As project manager, it is your job to pick these people or to work with the people assigned to you. Bring each on board, make sure that everyone understands the project, and guide each one in developing a work plan. As you bring the team together, they can also review the design specification and give you questions for the customer, help with the quality plan, and help with risk assessment.

- *Vendor representatives.* If you are considering buying part or all of the solution, then you will be working with vendor representatives to create demonstrations for your customers or customer representatives.

- *External resources*. Various groups, such as the audit department, the financial department, purchasing, or the legal department, may have some say in controls for the project process. It is best to contact these groups early. Internal auditors would much rather review your management methods for four hours now than spend 400 hours auditing you later. Proper handling of financial management can ensure capital funding or proper allocation of funds during the appropriate periods. Purchasing and the legal department have rules that need to be followed for purchases and vendor contracts. The easiest way to succeed with each of these groups is to get in touch early, and get their help in making their job easier.

Because of the focus on the customer and external groups during this stage, coordinating all of these people and their different perspectives on the project is the most important task of the project manager.

Inputs of the Analysis Stage

The outputs of the concept stage are the inputs of the analysis stage:

- A business case, including the statement of value and scope statement.
- A project overview with a defined purpose, a goal statement with inclusions and exclusions, a list of stakeholders, and as much other information as is already available.
- A schedule and budget for the analysis stage, and perhaps for the design stage as well.
- An initial plan describing the life cycle of the project—including whether the product or service will be developed in just one project, or implemented in full through two or more projects. The initial plan should include the deliverables of each stage.
- The context diagram, possibly with some details moving towards a set of data flow diagrams, and other technical specifications.
- A well-organized file of working notes.

Most of the work of the analysis stage will expand these documents to add detail and to make them more precise. Much of this work is done through iteration at finer levels of detail.

Process of the Analysis Stage

We can build a work plan for the analysis stage based on the following steps:

1. Choose a project overview format
2. Organize the project into stages, and multiple projects (if needed)
3. Plan and hold customer meetings (iterative)
4. Define the initial environment thoroughly
5. Define architectural requirements and one or more architectural solutions
6. Plan and hold peripheral stakeholder meetings (iterative)
7. Resolve peripheral stakeholder issues
8. Create the requirements specification with the customers (iterative)
9. Create the high-level project schedule and budget with the customers
10. Review all documents and resolve any open issues
11. Identify staffing needs and plan for the project team
12. Prepare a detailed plan and budget for the design stage
13. Present all documents to the customers, review and revise
14. Obtain formal approval to close the analysis stage and begin the design stage of the project

It is important to note that we can still cancel the project during the analysis stage. We hope we found any obvious project-killers during the concept stage, but sometimes we discover that, even though there is no one project-killer, the value does not exceed the cost, or there are simply too many risks, or some combination of the above. Sometimes, when we speak with peripheral stakeholders, we find a project-killer we missed earlier. Sometimes, customer needs or external situations change so that the project is not useful any more. If so, we cancel the project early, reducing sunk cost. *Sunk cost* is money already spent, so that if we cancel the project, it is gone with no value returned.

Discussed below are the details of each step we follow to bring the analysis stage to completion.

CHOOSE A PROJECT OVERVIEW FORMAT

The project overview is a flexible document. The form given in Chapter 5 works for most medium-sized projects. Below, in the section on tools, we introduce the quick project overview template for small projects. Here is how to think about project size in the analysis stage and how to decide which project overview to use.

- *Small projects* are projects where one end-user or manager knows almost everything you need to know from the customer side, and you, as project manager, fully understand the technical issues without needing outside expertise. If you manage many small projects, you will want to use the quick project overview (QPO). This one-page summary sheet will allow you to keep on top of each project's requirements and current status. So, if you work inside a department but do a lot of projects, alone or with just a few others, the QPO is an excellent tool.
- *Medium-sized projects* are those that require input from several users or user groups, or that require technical expertise held by several different people. The five-page project overview template has fields that will allow you to reconcile differences of opinion among stakeholders. Such projects typically take 1–6 months.
- *Medium-sized projects with additional technical specifications,* such as screen layouts and report formats for software development, or engineering plans, work best with the five-page template plus attachments detailing in full all the end-user requirements.
- *Large or complicated projects* that will take one year or more, or projects that are complicated because multiple stages, multiple locations, or multiple areas of expertise are involved, begin with the project overview template. At the beginning of the design stage, you and your team will build additional project overviews, one for each sub-project of the main project.

KEY POINT

Avoid Shortcuts

When we say that, during the analysis stage, you will specify all user requirements in detail, we mean it. Often, when I am teaching project management to computer professionals, a student asks me, "Can't we just make a list of the names of the reports, and save detailed report specification until later?"

The answer is no. That would be quite dangerous. And this is why. The name of a report does not tell you how long it will take to analyze or to prepare the report, or even if the data are in the database. Our research has shown that the range of time needed to complete a single typical report may range from 2 to 40 hours: a factor of 20. With several reports to prepare, there is no way of knowing how long analysis and design of those reports would take until they are fully analyzed. As a result, you could underestimate the time it will take to complete the project by several weeks. We have even seen some cases where the customer's idea of the report was so different from the project manager's idea that a hidden project-killer was missed.

These templates are extremely flexible. You might be in the middle of analysis, and discover that one particular peripheral stakeholder actually needs a custom menu with ten reports, and options on some of the reports. The easiest, and best, thing to do is obtain a QPO template, declare a sub-project, and track it as a small project that is part of your bigger project. It has its own purpose and goal, and it fits into the larger purpose and goal as well.

ORGANIZE THE PROJECT INTO STAGES, AND MULTIPLE PROJECTS (IF NEEDED)

Early in the analysis stage, we decide the details of the life cycle alternative we are going to use. Our recommendation is to follow the classic system development life cycle (SDLC) with one modification created by the author's company, QTI, which we call the Double Waterfall^{TM}, which is described later in this chapter, in the tools section. For the double waterfall, we define two delivery dates within one budget: the first delivery date is for essential core components, and the second adds enhancements shortly afterwards. This simple modification to the SDLC adds flexibility, simplifies management of customer expectations, and is easy to manage.

Whatever choice we make, we document it in the project overview, particularly on page 4, where we list stages and their deliverables. We can use a second copy of this page for the double waterfall.

PLAN AND HOLD CUSTOMER MEETINGS (ITERATIVE)

The customer meetings we hold during analysis are similar to the ones in the concept stage. Our job is to capture customer requirements in words and pictures. We have a series of meetings or show the write-ups of our meetings to the customers so that they can validate that the picture we are building is correct.

See for Yourself

Whenever you can, take a look at the initial situation yourself. This could be a site visit, a guided walk through, a physical examination of the product you are upgrading, or a viewing of the prior advertising campaign, which did not work. See for yourself how things are. See for yourself what is wrong. See for yourself what works. Then you will know exactly what to do and not to do on your project. That will define your specification with inclusions and exclusions.

This job boils down to answering a simple question: Exactly how many alligators are there in the swamp? While we are there, it might also be good to find poisonous snakes and cantankerous locals with rifles. The more we know about our starting point, the more likely we are to succeed. Here are some key areas you should investigate in detail.

- *Problem to be solved.* What problem exists now that will be solved by implementing the new system? What work cannot be done, or cannot be done well, until the new system is in place?
- *Business processes.* All current business systems that will be changed or replaced by the new system. The current form (manual or electronic, and in what formats) of information that the new system will hold.
- *Customer description.* If the customer is a separate company or companies, or a set of consumers, write a description of the customer as user, and buyer/decision-maker, and a description of any relevant elements of their business environment or life situation.
- *Computer systems and other equipment or facilities.* All systems that will be replaced by, or interact with, the new system. Include hardware platforms, operating systems, and data management systems. Also include user interfaces and systems that will receive or send data through import/export functions. If the existing systems are documented, a reference to those documents should be included here.
- *Risk evaluation.* What elements of the initial environment are undocumented or unknown? What things might we find that would create problems for the project?

When you have the answers, write them down in the initial situation section of the project overview. If it is too long, place a summary there, and attach detailed specifications. This review of the initial environment has a two-fold function. First of all, it allows us to define the starting point of any future process during the project. If, during design, a hardware technician asks for the specification of the equipment he or she is upgrading, we have it. Since we have defined the goal, he or she can create a work plan from start to finish. Secondly, when we know the existing system well, it reduces the chance of any surprises that could cost us time and money later on. To put it another way, any part of the existing system we have not reviewed and analyzed is a risk factor for the project.

DEFINE ARCHITECTURAL REQUIREMENTS AND ONE OR MORE ARCHITECTURAL SOLUTIONS

Earlier in this chapter, we defined architecture as the big picture of how the system will be built and what tools will be used. In some projects, the architecture is predefined. For example, if we are adding one new television advert to an existing campaign, then the architecture of the series—actors on stage, or cartoon, or voice-over, or whatever—will be the architecture for the one additional advert. In other projects, choosing the best architecture may be the biggest and most complicated choice in the entire project.

Once we have a good understanding of what the customer wants, and a clear understanding of the initial environment, we have most of what we need to define our architectural requirements and select an architecture or architectural options. We look at the possibilities and eliminate those that would not be reliable or offer sufficient quality of service. We also eliminate any that are too expensive or could not be implemented in time to meet the project delivery date.

If we are down to only one option, we cannot stop the architecture process and put this out as our proposal. We need evaluation of this choice by every stakeholder. We do not want to miss a project-killer.

What if we find that no architecture will work? We go back to the drawing board. We ask if there are any requirements we could change or drop that would make some architectural solution feasible. If so, we explain the problem to the stakeholders and seek to get their commitment to a solution that does not have all of the features that they want.

If we find that there is no suitable, reliable architectural solution, we should do some research to see if there will be one soon. If the project is urgent, we might consider relying on a new, untested approach. If we do, we are managing a high-risk project. We can also recommend delaying the project until a suitable solution arises.

If two or more solutions pass all of the basic requirements, we ask which one is better. Our first focus should be on proven reliability. After that, we

can compare features and cost of development and maintenance. We guide the project sponsor and key stakeholders through this decision process. When the decision is made, we follow through by also identifying weaknesses or risks in the architecture we have chosen.

PLAN AND HOLD PERIPHERAL STAKEHOLDER MEETINGS (ITERATIVE)

In the analysis stage, we must have some contact with every stakeholder group. That contact may be minimal, perhaps one short meeting and a follow-up e-mail. But we need to understand the needs of every person who will touch, use, support, or have something to say about the product or service we are creating. We need to specify their requirements in writing, and get their approval.

There is one group of stakeholders to whom we should listen closely. After the project is over, there will be some people who have the job of supporting the product or service. If we develop computer systems, then they will be the computer help desk and technical support staff. If we are developing a packaged product to sell for consumers, then they will be the call center staff who answer the telephone when people dial the number on the package.

Whoever these support people are, we should listen to them. We need to deliver documentation and training to them. We also need to lay out a plan for the last stage of the project, transition to production. And their knowledge of the current environment and the customers can save us a lot of time and increase the quality of our product.

The last group of peripheral stakeholders is a mixture of people and organizations that are involved in the project process or need to oversee and review it in some way. It can include internal auditors who will validate your project management and accounting methods. It can include the purchasing department and the legal department in relation to procurement and contracts. It can include people responsible for security, disaster recovery, insurance, and legal liability. It is much easier to get in touch with these people early and solicit their help than it is to turn to them later on, after a problem has already arisen. More than one project has been rejected during transition to production because the final system failed to meet a particular regulation or could not be installed without compromising security or disaster recovery procedures. If we contact these people and they tell us that our project does not raise any issues for their department, then we know we can move ahead with confidence. If they are concerned, we can get their help in clarifying matters easily and early, reducing project risk. In organizations that do a lot of projects, it makes sense to maintain a list of people and departments to contact for these issues.

RESOLVE PERIPHERAL STAKEHOLDER ISSUES

Whatever issues came up in the prior step should be fully resolved and documented.

- *Document all peripheral specifications.* Have them approved by the stakeholders. Arrange a time for review of the interface at the end of design or prototyping, and during production.
- *Prepare a draft of the test plan and the support plan.* You will complete them later. Arrange for help desk and support staff to be involved either throughout the project or during the transition to production stage.
- *Document and resolve all other issues.* Make sure that everything that was discussed is written down and approved.
- *If any issues cannot be fully resolved, identify the work to be done and the deliverable, and carry the work forward into design.* For example, if the security specialist needs you to research certain issues and present the results during the design, then keep track of that work.

CREATE THE REQUIREMENTS SPECIFICATION WITH THE CUSTOMERS (ITERATIVE)

The *requirements specification* is a set of documents that will include both functional and technical requirements. A functional requirement describes what the product or service will do for the user. A technical requirement describes how the product or service will interface with other systems. For example, for a computer program, "must print daily, weekly, monthly, quarterly, and annual sales reports" is a functional requirement. "Will provide data to the existing timesheet application" is a technical requirement. A complete requirements specification will describe all the data seen on the system, every user interface, all data transferred to and from other systems, and every interface with other devices, platforms, equipment, and applications. The requirements specification fully defines all interfaces, but it does not define the internal structure of the product or service. That is left to the design specification.

The work of creating the full requirements specification describes in detail the product or service as it will appear to users and interact with other systems. Methods for creating the requirements specification include interviewing, meeting, document reviews, and prototyping. The exact tools for describing the product or service depend on the nature of the goal, the tools with which teams are familiar, and the development tools that will be used later on. Here are some examples from different types of projects:

- Movies and television commercials use storyboards, either drawn by hand or laid out on a computer, to plot visual images.
- Computer analysts use data flow diagrams, entity relationship diagrams, and CASE (computer-aided software engineering) tools.
- Architects and engineers use CAD (computer-aided design) tools.
- Auditors develop an audit plan and make sure that the requirements conform to regulatory standards, such as the GAAS (generally accepted auditing standards) provided by the AICPA (American Institute of Certified Public Accountants).

It is important that requirements definition be an open, interactive process that comes to a clear, unambiguous resolution. In the early and middle stages, you present the customer with a view that says, "This is what we have thought of so far. Please correct it, improve it, and add more details. If you want it to be different, or if there are mistakes, now is the time we want to know." Encourage careful review and active participation. You will have to do a lot of rework later on if you do not have active, responsible customers or customer representatives now. If the customers think that you can do all the work, or that all you want is to write up what they said the first time and have them check it, then your analysis will not have enough depth. At the end of the analysis stage, the customers will be asked to confirm that the requirements specification is complete and correct. After the analysis stage, changes to the requirements specification require change control, which is costly. Lack of change control would allow scope creep, which is more than costly: It can be disastrous.

It is also important to prioritize the set of requirements. At a minimum, each requirement should be designated as either an essential core requirement or an optional enhancement.

The full list of documents should be maintained in the project overview, and the project manager should ensure that each document is built with both technical and customer input, and is reviewed and approved by the customer.

CREATE THE HIGH-LEVEL PROJECT SCHEDULE AND BUDGET WITH THE CUSTOMERS

Once the goal is clearly defined, you can make a reasonable estimate of the project effort and duration. This estimate will not be as accurate as the one you will create at the end of the design stage. But you will be able to define the planned end dates of each stage of the project and the milestones to be delivered at each of those times. Along with this, you can present a budget that is more accurate than the one you created at the end of the concept stage.

Putting all this together, you can calculate return on investment (ROI) and complete the business case and the project overview. Estimation techniques and ROI are discussed in Chapter 10.

REVIEW ALL DOCUMENTS AND RESOLVE ANY OPEN ISSUES

Review each document for clarity and completeness. Contact any stakeholder for additional information to complete the documentation.

To be completely thorough, it is best to use a review methodology appropriate to your industry. These advanced techniques are beyond the scope of this book, but are well worth mastering once you have basic project management under your belt.

IDENTIFY STAFFING NEEDS AND PLAN FOR THE PROJECT TEAM

At this point, you have a very clear picture of the project and the product or service you are creating. On a medium-sized or large project, you already have some members of your team. Now, it is time to define the team the project needs to succeed. Identify skills and abilities necessary to complete the project. Identify people (employees, consultants, or vendors) who can provide that expertise. Build an initial staffing plan.

PREPARE A DETAILED PLAN AND BUDGET FOR THE DESIGN STAGE

In analysis, we still cannot prepare a detailed work plan for the entire project. That does not come until we are designing the product or service and the

work to be done, in the design stage. But we can, and must, prepare a detailed plan and budget for the design stage itself. We define who we will need and make sure they are on the team. We create a detailed work breakdown structure, and build accurate time and cost estimates.

PRESENT ALL DOCUMENTS TO THE CUSTOMERS, REVIEW AND REVISE

Now it is time to present all project documents to the customer in a proposed final form. Each customer representative should review all documents relevant to the group he or she represents, as well as the general overview. Peripheral stakeholders should review only the documents relevant to the specification that affects them. The project sponsor should review and approve the overall project plan, budget, and schedule. If any changes are requested, make them and confirm them with other stakeholders.

During this review, some people will see the plan for the first time. Make sure they understand it and know how to work with it. Others will be seeing it a second time, having seen it during the concept stage. For them, be sure to note any significant changes in plan that have happened since they approved the concept.

OBTAIN FORMAL APPROVAL FOR THE END OF THE ANALYSIS AND THE BEGINNING OF THE DESIGN STAGE

When all changes are made, return to the project sponsor to get approval to move ahead with the project in the design stage. However, if the business case has faltered, and the project does not show sufficient value over cost, this is a good time to cancel the project.

Outputs of the Analysis Stage

At the end of the analysis stage, you have prepared a thorough, but high-level plan for the project. You have a complete, detailed requirements specification for the product or service. And you have a large number of supporting documents. Here is the complete list:

- A complete business case, including the statement of value and scope statement, supported by a cost/benefit analysis or return on investment (ROI) calculation.
- A complete project overview.
- A schedule and budget for the design stage.
- A stage and milestone plan for each project stage.
- A list of architectural requirements including: a decision on, or a set of questions to be resolved in design that will determine the conceptual architecture; a decision on, or a set of questions to be resolved in design that will determine the specific (brand name and physical) architecture.
- A functional and technical requirements specification including the context diagram, specifications appropriate to your project, and possibly a prototype.
- A draft support plan, or notes towards one.
- A draft training plan, or notes towards one.
- An initial risk plan, or notes towards one, including a record of risk management activities already performed.
- Notes towards a quality plan.
- A list of current and potential team members and their roles.
- A list of all stakeholders and contacts.
- A well-organized file of working notes.

We bring all of these for review by the sponsor, the customers or customer representatives, and the other stakeholders. When all is approved, and the sponsor allocates the budget and assigns the team members, we can begin the design stage.

Key Tools for the Analysis Stage

In analysis, we complete the project overview and the context diagram, as well as the other documents started in the concept stage. We also want to introduce two new tools, the quick project overview (QPO) and the Double Waterfall™ method of modifying the classic SDLC.

QUICK PROJECT OVERVIEW (QPO)

The QPO is a shorter, simpler version of the project overview that we introduced in the concept stage. The summary fits on one page, and you plan the whole project on the next few pages. It is excellent for simple projects where one customer makes a request and there are no divisive issues to resolve. You can use it to focus on the purpose and goal of the project and to track your work as you do it. The QPO can also be used for a small set of tasks within a larger project. Table 6-2 contains the QPO with field definitions.

Table 6-2   Quick project overview with field definitions.

Project name:	Descriptive name that indicates project purpose to all parties		
Project requested by:	Customer	**Project manager:**	IT manager of project
Imposed budget:	Amount desired or required by customer ($)		
Underline one:	**required limit**	**desired limit**	**not yet set**
Imposed delivery date:	Delivery date desired or required by customer		
Underline one:	**required**	**desired**	**not yet set**
Estimated cost:	Cost estimate from project team ($)		
Estimated delivery date:	Delivery date estimate from project team		

Purpose: (justification)
The reason the company, or a part of the company, should do the project. The value added to the company by the project. The business justification. The return on investment. See the seven types of value in Chapter 5
Initial situation:
The starting point. Description of the current system, the platform, and the problem to be solved

Table 6-2 Quick project overview with field definitions (*Continued*).

Current situation:
A status description of where the project is today. This is updated regularly during the project. Current situation is the initial situation plus completed steps
Goal: (detailed description)
The desired final state when the project is complete and the product is in use and supported. A careful, detailed, but non-technical description of what the system will do, who will use it, and how it will be supported. The scope and inclusions of the project
Steps:
Note: to create each task list below, review the process for each stage in Part Two. Adapt the generic steps to apply to the specific project. See also instructions for creating a Work Breakdown Structure (WBS) in Chapter 10.
Concept
List of tasks to complete the concept stage
Approval
List of tasks to get approval for the concept stage
Analysis
List of tasks to complete the analysis stage
Approval
List of tasks to get approval for the analysis stage
Design
List of tasks to complete the design stage
Approval
List of tasks to get approval for the design stage

Table 6-2   Quick project overview with field definitions (*Continued*).

Development
List of tasks to complete the development stage
Approval
List of tasks to get approval for the development stage
Transition to production
List of tasks to complete the transition to production
Approval
List of tasks to get approval for the transition to production stage
Project close
List of tasks to complete project close
Approval
List of tasks to get approval to close the project
The project is complete
Production
Brief description of support responsibilities in the production stage
Decommissioning
Description of events or dates that would cause this product or service to be in need of review for major upgrade or replacement

Using the QPO

Small projects can run into trouble if they are over-managed. We do not want to spend too much time tracking the project, we just want to get the work done. But small projects also have almost all the same dangers of failing as big ones do. There are three keys to succeeding on a small project:

- *Use a QPO*. Any project, no matter how small, needs a written plan and tracking system. And it works best if you break the plan up into stages. If you get interrupted and have to come back later, you want to know where you left off. If a small specification is needed, or a problem comes up, write down what you are doing.
- *Use the six keys to success*. These are just as important for a small project as they are for a big one (see Chapter 3).
- *Use common sense*. Do not feel that you have to deal with every field, or that you cannot add a field if you need one. For example, if a project is working internally within your department, and there is no need to track cost, just enter N/A (not applicable) on the cost fields. If you are working on something and realize that you cannot finish without asking the customer or asking an expert, add a page called "problems and solutions." Make the template work for you instead of locking yourself into a box and working for the template. Follow any helpful guidelines in this book, and use any tool or method that you know or find in this book if it makes the project easier.

Table 6-3 shows a QPO that was used to plan and implement a small wireless network for an office with three workers, two of whom needed to be able to move from room to room to do different work. This document comes from shortly after the analysis stage. Based on the research in the analysis stage, it was easy to select the system and vendor, and get approval. So the IT manager went ahead and ordered the equipment, doing some design steps and some development steps. He also went ahead and moved the printer and got it working on the computer that was going to stay on the landline network. In a sense, he broke the rules of the SDLC by proceeding with development tasks before getting approval on the design. But he knew what he was doing. He knew that this equipment was needed and approved, and that whatever other elements of network design might change, the printer would be on the landline network. Appropriately, he got that done.

One of the good features of the QPO is that it makes it easy to lay work aside and come back to it later. As much as we would like to get each job done, we are often pulled from task to task. Taking the extra two minutes to track where we are on each project saves a lot of time when we come back to the project and want to start up again. And this is as easy as typing the word "DONE" next to each step in the QPO when we finish it.

Table 6-3   Small office wireless network quick project overview.

Project name:	Small Office Wireless Network		
Project requested by:	Office manager	**Project manager:**	IT manager
Imposed budget:	$500 equipment budget, plus internal time		
Underline one:	required limit	<u>**Desired limit**</u>	not yet set
Imposed delivery date:	**10/1/2004**		
Underline one:	required	<u>**Desired**</u>	not yet set
Estimated cost:	$500, plus $10/month support fee		
Estimated delivery date:	Not yet set		
Purpose: (justification)			
To improve effectiveness of a small office with three people doing many different types of work at all hours, it would be useful to allow two of the workers to go to any room of the house. An author or researcher who wanted quiet could take a laptop to a different room, and still have file server, e-mail, and internet access.			
Initial situation:			
A messy office with a peer-to-peer network of a desktop, and a laptop with a printer. Only the laptop can use the DSL connection. A third laptop is in use, but not networked.			
Current situation:			
Equipment for a wireless network has arrived from the DSL provider, including a wireless hub and two wireless network cards.			
The DSL link has been upgraded (at $10/month) to support multiple users once the router and wireless hub are installed.			
The box has not been unpacked.			
Crucial office files are primarily on the laptop, and some are backed up to the desktop.			
All computers have all needed software installed and are working properly.			

Table 6-3 Small office wireless network quick project overview (*Continued*).

Goal: (detailed description)
A wireless network connecting a desktop computer with local printer on a peer network with two laptops. All three computers have internet access for browser and e-mail through a shared DSL connection. The network is configured using equipment from the DSL provider and installed according to their specifications, so that they will support the network.
Steps:
Concept
DONE Get idea for wireless network
DONE Research cost options
DONE See advertisement from current ISP
DONE Get everyone's opinion that it is a good idea
Approval
DONE Office manager says go ahead
Analysis
DONE Determine user needs
DONE Confirm equipment order and support from ISP
Approval
DONE Get approval for increase in monthly service charges and equipment order
Design
Draw up network design
Identify components
DONE Plan procurement
DONE Estimate time and cost
Approval
DONE President approves installation plan and purchase plan, time and cost

Table 6-3   Small office wireless network quick project overview (*Continued*).

Development
DONE Place order for new service and equipment
DONE Clean office
DONE Relocate printer to desktop computer, reconfigure print sharing
DONE Test print sharing
DONE Receive order
Unpack and check equipment
Install equipment with drivers
wired LAN
wireless LAN hub
wireless LAN cards in two laptops
Install internet service upgrade
Approval
test LAN
test wireless LAN
test internet connection, all services, all systems
Transition to production
Use network for 2 weeks with both laptops in all useful rooms and locations with all services
Approval
all users approve
president approves
Production
Approval
Decommissioning
Approval

Organizing Too Much Work

A network manager for a construction company was responsible for supporting 200 users and performing all projects to grow the network aggressively. This construction company was committed to developing and using the best technology for construction estimation, engineering, and project management, and as a result had cutting-edge IT systems. It was one of the first medium-sized construction companies to consider and implement wireless technology.

The network manager, Glenn, felt he had too much work to do. His boss, the COO, thought that Glenn was not very effective. Glenn decided to use the method in this book to organize his work. He identified each project on which he was working, and, with a bit of help, wrote a quick project overview for each one. He was working on 42 projects all by himself, as well as keeping everything running!

He built a spreadsheet as a master list of projects. Evaluating what he had written, he realized that there were a number of projects he thought he had finished, but the customer did not know he was finished. He had trouble with the sixth key to success: follow through. He quickly took the last steps on ten projects, and the COO changed his mind and thought that Glenn was extremely effective. Glenn then analyzed his project work and budgets. He identified some management and financial reporting problems that were not under his control. Using his new reputation, he went to the COO to suggest some changes. This COO could be hard to convince. In this case, though, Glenn made his point. The way finances were managed for IT was changed, and the COO hired a new, full-time assistant network manager. Glenn had been lobbying for that for three years, but until he could prove that he was not the problem, and that the workload was the problem, he got nowhere. Organizing his projects with QPOs helped him get his work done, show what a good worker and manager he was, and get the support and resources he needed from his boss.

You, too, can use these methods to get organized, solve real problems, gain influence, and get the support you need.

THE DOUBLE WATERFALL

During the analysis stage we often find that the customers do not know everything that they will want. This is especially true if we are bringing in new technology. Until they get their hands on it and try to use it, they will not know all the features that they want. How, then, can we define a project that gives them a clear defined result, when they do not know what will satisfy them?

In cases like this, the classic SDLC needs some modification. We cannot specify all the features in analysis, because no one can think of them. If we tried to use the classic SDLC, we would either deliver a result that did not really do what the customer wanted, or find ourselves handling a pile of expensive, time-consuming change requests. This is called scope creep, because one small item after another creeps into the scope, and the delivery date creeps out longer and longer. Scope creep gives many project managers a bad reputation.

There is a solution. We call it the double waterfall and it gives an easy solution to the problem of scope creep.

Explaining scope creep and change management to customers

Since changes are inevitable, it is crucial that everyone in the project understand the consequences of changes. Everyone needs to understand how changes will be handled, and why.

The "why" is simple. If changes are not handled well, the project cost and schedule will spiral out of control. *Scope creep* is a term for how extra requirements creep into the project, so that the scope grows, and then the delivery date creeps ever later while the total cost creeps upwards.

The "how" is tricky. Customers who are not familiar with project management will think that you are being draconian when you tell them what the rules are. It is a good idea to have some scary stories to make your point. Here are some general rules for change control:

- Time and budget estimates are all subject to revision if a change is made to the plan.
- The project manager, and not the customer, has final say regarding whether or not a given change will be allowed to be added to the project, rather than held off to a later version.
- The costs for redesign and planning cost, time, and risk management for the change will all be billed to the customer, in addition to the costs of developing the change itself.

Even with these dire warnings, it is essential that you encourage the customer to request all changes that any stakeholder raises as desirable. If you do not, then the customer may withhold some crucial requirement that must be met, throwing the actual value of the whole project into jeopardy. We do not want to stifle communication or create an environment where customer expectations can veer away from the project plan. Therefore, follow these steps, called *Change Control Procedures*:

- The customer is responsible for raising any issues that may require a change to the product, or the project time, cost, or delivery date at the earliest possible time.
- The customer is responsible for reading the project overview and design documentation and raising any issues about anything that is not clear.
- The project manager will respond to each issue raised. The project manager will make a list of proposed changes that cover all the issues raised. Each change will be tracked in a separate *change request*.
- Each proposed change will be evaluated. The criterion for evaluation is: Is this change essential to the success of the project? If it is essential, then it is included in the first life cycle and delivered with the first version.
- If the change is essential to the success of the project, a change control document, defining the change to the project and the product, will be written. This document will define the change, define the project steps that are changing, and define the changes to the cost estimates and the schedule.
- The change control document will be completed and delivered in a timely fashion, so that all involved can approve it before any step of the project that is changed needs to be delayed pending approval.
- The customer, the project manager, and all team leaders affected by the change will sign that they understand and approve the change control document.
- If a change request is an item that is of value, but not core to the project, it will be included in a second small project, delivered on the second version delivery date, and be worked on in the second waterfall of the life cycle.
- If the requested change cannot be implemented without reducing the quality and reliability of the system, or its value does not exceed its cost, then the project manager will explain the reason the change has been rejected on the change request form, and contact the requestor.

Introducing the double waterfall

If the customer or the project team thinks of something that is valuable to the customer, but not essential to the success of the product, it is much better to do it as a follow-up project than to perform change control on the main project. Here are the advantages:

- Not changing the project reduces confusion and error.
- Not changing the product ensures that your test procedures will be valid. If the product specifications are changed, it is much more likely that errors will creep through testing and end up in the final product.
- Change control itself is time-consuming and costly.
- If one stakeholder demands a change, and another one resists it, the conflict could create problems for the project.

The best way to handle all of these issues is to create a follow-up project for enhancements. Figure 6-2 illustrates the benefits of this approach. If we call the original product "System 1.0," then adding a follow-up project does not change the original product delivery date, and the customer can begin using Version 1.0 at time T1 and realizing value from it. The follow-up project can begin, and can deliver a working "Upgrade 1.1" by time T2. There are several benefits to the double waterfall:

- The double waterfall encourages the customers and stakeholders to tell us as much as they can during analysis, so that they can get more in the first-stage delivery.

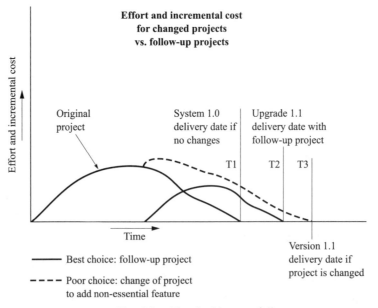

Fig. 6-2. The double waterfall.

- At the same time, it also encourages users to tell us things that they think of later. We have committed to listen and to give them whatever will really help them, either in stage one, or in stage two.
- The double waterfall reduces the chances that we will need to delay a delivery date and fail to satisfy our customers.
- It reduces the time and effort spent on change control. As each change request comes in after the analysis stage, we can quickly decide whether to place it in the first project and do essential change control, or to set it aside for the second waterfall. When the first waterfall is in the middle of development, we can design a new project overview and schedule for the second waterfall, including all open change requests in the second stage of the project.
- It reduces time and cost on testing. Test plans can be built early in development, and developers can test against them as components are developed. The second-stage tests are very simple; we can test the upgrades to the system.
- It reduces the risk of a major error due to misunderstandings of project change. If too many changes are brought in, there is a chance that different groups will be working on different parts of the project plan. The result can be a project with the head of a horse and the rear end of a donkey: things just do not fit together as they should. Moving most change requests to the second stage keeps the plans more stable, reducing the chances of this error.

The double waterfall reduces project risk, decreases cost, and delivers value sooner. For many projects, using a single SDLC leaves everyone worse off. We can see that by following the dotted line in Fig. 6-2. Using a single waterfall, System 1.0 would never be delivered. The first usable version would be Version 1.1. And, due to the confusion, error, time, and cost of change control, it is likely to arrive even later than Upgrade 1.1 would have arrived if we had stuck to the original project and added a separate follow-up project.

We recommend that one project budget be used for the entire project, including all the work leading to delivery of the first version and the upgrade. We need the resources committed up front to succeed at delivering what the customer wants and needs. The double waterfall is a way of managing deliverables, time, and communications, but it usually works best to secure full financing up front.

The double waterfall is very good for new systems and major upgrades. For small projects, and for projects that are enhancements of existing products or services, the standard SDLC is likely to be sufficient and easier to manage.

The double waterfall was created particularly to solve problems in the computer development arena, but it can also apply to other projects. If a customer is building their dream home, we could finish the exterior and the interior walls, and then let them see the space before putting in furnishings and fixtures. But there are some times when we do not want to use the double waterfall. Do not use the double waterfall in the following cases:

- When getting it right the first time is essential. If you are putting a new satellite into orbit or putting an advert on television during a specific sporting event, do not use the double waterfall.
- When the product is going to thousands of customers. Here, you could release an early version to a few customers, but the best version should go into production.
- When retooling production is expensive. Car manufacturing is a good example here. Changing features of a car requires retooling an assembly line, which is an expensive proposition. So it is better to finish the design of the final car and final production line before going into production.

In these cases, there are other solutions. For example, one can work with extensive prototyping throughout design and development, involving the customer throughout the life cycle. This ensures that we will continue to identify and adopt customer improvements throughout the project. The best companies that do this kind of work, such as Hewlett-Packard, the Saturn division of GM, and the group that developed the Plymouth/Dodge Neon, have highly structured, advanced project life cycles and change control procedures that make this work.

Key Concepts for the Analysis Stage

Project communications management and scope definition are the most essential processes in the concept stage. We also begin to work with issues of time, cost, and quality more extensively. It is definitely valuable to begin risk assessment for the whole project, and to manage the risks inherent in the analysis process itself. The biggest risks in analysis are:

- *Lack of sufficient communication with customers*, resulting in a requirements specification that does not describe what the customer wants and needs. We can prevent this by using effective methods of communication, reliable requirements gathering techniques, and good tools such as data flow diagrams and prototyping.

- *Failure to identify key stakeholders*, leading to a requirements specification that is missing a key project component.
- *Political conflict about the value of the project.* Methods for bringing everyone onto the same page are found in Chapter 3.

Case Study: The Historic Battle of the Cellular Base Station

A wireless engineer involved in setting up a cellular telephone network in a rural area of the USA with historic battlefields, found himself managing a battle instead of managing a project. Conflicts over the location of a cellular telephone base station and tower led to major problems and delays. But the project manager stuck with a cooperative approach, and eventually succeeded. The case study is summarized in Table 6-4.

WHAT THIS MEANS FOR YOUR PROJECT

I would like to say that people have learned lessons from problems like those illustrated in Table 6-4. However, a recent case involved the building of wind generator farms in western New York State. The project manager thought he had done a good job communicating with the public. But he ran into the same kinds of barriers. The lesson: being a good project manager requires getting along with everyone who might care about a project, and getting their support from the very beginning.

Most projects do not turn into court battles or controversies on television. However, a small, internal conflict can finish or hinder a project for a customer or an internal project just as easily as a public battle can finish a public project. The solution is to use the communications and political skills that the project manager demonstrated every time right from the start of the project discussed in Table 6-4. Had this happened, the National Parks flagpole, which provided full coverage at the lowest cost and required no county zoning permit, might have been chosen first. And the Park Service might not have backed out if there was no controversy. Or the first plan would have worked, because the owner of the nearby land would have made his complaint at the hearing, and then he would have had no basis for a lawsuit.

Table 6-4   The historic battle of the cellular base station.

Stage: Analysis
This case study is: Overcoming a challenge
Initial situation

A growing cellular company had received the license for frequency allocation to serve a rural area including a town famous for being near a US Civil War battlefield that was also a county seat. Customers wanted service, and the project manager discussed options with local landowners and proposed an option based on leasing property from one landowner. Prior to the meeting, everyone seemed satisfied.
 	
    In preparing the deal, the land acquisition company (representing the cellular provider) negotiated with more than one landowner. They took the best offer and arranged an option to buy a tower location 500 feet outside the town area. The cellular company proposed a 250-foot self-supporting tower. The high tower was needed because the site was just below a ridge. The first 150 feet of tower reached the level of the ridge, and the top 100 feet gave enough clearance to serve the town.
 	
    County public hearings had only a normal amount of opposition. There was no unusual political noise, and no historical issues were raised. No view shed issue (degradation of view, especially relevant for historical areas) was raised. As a result the vendor received the county permit for construction.

Problem

A lawsuit was filed in the county seat challenging the permit. The cellular company and the project manager were taken completely by surprise.
 	
    The people who filed the lawsuit had not spoken up or raised any issues at the hearing. The suit was filed in the name of the owner of an adjacent piece of land. His complaint was about reduction in property value, but property value was not really the issue. He wanted the tower on his property; he was challenging the permit because he did not get the deal.
 	
    The issues set forth in the lawsuit were reduction of property values and view shed. The lawsuit claimed that the board had erred in consideration of the facts.
 	
    Several politically connected parties became involved in the negotiations that followed. Three were generally supportive of the cellular provider's efforts: The landowner who would sell the land according to the original plan, the county supervisor, and the Appalachian Trail Council, which saw value in cell phone coverage for hiker safety.

Table 6-4   The historic battle of the cellular base station (*Continued*).

Other key parties who became involved were the US Parks Department, which, at the time, had oversight of Civil War battlefields, and an individual who lived nearby and was connected to a Congressional oversight agency, who opposed the original plan.
Action or method used
The project manager decided to take action. Rather than wait for the resolution of the lawsuit, he decided to build public support, and also to actively seek alternative locations for placing the base station and cellular tower. He arranged and held a number of public and private meetings. The public meetings were held at a motel owned by the man who had filed the lawsuit, and the cellular company paid for its use. This choice made it clear that the cellular provider did not want a fight, and that they wanted everyone to benefit. The private meetings included dozens of hours of conversations with interested parties, including the mayor of the town, who was concerned about issues of historical preservation.   The legal conflict went back and forth between the courts and the planning board for two months before the permit was reissued.   Parties opposed to the cellular site plan moved the battle from the courts to the media, going for press and television coverage and publicity in trade magazines and regional newspapers.   The cellular provider began discussions with the National Park Service, but this was before the US president wrote a letter asking the Park Service to support deployment of cellular towers. Working with the Park Service, the cellular provider proposed a 120-foot flagpole at the park with an antenna hidden inside. After six weeks the Park Service backed out of the plan, but no reason was given.   The friend of the plaintiff who had links with the Congressional oversight committee became more polarized. He saw no acceptable solution and wanted to stop deployment of the cellular service completely.   The project manager continued conversations with local politicians, including the mayor, and got the mayor to support the cellular provider. Other parties all wanted a good solution. Some of them helped placate more contentious people. Private meetings were generally between the cellular provider and one to three other parties, in order to support effective brainstorming.   The cellular company found and proposed a third location in an adjacent township on top of a ridge that overlooked the entire town. The ridge was itself considered a historic location in the Civil War, but no shots had been fired there, even though it changed hands several times. There were already two or three water tanks located at the top of the ridge, and the town had already installed a microwave dish below the treeline to provide local access to cable television.

Table 6-4   The historic battle of the cellular base station (*Continued*).

The proposal was for renting space for the cellular base station as long as the cellular antennas were not visible and the microwave installation for connection to the cellular network was behind the water towers. Planning the microwave location was easy. For the cellular antenna, it was mounted on two 30-foot wooden poles painted the same color as the water tower. The two poles provided spatial diversity for the antennas, preventing signal fading and maintaining high-quality cellular calls.

The whole process took six months, but the final plan was acceptable to almost everyone, required no local or county zoning, and worked at low cost.

Result

The cellular tower was built near the water tower on the ridge.

This solution covered the town well, but reduced coverage to rural areas nearby. The coverage area was about 40% of what it would have been with the first plan, but it covered the business district and the most concentrated residential districts.

Construction cost was much lower, as two 30-foot poles cost a lot less than a 250-foot tower, but the cost of the conflict well exceeded the savings on the construction costs.

The cellular base station became operational in about 1998, and is still in use. The town has good coverage from that tower. Coverage was created for the surrounding area, with service by three small towers. To date, only one or two have been installed.

Lesson learned

All politics are local. Even with federal departments and national organizations involved, the solution is found by cooperation with the people most involved.

The more quickly you can reach a compromise, the more quickly and more effectively you will complete the project. This will lead to higher quality at lower cost with an earlier delivery date.

When there is a conflict, understand who your opposition is.

To gain cooperation, solicit views of all possible stakeholders at the beginning of the process. The cellular provider's original error was to assume that, just because no one spoke up at the zoning meeting, they had no opposition.

Cast a wide net to find all stakeholders.

The results of any particular conflict or project have a long-term effect on quality of service. (Over a decade later, people are living with lower coverage and the vendor has less revenue.)

Or the third option might have had more flexibility, such as the ability to put the cellular antennas slightly higher, increasing coverage.

The point is that the less conflict there is, the more options you have, and the sooner everything is resolved in the best way possible. If we work to create cooperation from the beginning, we will not have to struggle to resolve conflicts later on.

Also, if we are involved in a conflict, we succeed by not becoming polarized ourselves. As long as we continue to work towards the best solution for everyone, we have the best possible chance of long-term success.

Conclusion

If the work during analysis is done well, we have a clear picture of what we are going to make, and we are started on the spiral of success described in Chapter 1. At the conclusion of the analysis stage, the project overview and the requirements specification that lists all required and desired customer features are locked down. For these documents, any future changes require change control.

As a general rule, we manage projects well and prevent scope creep by keeping things very flexible in the early stages, and then locking them down very tightly at a certain point. What determines that point? We lock an item down when we begin to work on tasks that depend on that item for input. In the design stage, we will build our project plan, including the work breakdown structure, the detailed schedule and budget, and the quality and risk plans. These all have the project overview and the requirements specification as inputs. A change to any of these documents requires a lot of time spent reworking the activities of the design stage. In addition, the design specification depends on the requirements specification. To prevent this rework, we lock down the analysis deliverables once they are approved at the end of the analysis stage.

Once analysis is complete, we can think of the project overview as a project charter. It defines our mission. There will be changes, but there should be few or no changes that redefine the mission, that change the scope of the project at a large level. Our goal in the design stage is to design a product or service that will fulfill the needs, requirements, and added benefits discovered in the design stage. We design to meet the requirements specification.

During design, therefore, the requirements specification and the project work plan are all very flexible. These will not be locked down until the end of the design stage.

In the design stage, we build and manage the project team, and turn our attention to them. The team creates the design specification, and we prepare the documents that will guide the project and ensure success.

Our Case Study: Hi-tech Home Theater

How do you get more for your money? Talk to experts. Our first experts were friends who love to watch television. From them, I learned that a lot of my favorite television can be found on the internet, ready for download, in case we miss an episode. That would be excellent.

When a project manager hears a customer say, "Boy, that would be great!" his or her first reaction should be fear: "Scope creep! You're adding more to the project." And we were. But, since we were still in analysis, there was a chance we could make it succeed. After all, with a home business, a computer with a DVD burner is a business expense, not an additional cost on the home theater project. Still, bringing the computer into the picture makes the project more complicated. To avoid trouble, it was time to introduce the double waterfall. First, get the home theater set up with DVD, video recorder, and surround-sound stereo. Then, for the second waterfall, we will add on downloading television shows, learning all about codecs—coder-decoders, the software that plays different audio and video formats—and either burning DVDs that the DVD player can read or connecting the computer to the home theater system. How did I learn we needed to do all that? More talking to experts.

When I read the previous paragraph, I see a lot of architectural thinking. In fact, creative architectural work is the backbone of this project. Because we are choosing to integrate components ourselves, we are able to do the project for about $2,000, instead of $10,000 to $25,000, which would be the cost of buying a complete system. Keeping some old components and linking the pieces together ourselves is what we are doing. The architectural term is integration.

So, combining brainstorming for additional value, talking to experts, bringing in the double waterfall to avoid scope creep, and refining our architectural plan, we have set up the project for success.

Your Project for Learning

Now is the time for you to complete the analysis stage of your project for learning. Begin by reviewing the results of the concept stage. Then go through this chapter, reviewing inputs, process, outputs, and tools. Use as many of the tools as you can, even if they seem inappropriate for your particular project. For example, you might use the full-sized project overview form, even though this project really only needs a quick project overview. Or you might prepare for a stakeholder meeting with yourself, have an agenda with questions, talk to yourself, and write up the results as a specifications document. Remember, you have two goals. One is to complete the project, and the other is to get comfortable with using the tools of project management.

For your end-of-stage review, compare what you created with the list of outputs for the analysis stage, discussed above. If anything is missing or not completely clear, send it back to yourself for rework!

When you have completed the analysis stage, you are ready to read the next chapter and design your project for learning.

Questions for Learning

Being a project manager requires a lot of flexibility. See if you can think of several ways to handle each of the following situations. If you cannot think of at least three approaches to each problem, make a note to read the chapter or chapters listed in parentheses after each item.

- The project on which you are working requires a new piece of equipment that is due out in three months from the vendor, but may be delayed. The project is on a short deadline. (Chapter 12)
- You are replacing an existing office system, and two different customer groups have very different needs. One finds the current system unusable, and needs a quick solution, even if it has only basic features. The other is satisfied with the current system, and will not use the new system unless it has much better features, including a long list of improvements for which the group is more than willing to pay. (Chapter 12)

- The project sponsor leaves the company unexpectedly. The sponsor's successor does not know anything about what you are doing. (Chapters 3 and 12)
- Think about a project you know about or were involved in that failed or ran into a lot of trouble. Did it suffer from any of the mistakes listed in Table 6-1? If so, what were they? How would you manage that project if you were in charge? (Chapter 6)
- You have been asked to implement changes to the way the analysis stage is done at your company. Which changes would you implement first? What training would be needed? Prepare a case demonstrating the value of these improvements. (Chapters 3 and 6)

CHAPTER

Design: What Are We Making? How Will We Do It?

In the design stage, the project team takes on the challenge of designing the product or service, while the project manger faces these three tasks:

- Creating the team, and leading it to complete its work.
- Planning the rest of the project, including the work plan, schedule, budget, risk plan, quality plan, and more.
- Keeping the customer and the sponsor informed, managing expectations, and getting approval for the design and the entire project schedule, budget, and work plan.

This chapter is relatively short for two reasons. Firstly, we have defined many of the most important tools and concepts already, and now we need only make reference to them. Secondly, during the design stage, our work is widening out. In the concept and analysis stages, we focused on the customer, and worked

mostly with communications and scope definition. In the design stage, our focus turns inwards towards what the team will do, and how we will do it. But we need to plan all aspects of how the team will bring the project to successful completion: time, cost, quality, risk, and more. So you will not find most of the tools for the design stage in this chapter. They are in Part Three.

In This Chapter

- Key points of the design stage
- Resources assigned to the design stage
- Roles in the design stage
- Inputs of the design stage
- Process of the design stage
- Outputs of the design stage
- Conclusion
- Our case study: Putting the pieces together
- Your project for learning
- Questions for learning

Key Points of the Design Stage

As we begin design, the purpose and goal of the project are clear. They are defined in the project overview and the business case, and detailed in the customer's requirements specification. Now the question is: How will we get there? For the technical team, that is mostly a matter of deciding what we will build that will do what the user wants it to do. As project managers, we chart the work path to our target.

KEY POINT

The Core of Project Design
Even if we are managing a simple project where the work is routine for the team, the three things we want to create are a work breakdown structure (WBS), a schedule, and a budget. The WBS comes first, because an accurate schedule and budget, and all the other plans as well, are built from a good WBS. Be sure to read Chapter 10 and practice creating work breakdown structures with your team.

There are eight elements to our work in the design stage:

- *Building the team.* Some people say that the key to project success is defining the right job and then getting the right people to do it. There is a lot of truth in that. Now that we know what we are making, we can define the skills needed for the job. Using the techniques in Chapter 12 we can create the best team of staff and consultants for the job.
- *Creating the design specification* is actually the work of the project, not the work of managing the project. But we should understand what it is our team is doing.
- *Communications: How much should the sponsor and customers be involved?* Traditionally, technical project teams would finish analysis and wave goodbye to the customer, saying, "Now, we know what you want. Leave us alone to design and build it. We'll see you when it's ready for testing." Experience has shown that this does not work. We need to keep in touch with our customers.
- *Preparing a work breakdown structure* is our most important planning task. A careful, detailed WBS will increase the accuracy of our time and cost estimates, and simplify and improve the quality of our quality, risk, and procurement plans.
- *Detailed time and cost estimation* is possible once the WBS is complete.
- *Planning for quality control and quality assurance* during design is key to project success.
- *Risk assessment and risk planning* are a team effort during the design stage.
- *Making procurement decisions* is done during the design stage.

Let us look at each of these items more closely.

BUILDING THE TEAM

Gordon Bethune, the CEO who took Continental Airlines from the brink of its second bankruptcy to the USA's first airline to become one of Fortune's 100 best companies to work for, defines management as: Defining the job; getting the right people; getting out of their way, and keeping everything else out of their way. If we apply that to project management, then we defined the job in the concept and analysis stages. We get the right people in the design stage. If people are assigned to us, then we assess them and close any gaps, either through training, or through retention of additional staff or consultants. Then we get out of their way. We set up structures for effective team communications and let the team get to work while we do our job. What is our job? Keeping everything else out of their way. We plan ahead, defining the course of the rest of the project and clearing away obstacles so that they will be able to work smoothly through to a successful finish.

In some fields, it is easy to see the difference between design and development. In construction, an architectural engineer creates drawings, and construction workers build the building. In making a movie, a conceptual artist draws storyboards, a director with camera operators, actors, and crew shoots the actual scenes.

However, when we develop products or services that are all in computer programs or in writing, it can be harder to distinguish design work from development work. Nonetheless, the skills really are different, and we need to recognize the difference. The skills of designing a good computer program, skills such as data flow diagramming, data modeling, interface design and specification, and logical design, are entirely different from the skills involved in writing program code and testing it. Those skills include: coding in a particular language, effective module design, high-quality documentation, and testing and debugging.

As a result, the people we need for design may not be the same as the people we need for development. Yet most projects build a team of programmers or engineers, and assume that they can do all the necessary tasks. We need to take a more careful approach. We need to assess each team member's skills at doing each of the jobs that need to be done, and then close the gaps. And we also need to assess and improve the team's ability to work as a team.

EXERCISE

Evaluating Design and Development Skills

Whatever field you are in, take some time aside to make a list of the skills someone needs to complete the design for a project, and a separate list of the skills needed to develop the product or service. Then evaluate yourself and each member of your team. Does each person have the skills he or she needs for each stage? If not, could someone help them out? Do they need training? Does the project need additional staff?

CREATING THE DESIGN SPECIFICATION

Our team has a piece of technical work to do, converting the requirements specification into a design specification. The requirements specification is the outer face of the product or service we are creating, the face it shows to customers (the user interface) and the face it shows to all other users and systems in the context diagram. The design specification is the inner face of the product or service. It defines the internal structure, the subsystems and components. It also defines the inner process flow, the communication across each interface between internal components. Whatever your team is creating, the creative challenge is to design a system with the outer face defined by the requirements specification, and the inner face designed for reliable, effective, and efficient operation using existing technology and means of production.

If we want to explain this to users, we can return to the analogy of architecture and building design. In a building, users specify the purpose of a room, for example, a banquet hall. The architect designs the building to create the space the user defines. After this, the architectural plan is passed on to an architectural engineering group. The architectural engineering group estimates the amount of heating and air conditioning needed for a banquet hall of a certain size (specified by the architect) and a certain number of people (specified by the customer), all of whom generate heat. The architectural engineering group then selects appropriate components (heaters, air conditioners, fans, ductwork) and creates engineering diagrams that specify how they will work together within the architecture to meet user requirements.

In a similar way, on any project, the user defines the need and the architects and engineers design a system to meet that need in the design stage, and build it in the development stage.

COMMUNICATIONS: HOW MUCH SHOULD THE SPONSOR AND CUSTOMERS BE INVOLVED?

If we say farewell to the customers at the beginning of design, they will start dreaming. They will dream of delivery day, when they will have the perfect system and all of their problems will be resolved. And they will be sadly disappointed, because they will have drifted off and imagined far more features than they asked us to include. We need to maintain enough communication to manage customer expectations. On the other hand, we do not want them over-involved. We do not want to waste their time, nor do we want to be micromanaged.

The right level of communication will depend on a number of factors, from the corporate culture to the types of tools used in design. If the design tools include prototyping tools, we can actively include the customer representatives on a weekly, or even daily, basis. At a minimum, we should provide weekly status reports to the customer and the sponsor, and also verify any questions any team members have about the requirements specification. Some clarification is almost always needed as a technician actually begins to work from a specification.

In addition, we should contact peripheral stakeholders as needed. When an engineer, technician, or programmer begins to create the design specification from the requirements specification for a particular stakeholder, he or she should make contact with the stakeholder and arrange as many phone calls, meetings, or e-mails as are needed to ensure that there is mutual understanding of the job being done.

PREPARING A WORK BREAKDOWN STRUCTURE

Work breakdown structuring is a skill all project managers should master. We should not only be able to do it well ourselves; we should also be able to guide others through the process. As we will see in Chapter 10, the very best WBS is built by a two-person team process. The person who will be doing the work imagines doing it and walks through it while the project manager guides the process with specific questions and takes notes. This results in a high-quality WBS, which leads to more accurate time and cost estimates and better plans altogether.

DETAILED TIME AND COST ESTIMATION

Once we have the WBS in hand, it is time to use the Project Evaluation and Review Technique (PERT) to create our work schedule. From the schedule and the procurement plan we can complete the budget. If the schedule and budget created by these methods differ widely from the schedule and budget prepared by the methods we could use in the analysis stage, then we must perform gap analysis and gap reconciliation. If we cannot reconcile the gap ourselves, we need to prepare alternatives and meet with the sponsor and the customer and work with them to decide what to do.

PLANNING FOR QUALITY CONTROL AND QUALITY ASSURANCE

During the design stage, we create the quality plan. The customer's requirements specification is our definition of quality; our goal is conformance to the specification. Now, we need to decide how we are going to get there, and how we are going to make sure that we have done it right. Preparing the quality plan means planning for quality control and quality assurance.

Quality control refers to ongoing quality management and review of the process of doing the work of the project. *Quality assurance* refers to the actual testing of product components and the entire product before and during delivery. These terms are sometimes confusing, and used in different ways in some texts. Here is an easy way to remember:

KEY POINT

Quality Control, Quality Assurance, and Dental Hygiene

Do you brush your teeth every day? Do you spend at least five minutes? Do you floss? If you ask these questions every day, you are doing quality control. You are controlling the process of cleaning your teeth, ensuring that the process is done right. But a good process creates a good product. If the answer to your questions is yes, then that ensures good results.

When you get to the dentist's office and the hygienist asks you to open your mouth, takes a look and says either "Yuck" or "Good job," that is quality assurance. And if you did quality control and good quality work, then you will hear, "Good job." Also, your dental costs will be lower, and you will be out of the office sooner with less pain. Quality control as we do our work reduces cost, time, and risk. Quality assurance, testing of the intermediate deliverables and actual results as we go along and when we finish, assures a quality product or service.

We also introduce our team to methods of quality teamwork.

RISK ASSESSMENT AND RISK PLANNING

The time, cost, and quality plan defines what we will do, how much it will cost, and when we will finish if we do not encounter any problems. But we will encounter problems. *Risk management* addresses the questions: What problems will we encounter? How will we handle them? The goals of risk management are:

- Whenever a problem comes up, we want to be able to say, "We thought that might happen. Here is what we can do about it."
- We want to see some of the problems coming, and prevent them.
- We want to reduce the costs and delays associated with problems that do come up.

- We want to communicate before the problems occur, ensuring that the sponsor understands the level of risk the project entails, and is ready to provide support as needed.
- We want to communicate when problems are happening, managing the situation and getting help if we need it, while keeping the project going at the same time.

As part of risk management, we may arrange for additional time to be allotted for new customer requests, for events that increase time and cost, or both. These are *contingencies* to be used if needed. We manage their use through written change control. Methods for setting up time contingencies and a contingency fund, and for written change control are given in Chapter 11.

MAKING PROCUREMENT DECISIONS

Procurement, acquiring physical components and equipment, tools for the job, and contract labor or consulting expertise, is a major part of some projects, a small part of others, and sometimes not at all an issue. In the design stage, we will create a procurement plan if the project needs one, and begin to put it into action.

As we move ahead with design, we complete the conceptual and specific (physical) architecture decisions. This paves the way for making a choice of vendor and product on all purchasing decisions. We perform research into the quality and suitability of products, services, and vendors, get quotes, and maybe put parts of the project out to bid. We evaluate the quotes and proposals and make decisions. We get those decisions and the funding approved.

Placing an order or signing a contract is actually a step that launches development. However, it can be appropriate to move ahead with this step even if some other aspects of the design specification or project plan are not yet complete. If the team, the sponsor, and the customer have all accepted a procurement decision, we can save time and speed up the project by acquiring it during the design stage, so that it is ready for our team to work with as soon as the development stage begins.

Resources Assigned to the Design Stage

The amount and type of resources assigned to the design stage varies greatly with the type of work involved in the project, and especially with who will be doing the work.

Projects using newer, cutting-edge technology require more risk management and a stronger human resources effort to get the right team. Projects in rapidly changing environments, and those with customers who demand a lot or do not listen well, require more effort in scope and communications management.

On every project, we seek to balance our focus on managing time, cost, and quality, but one of these will be the most important, and we call it the *driver* of the project. Be sure you and your customer agree on what the driver is. For example, if the customer is thinking, "I absolutely cannot go over budget," and you are telling the team, "Let us do the best job we can," then the project may be headed for trouble. However, we cannot focus solely on the driver and forget the other two key project elements. Remember that attention to quality early on and throughout the process helps ensure on-time, on-budget delivery.

If your company is not familiar with project management methods, or if you are trying a new method, or introducing the life cycle, or bringing in a new set of project management tools, then expect to spend more time on the coordination of the project itself.

You can start the design stage by making this evaluation yourself. You have a good definition of the project and its drivers in the business case and project overview. Evaluate the situation and decide where to focus your efforts. Also, perform a gap analysis on yourself. Are their any project management skills that you need to exercise better than you have before? Are there any technical areas where you need an expert to talk to, or you need to do some study? Then, sit down and build yourself a work breakdown structure of the project management work to be done in the design stage. Assign the tasks to yourself and your team, and go ahead.

Roles in the Design Stage

The same roles apply here as they apply in the analysis stage, but the work done by people in each role is different.

- *The project manager* builds and guides the team while writing the project plan, as discussed earlier in this chapter.
- *The project sponsor* is available, and we need to keep him or her updated on progress. The sponsor continues with efforts to promote the project and helps in managing customer expectations. The sponsor

is available to resolve conflicts and to provide resources and ideas for solving problems that cannot be solved at lower levels.

- *Customer representatives and business analysts.* The customer representative becomes the voice of the customer. We check with the representative to ensure that we understand the requirements specification correctly. The representative has the authority to speak for the customer regarding any clarification or decision, but must use that authority wisely and not simply set forth his or her own preferences. The business analyst may be assigned full-time to the project, or may return to more routine production work. In the latter case, the analyst should be available to clarify questions about the requirements specification and to do additional research or verification as needed.

- *Customer service and support staff* have relatively little involvement during the design stage. The support staff may be able to help us with details of the current operating environment. Both groups should be involved in our work of designing the transition to production stage, and can help with risk planning.

- *The users.* We will deal with them mostly through representatives during the design stage. But it may be appropriate to meet with focus groups, particularly if we are developing prototypes. If user acceptance of the new product or service is an issue, we should begin our promotional campaign now.

- *Other stakeholders.* Different peripheral stakeholders have concerns about particular components. We should verify the component about which each stakeholder is concerned with that stakeholder.

- *Technical and engineering staff.* This is our project team. They will be developing the design specification. As much as possible, help each of them become more independent and self-managed, and also a better team player. Also, as much as you can, include them in work breakdown structuring and risk planning.

- *Vendor representatives* will be preparing proposals or bids. We will be evaluating them, as well as their products or services, and we should do due diligence by contacting prior and current customers.

- *External resources.* Various groups, such as the audit department, the financial department, purchasing, or the legal department, may have some say in controls for the project process. For the most part, these groups will not be very involved during the design stage. However, sometimes designs need to be verified as meeting particular standards, or project plans (especially for projects exceeding a particular dollar value or using capital funds) need to be filed appropriately.

Although we should keep in touch with everyone, our focus should be on the team and on the future work of the project.

Inputs of the Design Stage

The outputs of the analysis stage are the inputs of the design stage:

- A complete business case, including the statement of value and scope statement, supported by a cost/benefit analysis or return on investment (ROI) calculation.
- A complete project overview.
- A schedule and budget for the design stage.
- A stage and gate plan for each project stage.
- A list of architectural requirements. A decision on, or a set of questions to be resolved in design that will determine, the conceptual architecture. A decision on, or a set of questions to be resolved in design that will determine, the specific (brand name and physical) architecture.
- A functional and technical requirements specification including the context diagram, a set of data flow diagrams, screen and report designs, possibly prototypes, and other technical specifications.
- A draft support plan, or notes towards one.
- A draft training plan, or notes towards one.
- An initial risk plan, or notes towards one. A record of risk management activities already performed.
- Notes towards a quality plan.
- A list of potential team members.
- A list of all stakeholders and contacts.
- A well-organized file of working notes.

The more business-oriented documents, such as the financial justification, are kept available in case they are needed. The requirements specification is the starting point for your team's work developing the design specification. The project overview, supported by the other items, is the starting point you need for creating the WBS and the rest of the project plan. In the design stage, we will complete all the plans we began during analysis, and more.

Process of the Design Stage

The following are the steps of the design stage:

1. Create the team. (Chapter 12)
2. Create the WBS with your team. (Chapter 10)
3. Create a communications plan from the list of stakeholders and contacts. (Chapter 12)
4. Support the team in understanding the project and working together as a team (ongoing). (Chapter 12)
5. The team builds a design specification in response to the requirements specification, and also expands and improves the support plan and the training plan.
6. Build a PERT chart and project schedule. (Chapter 10)
7. Assign tasks for the entire project to team members. (Chapters 10 and 12)
8. Complete the project schedule. (Chapter 10)
9. Create the detail budget for effort (employee and consultant work time). (Chapter 10)
10. Create the quality plan, and have your team review it. (Chapter 13)
11. Work with the team to create the high-level test plan, and prepare data and tools that will be used in testing. (Chapter 9)
12. Create the risk plan, including your team in risk assessment and risk planning. (Chapter 11)
13. Make all final procurement decisions, and write the procurement plan. (Chapter 10)
14. Complete the budget by adding the purchased items. (Chapter 10)
15. Review the WBS, schedule, and budget with your team. (Chapter 10)
16. Compare the schedule and budget prepared in design with the schedule and budget approved by the customers and sponsor. Resolve any gaps.
17. Meet with the sponsor and customer regarding any gaps you cannot resolve on your own.
18. Perform validation, reviews, or other quality control and quality assurance checks on the design process and design specification. (Chapter 13)
19. Meet with the sponsor and customers to review the entire project plan. Make any requested changes (iterative).
20. Meet with the sponsor and customers to validate, or at least review, the design specification. Make any requested changes (iterative).

21. Get approval for the project plan and design specification from the project sponsor and customers.
22. Get approval of funding for procurement and for the remainder of the project from the sponsor.

When all of these steps are done, you are ready to launch the development stage.

There is a chance that the budget or schedule you create in the design stage will indicate that there is a very large gap between what everyone thought was possible at the end of analysis and what is realistic now that we know the whole picture in detail. If this happens, it may be necessary to cancel the project. Or, it may be possible to go back to the drawing board and reduce the scale of the project to an affordable size.

In some cases, our work in risk assessment uncovers a hidden project-killer. Very rarely—I have only heard of two cases in my entire career—a technical point discovered in the design stage cannot be resolved, and the project must be canceled.

Such events should be rare. But, if they do happen, and there is no way to resolve the problem, it is better to cancel the project than it is to move ahead towards certain failure. Karl E. Wiegers, in *Creating a Software Engineering Culture*, puts it this way: "Never let your boss or your customer talk you into doing a bad job."

The design stage has many steps, but we have already discussed some of them, and many have methods fully described in Part Three.

Outputs of the Design Stage

When the design stage is complete, we have a complete project plan and a complete design specification. The project plan has these elements:

- A validated project overview, with any changes resulting from change control integrated.
- The business case, with the cost budget and delivery dates validated through PERT estimation.
- A communications plan.
- The project schedule, created by the WBS process and PERT, and probably maintained in a project management software tool.
- The project budget, in detail.

- The procurement plan, including what products and services we will acquire, what bidding or acquisition policies we will follow, and what vendors we will use or are likely to use.
- The quality plan.
- The risk plan.
- A staffing plan, if needed.

The design specification has these elements:

- A fully specified conceptual and specific (physical) architecture.
- The design specification for the product or service, validated to the requirements specification.
- The high-level test plan.
- A test bed, test cases, and test data files or other materials for testing.
- A draft support plan.
- A draft training plan.

This list will vary depending on the type of product or service you are creating. For example, if you are making a Hollywood movie, you hardly need a training plan for your customers. And different industries will have different standard tools for performing this work and validating it. For example, software development can use a technique called *use cases* for validating a design specification against customer requirements. But in making a movie, there is less need to have a formal review comparing the storyboard to the script. Rather, the key is that the storyboard be satisfactory to the director and his or her team.

As we discussed above, as the team does the work, we create and follow the project plan to keep it on course. We interact with the team a great deal, especially on quality and risk issues.

Conclusion

In one way, the project is more than half finished. But if you look at it another way, it has not started yet. We have completed all of the planning: All of the items that fit into the "1" of the 1:10:100 rule are done. Depending on the project, that could be anywhere from 30 to 90% of project effort. Typically, though, it is about 60%. That may sound high, but remember: anything we have not done well by this point will cost us ten times as much to fix in the development or transition to production stages.

We have charted our course. In development, the team will work on building the system, documenting it, and testing it. We will do everything we can to clear the way and keep the team on track.

Our Case Study: Putting the Pieces Together

Our home theater project is small, and it made sense to keep our focus on managing the most important parts of the project. For example, buying and installing the system should only take a couple of days, and if it takes twice as long, well, that is a weekend used up. But that is not so bad. So time management was not critical.

Cost control was critical because we are aiming for big results from a small investment. And technical issues are important. If we buy a new component that does not work with our old components, then we will either lose value, or run into expensive, time-consuming returns and trade-ins.

The technical issues were more complicated, so we tackled those first. A quick diagram of the components showed that all of the sound signals would go through the receiver out to the speakers. That raises two questions:

- Will the sound for the television input devices, the video recorder, the DVD player, and the cable television box, go directly from those devices to the receiver, or will it pass through the television? The answer turned out to be that the system would deliver the best sound if the DVD player and video recorder each connected straight to the receiver. But it is better to connect the cable television box through the video recorder, so that we can record shows. So the video recorder will carry sound from cable television to the receiver. There is one more item. It is in our second waterfall, but can we connect the computer to the receiver? We do not want to have to buy a new receiver to finish the project. Good news: we can.
- What are all of the devices that will connect to the receiver? Our complete list has five input items: video recorder (carrying cable television with it), DVD player, CD player, tape cassette player (with a two-way connection for recording), and phonograph. And the receiver connects to a 5.1 speaker system, with five speakers and a subwoofer.

With help from a few people who are technically minded, we have a plan. We also did a similar diagram for the television. This picture of the whole system gave us the technical specifications (inputs and outputs, or interface requirements) for each piece of equipment. With all that in hand, it is time to go to the video store and consider brands, models, and cost.

Going to the store at this point is still part of the design, so it is probably a good idea not to buy anything at this stage. This trip to the store is technical research, not purchasing, which would be in the development stage. To give one example, we learned that the phonograph was a key issue. Lower-end receivers no longer have phonograph inputs. But, if we got a system with a phonograph input, it would have all the other inputs that we needed. We also learned some interesting things about optical cables and power strips that come with insurance for the equipment.

Putting all this information together gave us a purchasing plan with specific equipment to choose from. It was time to reconsider cost. Could we still do it for under $2,000? Yes, but there would be some trade-offs. Getting the receiver we really wanted meant buying some used speakers, but we found a good deal. The deal on the speakers meant we could get the better receiver, along with the television we had selected.

Are we done? Not quite. Knowing what we want, it is time to start price hunting. But that is in development.

One more thing: What about a risk plan? Well, we noticed one risk issue. Every time we go to the video store, we keep watching the giant, flat-screen, cinema-style plasma television with a price tag of over $10,000. Well, maybe next year.

Your Project for Learning

It is time to design your project for learning. Begin with the WBS. From that, use PERT to derive the schedule, then create the budget. Create quality and risk plans as well. Jump ahead to Part Three and read any chapters and use any tools that will help. As you create the plans, develop templates for each of these plans that you can use on future projects.

To validate your design stage, do the following:

- Compare your outputs to the list of outputs in each chapter.
- Compare your outputs to the inputs. Did the design stage introduce any surprises that changed the project plan in a significant way?
- Review the outputs. Do they satisfy you? In particular, do you have a clear work plan for the development stage for you and your team?
- Make notes regarding which tools you think are most valuable for future projects in your field.

When I teach project management classes, I find many project managers have already been trained in PERT for time estimation, but almost none of them use it on a regular basis. That is an example of how we rush through planning, hoping to save time, and then lose out in the long run. I hope you will take the time to become comfortable with the tools in this book. It takes effort to learn new skills. But these tools are here because they have been proven to reduce the risk of project failure and improve project results. Your practice will pay off.

Questions for Learning

- Describe the most important tasks of the project manager during the design stage in your own words.
- Describe the work of the project team during the design stage in your own words.
- Take a look at the list you created when you answered the previous question. Highlight the two or three items you do well, and teach them to someone else. Highlight the one or two items you need to learn most. Read about them in this book. Then make a plan for learning and practicing them.

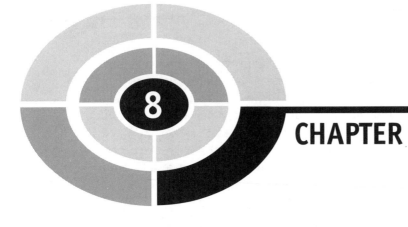

CHAPTER

8

Development: Keeping on Track and Managing Change

In the development stage, the team creates the product or service that the customer wants. They also complete related items, such as the documentation and the training plan. In addition, they develop the test plan and the test system, and test the product or service as it is developed. We can view the work of the team as the creation, testing, and assembly of components that come together to be the resulting system, the product or service we will deliver. We use the term *component* generically to mean a part of the finished system. A component may be a physical item such as a single computer chip, a physical device such as a tennis ball, a computer program, a television advert, a written document such as a user manual or quick start guide, or a subsystem made up of other components of any type.

What do we do as project managers? We make sure that the team can do their work as well and as smoothly as possible. We focus on achieving quality results through quality management and risk reduction. Using management skills from most of the nine knowledge areas, we track progress and then take action to keep the project on track. You will find many additional tools for tracking development and staying on course, such as team meetings and quality management, in Part Three.

Where should our main focus be? It depends on the project. We may already know that finishing the project on time or under budget will be a real challenge, making time or cost the driver. Or we may know we are fixing a shoddy product, and the focus should be on quality. Occasionally, another issue takes the fore. In fields where human life is in danger as the team does the work, risk is likely to be the central focus of our work. On a project where everyone involved is an outside consultant and we are managing people from many vendors, our focus may be on procurement. Be sure to evaluate the project and the customer's concerns so that you know where to keep your focus.

As a general rule, by focusing on quality early on in development, while keeping an eye on everything else, we ensure project success.

In This Chapter

- Key points of the development stage
- Resources assigned to the development stage
- Roles in the development stage
- Inputs of the development stage
- Process of the development stage
- Outputs of the development stage
- Tools for the development stage
- Key concepts for the development stage
- Case studies: Management matters
- Conclusion
- Our case study: Negotiating and closing the deal
- Your project for learning
- Questions for learning

Key Points of the Development Stage

There are seven important points to keep in mind as we prepare for and manage the development stage:

- Test planning and testing should be independent of development.
- Although the product or service itself is important, related items such as the support documentation and the training plan can be equally important. Projects have failed because good systems were introduced without good support.
- The project manager's primary job is to track status, adjust things to keep everything on track, and escalate issues when necessary.
- If each team member gives high-quality deliverables to other team members, then each subsequent step can get off to a good start. High-quality deliverables within the team are essential to team success and to keeping the project on schedule.
- Risk management should be proactive.
- Procurement management must meet the project's needs.
- The testing process is cyclical, not linear, because we have to fix things when they fail the tests and then retest.

Let us take a closer look at each of these points.

THE INDEPENDENCE OF TESTING

Many project teams design their tests as they complete each module, or even as they complete the product. This does not work. At this stage, the team has in mind the functionality that they built into the product, not the functionality requested by the user. As a result, they build tests that only confirm that the product works the way the team thinks it should work, and customer requirements become lost or forgotten. By building the test plan, test data, and test bed from requirements, and not from the product or service under development, we avoid the following hazards:

- If the team misunderstood or forgot a user requirement (and we all do that sometimes), then that requirement is left out of testing, just as it is left out of the product.
- If the team makes the same assumptions in designing the module as they make in designing the tests, then those assumptions never get tested, and the product or service may be flawed. This was the primary reason that the Hubble Space Telescope went into orbit with a wrongly focused mirror. The primary device used for testing the roundness of the mirror was the same device that was used to cut the mirror. It was out of alignment, and so was the mirror. But the mirror image of the

error in the cutting/testing device reversed the error, making everything look fine.

- Developing test beds and test data at the last minute is often a rush that leads to delay in delivery or reduced quality of testing.

There is a better way. We should have our team build the test plan, test bed, and test data at the end of design, or early in the development stage. The test plan and data sets should be based on user requirements and the design specification, before the actual work of building—whether it is writing computer code, constructing a building, or filming a movie—begins to interfere with the picture. This makes for more reliable testing, and it also reduces rush and difficulties at the end of the process.

CREATING RELATED COMPONENTS AND DOCUMENTS

Sometimes it is hard to keep a technical team focused on the customer. Programmers want their programs to work, and engineers want their boxes to do the right thing. There is nothing wrong with that. It is just not enough. At least some members of the team must focus on the peripheral aspects of the customer's needs, including the documentation and training that will make it possible for the customer to use the product or service effectively and receive value, and to make the life of the product or service longer with lower maintenance costs. The team members who focus on documentation, training, and the needs of the customers, support staff, and help desk are going to need cooperation and support from the more technical members of the team who are focusing on creating the product itself. It is your job to encourage that cooperation.

One very simple approach is to ask each person on the team to picture the system, or the part of the system they are using, from the perspective of the user. We can take those old jokes that engineers have about non-technical people and use them to get the engineers to understand what it is really like to use products and services without a clue as to what is going on inside them. From this, we can help our team understand their customers and work to serve them.

TRACKING, CORRECTING, AND ESCALATING

We *track* time and cost through routine procedures and weekly status meetings as described in Chapters 10 and 12. As part of this, we track the status of each task. At the weekly status meeting, we also track quality and risk. We track quality by following the quality plan we created during design, and by asking the team to discuss the quality of every task and deliverable as it nears completion. Managing the quality of tasks is quality control. Managing the quality of deliverables is quality assurance. We also track risk by reviewing the risk plan.

What does it mean to *track* something? It means we compare the actual situation to the plan we created, and note the difference. Is the work on course, or off course? Is it ahead of schedule, or behind? Is it as good as we want it to be, better, or not as good? Are there any boulders lying in the road ahead?

It is important to separate tracking from adjusting the course. In tracking, we want to find out one thing, the truth. We want the truth, whether it is good or bad. As a result, we should always thank anyone who tells us what is going on, and thank them equally for bad news and for good. Only after we have received the news and tracked the present situation against the plan do we respond with a change to the way the team is working, or, if necessary, a change to the plan.

The no-blame environment

To track things, we need to see things as they are, and to receive accurate reports of the status of work. Unfortunately, managers often do things that make it hard for employees to be clear and honest. We are often too quick to praise or criticize based on the news we hear without first praising the fact that we heard accurate news at all.

An environment of blame is a barrier to communications, and a barrier to accurate status reports. It is essential to remember that we work with people, and we manage the project. People change through encouragement and clear correction in a supportive environment, not through blame and criticism.

Creating a *no-blame environment* does not mean playing tennis with the net down. As we discussed in Chapter 2, it means holding people accountable and responsible for solving problems, improving, and delivering the best work they can on time.

Correcting the problem

If anger and blame are ineffective, how do we respond to problems? We respond most effectively by identifying the gap and finding a way to close it. If reality is not meeting the plan, then we change the way we are working so that it does. And if what is necessary is to have a team member change the way he or she is working, then we clearly define the reason for the change and the change that is needed. Then we work with them to help them achieve the necessary results.

Working in this way, we encourage our team to give us all the news, good or bad. And the sooner we get news about what is happening, the sooner we see the gap between the plan and the reality. The sooner we see the gap, the easier it is to make a course correction.

Sometimes there is no way to adjust the work to match the original plan. Either the plan contained an error, or something unforeseen has happened. In that case, closing the gap between reality and the plan requires changing the plan. And that brings us to our next topic, change control.

Written change control

If we need to make a change to the requirements specification or the design specification, written change control is essential. In those cases, we also need to ensure that the test plan is adjusted appropriately.

We should also use written change control if the change alters time or cost to a degree that makes it likely that we will need to delay delivery or that we will exceed our budget. If our project method includes contingencies for additional funds or time that are already under our control, then we are less likely to need to involve the customer or sponsor. For a more detailed explanation of contingencies, see Chapter 11.

Changes that can be made within the available time and budget, and also routine handling of risk events, all do need to be tracked in the project plan, but they do not require use of the separate change control process.

Escalation

What if a problem comes up that is too big for us to handle? There is a specific process for managing those kinds of situations, called *escalation*, discussed in Chapter 12.

DELIVERING QUALITY WITHIN THE TEAM

Quality is not just a result for the customer. Quality is a measurable factor that we can see and feel every day of the project. Every time a team member starts a new task, there is an opportunity to measure the quality of the previous task and deliverable. Can the team member do this next task without running into trouble? Is every input available, right where it is supposed to be? Each input is a deliverable from a prior task. If that task was done well and completed correctly, then the team member should be able to start work on his or her own, without having to call anyone and ask questions. Whatever the deliverable is, it should be complete, functional, and well documented. If each piece of the project is built well, then the whole project can come together well, and the final product or service will be excellent.

PROACTIVE RISK MANAGEMENT

Different companies and different project managers take varying approaches to risk management. Some organizations make risk management the first and foremost priority on every project. If this is done in a clear way, it can be effective. However, we have also seen some organizations that tried to define risk before they had a schedule and a budget. That does not work: If nothing is defined, everything gets called a risk.

We define risk after we define the plan. A *risk* is anything that decreases the chances of any aspect of project success. A risk might cause the project to fail, to be over budget, or to be delayed, or might reduce the quality or value of the resulting product or service.

On the other hand, it does not work to create a plan and then just hope everything will proceed smoothly. And it does not work either to write a risk plan and store it away and pull it out when an emergency happens. (There is an episode of a television hospital drama in which there is a toxic spill in the emergency room, and no one can find the emergency evacuation plan.)

We recommend a compromise approach. We clearly define the plan, developing plans from all nine areas of project management knowledge. Anything that might cause reality to deviate from that plan significantly is a risk. If your project team takes part in a lottery pool every week then that is a risk. If they all win the jackpot, they all quit. (That actually happened. Over half the police force of a small town in New Jersey, USA, split a lottery pot for $45 million and quit their jobs.)

To start risk planning, we work with the team to think of everything that might go wrong. This is an exercise in proactive worry. We write down that list of risk events, and evaluate each one for its likelihood and its consequences. Then we find ways to make each one less likely to happen. Then we decide what we will do if each one of them does happen. During the development stage, we track the list of risks and take care of anything as soon as it is looming on the horizon. If the problem grows beyond the resources of the team, we escalate the issue to the project sponsor for assistance. For more on managing risk, see Chapter 11.

APPROPRIATE PROCUREMENT MANAGEMENT

On some projects, procurement is a small job. We fill out a few purchase orders, and check the equipment when it comes in. On others, procurement is the biggest part of project management. If we are relying on a vendor to provide equipment, customization, and installation, then managing that contract can be a full-time job.

When procuring equipment, it is important to plan for inspection of items, shipping documents, and invoices. We must catch flawed equipment or erroneous orders quickly, or we will not be able to keep the project on schedule.

When procuring services, such as installation of equipment or communications lines, it helps to have in-depth technical experience in vendor requirements and operations.

When procuring consulting work, such as programming or customization, we need to make a strong effort to integrate people who work for the vendor or vendors with the project team and our company. In addition to general team management, we need to pay attention to differences in corporate cultural attitudes and approach. In certain circumstances, we need to do even more. Sometimes, the incentive for the vendor as a company is at odds with the goals of our project. For example, if the vendor's team is operating on a fixed-price contract, and the money is running out before the work is done, the vendor may be pressing its employees, that is, your team, to finish the job quickly even if it means taking shortcuts that risk creating problems for the project, or later on in production. In that case, we need to manage the vendor relationship while also managing the team that works for the vendor.

THE CYCLE OF TESTING, DIAGNOSING, AND FIXING

In the development stage, we are building and testing the product. But, if we are testing something, it might fail. Then what?

Then we need to diagnose the problem and repair it. The consequences of this *test–diagnose–rework–retest cycle* are illustrated in the lower part of Fig. 8-1. Diagnosis and repair add tasks and time to our work schedule. And, when we are finished, we still have to run the test again. If the component does not pass, we go around the cycle again, as many times as necessary. When the component (finally) does pass the second (or third, or fourth...) time, then we still face more work. The component we changed is now in a new version, and that version has not passed any earlier tests in the series of tests for this component. We need to restart the entire test series.

Iteration is a term that refers to any process that does, or might, repeat itself. Therefore, we see the test cycle as cyclic, or iterative.

The test–diagnose–rework–retest cycle is iterative, and that is why we do not have a test phase or stage in our methodology. The terms phase and stage refer to a set of related tasks done in parallel and in series, moving through time in a linear way towards a target date when we deliver the milestone. The linear progression of phases is illustrated in the upper part of Fig. 8-1. If we plan a test phase, we fool ourselves into thinking we know when testing will be done, when we will get out of the maze. But the very nature of a maze is that we cannot see its winding course. And the very nature of testing is that we do not know if the component will pass the tests, so we do not know what tasks we will have to do next.

Testing is the process of ensuring that a component performs to both design and requirements specifications. *Quality management* includes the processes required to ensure that the project will satisfy the needs for which it was undertaken. Therefore, in quality planning, we define and prepare the test plan, and we also define other procedures that help ensure quality process and quality results. Testing does not begin until the development stage, because there are no components to test until the team builds them. However,

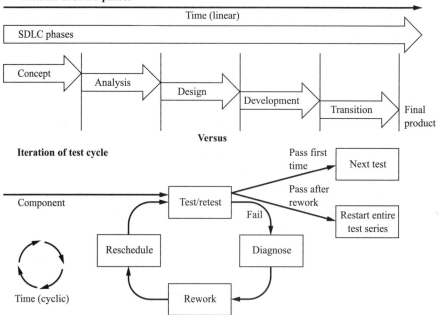

Fig. 8-1. Linear time in phases or stages vs. cyclic time in testing.

there is a process similar to testing in earlier stages. It is called review, and it is also cyclical. However, the review cycle is generally faster than the test–diagnose–rework–retest cycle. When we evaluate written documents in review, we can usually see immediately what is wrong. Often, we can also make an appropriate fix right away. When testing physical devices, software components, or other parts of a product or service, we are rarely so lucky. Diagnosis is usually a separate task, and rework almost always is.

Testing begins during development, but review occurs in every stage because all documents should be reviewed. In concept, analysis, and design, all deliverables are documents, and all should pass review. That is why we allow time for the gates at the end of each of these stages, and include the possibility of rework. But if we want to pass through the gate easily, we should include a review cycle in our own schedule, before the gate. In development and transition to production, components should be tested, and documents such as the training plan, the user manual, any software code, and the software code documentation should be reviewed. Software code is an interesting case, because we can both review it as a written document and test it as a component. Generally, we should review it first, because catching the errors in review will save a lot of time in testing.

As we move through development, there is more and more testing. There is even more in transition to production. Also, as we put pieces together, we have to perform *integration tests* to make sure that they work together. With every test, our schedule has two elements of uncertainty: Will we need to do rework? How much retesting will we have to do?

The uncertainty of the test cycle creates a management problem. We have the most uncertainty about the schedule near the end, when we have little time available before our delivery date. There is almost always a rush at the end. But there are several things that we, as managers, can do to handle the workload:

- We can know that testing is cyclical, and build in extra time. How much time should we build in? During analysis and design, it is not possible to estimate accurately the length of time rework and retesting will add to a project. We propose a rule of thumb, called the *multiply by pi rule:* General studies have shown that the average length of time for the testing phase is 3.2 times longer than the time it would take if all tests ran and no errors were discovered. Therefore, we suggest that you use a project tracking tool to arrange the test schedule and calculate the duration based on successful completion of all tests. Multiply this duration by 3.2 and allow that much time for the test–diagnose–rework–retest cycle. Calling this "multiply by pi" reminds us of the

figure (3.2 is very close to the value of pi, the ratio of the circumference to the diameter of a circle) and also the reason for it: it is the cyclical, circular nature of the process that adds the time.

- We can estimate the length of the testing cycle early in development.
- We can build in some leeway when we set the date of the pilot test and the delivery date for the product or service with our customers.
- We can have our team prepare the test bed, the test data, and the high-level test plan during design or early in development.
- We can encourage quality all the way through, and have team members check deliverables and inputs closely when a task is completed.

Chapter 13 provides tools that help us manage quality and deliver on time.

Resources Assigned to the Development Stage

Most of the resources assigned to the project during the development stage should be on the work of the project. Project management should take a supportive role. However, each team member plays a part in the project management process by reporting time, quality, and cost status promptly and by participating in weekly meetings and risk management activities.

The project manager takes care of everything else, clearing the way for the team. On large projects, the manager may need an assistant who works with a project tracking tool. Very large projects may be broken into sub-projects. Each sub-project will have its own manager or team leader. Depending on the size of the sub-project, the manager or team leader may also be doing some of the development work, or may be managing multiple sub-projects, or parts of several projects.

The resources are defined in the plans created during the design stage, the work breakdown structure, with each task assigned to a team member or another party, the schedule, and the budget.

Roles in the Development Stage

Here is the work to be done by people in each role during the development stage:

- *The project manager* tracks work, time, and cost. We also manage quality and risk, and procurement as needed. We prevent and resolve problems, or escalate them as necessary. We maintain communications with all stakeholders.
- *The project sponsor* is available, and we need to keep him or her posted on progress. The sponsor continues with efforts to promote the project and helps in managing customer expectations. The sponsor is available to resolve conflicts and to provide resources and ideas for solving problems that cannot be solved at lower levels.
- *Customer representatives and business analysts.* The customer representative continues to be the voice of the customer. In a project following the classic SDLC, he or she might be less involved in this stage, at least until testing begins. However, with the advent of modular systems, it is possible to use life cycle alternatives that keep the customer in close contact with the product or service as it develops. The customer representative should also guide the development of user documentation and training materials. The business analyst may be assigned full-time to the project especially if he or she has skills that serve the development team, or may return to more routine production work. In the latter case, the analyst should be available to clarify questions about the requirements specification and to do additional research or verification as needed.
- *Customer service and support staff* reduce their involvement in the project after contributing to the analysis and design stages, and have relatively little involvement early in the development stage. However, the end of development overlaps with transition to production, when representatives of both these groups actually join the project team.
- *The users.* We will deal with them mostly through representatives during the early part of the development stage. However, depending on the project or service we are developing, it will become possible to include them at some point during testing and transition to production. The earlier we can involve them and get their response to the product or service, the greater likelihood the project has for success. Promotional effort should prepare the users for the day we go into production, aiming for them to have high hopes, but not excessive expectations.
- *Other stakeholders.* We should verify the component about which each stakeholder is concerned with that stakeholder and have him or her test the component.
- *Technical and engineering staff.* This is our project team. They will be developing the product or service and related items. As much as possible, help each of them become more independent and self-managed,

and also a better team player. Also, as much as you can, include them in quality and risk management.

- *Vendors* will now be represented by consultants we have retained, technicians performing installations or service, or post-sales customer service representatives. We should inform each person of his or her role in helping the project succeed.
- *External resources.* Various groups, such as the audit department, the financial department, purchasing, or the legal department, may have some say in controls for the project process. For the most part, these groups will not be very involved during the development stage.

Inputs of the Development Stage

You probably are not surprised to hear that the inputs of the development stage are the outputs of the design stage.

The complete project plan describes our work during the development stage. It describes what we will do as project managers, and it provides the schedule and budget, the reference point for tracking the work of the team. The WBS describes the work the team will do in detail. If tasks in the WBS have not already been assigned to specific workers during design, they can be assigned as they come up, or reassigned as needed. The tasks are mostly done by the team, but we also include tasks to be done by customers, vendors, and other stakeholders, as needed.

- A validated project overview, with any changes resulting from change control integrated.
- The business case, with the cost budget and delivery dates validated through PERT estimation.
- A communications plan.
- The project schedule, created by the WBS process and PERT, and probably maintained in a project management software tool.
- The project budget, in detail.
- The procurement plan.
- The quality plan.
- The risk plan.
- A staffing plan, if needed.

The design specification is the starting point for the development team. Their work is to build a product or service to meet or exceed this specification. If the design specification is correct, then the product or service they create will also meet the requirements specification, and therefore provide the functionality that the user has requested. The design specification includes:

- A fully specified conceptual and specific (physical) architecture.
- The design specification for the product or service, validated to the requirements specification.
- The high-level test plan.
- A test bed and test data files or test cases.
- A draft support plan.
- A draft training plan.

Process of the Development Stage

We need to describe project management in the development stage a bit differently from that in earlier stages. In earlier stages, we provided a list of management and project tasks that were more or less sequential. In this stage, most management work is ongoing. We are not creating one plan after another. We are tracking the project using all of the plans all at once. However, our focus does shift from the beginning of the stage, through the middle, to the end.

PERIODS WITHIN THE DEVELOPMENT STAGE

In the early part of development, our focus should be on getting things started. People should be brought on board and up to speed. Tasks should be launched. Orders should be placed. One very good practical habit is to do the work of communications first, assigning tasks and getting everyone else moving, and then sit down and do our own work. We should also keep our eye out for parts of the project that seem to be getting off to a slow start. If there is lack of clarity about the work, then plans should be reviewed. If there is a specific barrier to getting work done, such as a team member whose skills are not strong enough for the job, then we need to identify the issue, then provide support or develop another solution.

In the middle of the development period, we try to keep things moving smoothly. Our focus should be on risk and quality. Managing risk means looking for trouble and fixing anything troublesome while it is still small. We focus on quality because we do not want to be allowing many small errors to

pile up. There are always errors, but the more of them that reach testing, the more trouble we will have delivering the project on time. We also track time and cost. If it looks like we will not be able to keep on schedule or stay within budget for any reason, then that is a risk event in itself. If one part of the project is running behind schedule or over budget, we need to pay attention to the issues there. If we cannot resolve the issue and keep the project on schedule and within budget, we need to escalate the issue and get assistance as described in Chapter 12.

As we approach the end of the development stage, we should focus on completion. Any tasks that are nearly done should be finished and tested. Tasks that were set aside should be addressed. Team members should be supported in focusing on seeing how their contribution fits into the whole product or service, and how the customer will use it.

TESTING DURING THE DEVELOPMENT STAGE

The work of testing is split between development and transition to production. The basic difference is that, during development, we test parts of the product or service, and then the whole product or service. During transition, we test the product or service in actual use, in relationship to customers, other equipment, and systems, and it is a very complex and changing real-world environment. In development, we should plan to complete the tests listed below. As we discussed earlier, this means planning for the test, diagnosis, rework, and as much retesting as necessary.

- Each component should pass its low-level and high-level tests.
- Product integration testing should ensure that all components work together. Integration testing is done progressively as each component is finished.
- End-to-end testing ensures that the system works in its environment.

Many more tests are still to come during transition to production. It is essential that we have a reliable product or service at the end of development. Otherwise, transition to production will be delayed by rework, customers will be dismayed by what they see, and the project may fail.

For more information about testing and test schedules, see Chapter 9.

Outputs of the Development Stage

At last we have something, an actual product or service, to show for all the work we have done. At the end of the development stage, the team will deliver:

- A product or service that has been tested and meets the requirements specification and design specification, as modified by change control.
- A nearly final user manual or help system.
- Technical specifications to be used by future teams for support and modifications, such as software code documentation and hardware technical specifications designed to be used by future programmers and engineers who will support and modify the system.
- A proposed final support plan.
- A proposed final training plan.
- A complete high-level and low-level test plan.
- A test bed and test data files or test cases.
- Documentation of all test results.
- Documentation of any open issues.
- A draft training plan.

Of course, not all of these will be needed on every project. In the design stage, we determined what products and services would be of value to the customer, and that is the actual, specific list of outputs for the project you are managing.

As project managers, we will deliver:

- A plan for transition to production and deployment, covering all steps to be taken and the management of issues from all nine areas of knowledge.
- A validated project overview, with any changes resulting from change control integrated.
- The business case, with the cost budget and delivery dates validated through PERT estimation.
- The project schedule, created by the WBS process and PERT, showing estimated vs. actual results and incorporating project change, probably maintained in a project management software tool.
- The project budget, in detail, with estimated vs. actual results to date.
- A risk plan for the remainder of the project.

We may have one other set of deliverables: presentations or demonstrations of the system for the sponsor and the customers. Since we have something to show for all of our work, we should show it!

Table 8-1   Document checklist for projects.

Title	Complete in stage	Length and format	Contents and purpose
Project overview	Analysis	Standard is 5-page minimum	Purpose, goal, starting point, and customer information. Sets project scope and guides project to meet user objectives
		Small project, 1-page overview form	
		Large project, each sub-project has its own 5-page overview	
Project design	Design	Large detailed design of product	A detailed description of what will be created, which also serves as the technical specification of the product during its life
		Project WBS, schedule, and budget, perhaps in Microsoft Project®	The steps it will take to do the project, the time and budget required
Quality plan	Early development	A few pages. May be appendix to design	Description of quality control and quality assurance issues, and how they will be managed
Risk management plan	Early development	A few pages. Lists risks to project success and how each risk will be handled	Put it in the file and retrieve it if you need it
User guide	Development	Varies. Optional. Written to level of user	Instructs user in use of the system so that they can use it with little or no support
Security plan	Development	Optional. May be separate non-technical overview and technical detail plan	Addresses issues of how the product will interact with or affect organizational security
Implementation plan	Early transition	Length depends on complexity of deployment	Describes what is to be deployed where. Explains multiple components, multiple target platforms, and multiple locations

Table 8-1   Document checklist for projects (*Continued*).

Installation guides and checklists	Early transition	Short checklist and installation guide for each component to be installed. Written to level of expertise of installer. Includes un-installation guides. One for each component to be installed	Allows IT support to install, uninstall system without relying on project team, during deployment and for the life of the system
Test schedule	Early transition	Description of each test and calendar of all tests	Makes sure all tests are done. Schedules time for testing and possible rework
Support plan	Early transition	Sections for network support and customer support. Contains standard operating procedures (SOP)	Allows network support to maintain system, and customer support to support users, for the life of the product, without calling on project team
Pilot test lessons learned	Late transition	Short	Results of pilot test. Report to customer. Guides remaining steps of transition
Known problems and issues	Throughout transition	Multiple sections (see Chapter 8)	Guides transition stage, makes sure nothing is left out
Rollout schedule	Late transition	Calendar	Calendar of deployment to each target location, coordinated with user departments and training
Deployment results and version tracking	End of transition	Tabular	Identifies who has the system, and multiple versions if version changes occurred during deployment
Project lessons learned	Project close	Bulleted list of points	Identifies ways any project manager or team member can do better on future projects by emulating success or avoiding errors

Tools for the Development Stage

Since we need to create many project documents, it is good to have a list of all of them with definitions. We present this in Table 8-1.

Here are a few notes about project documents:

- Table 8-1 includes only project management documents and deliverables to the customer. Technical plans and design documents, such as the context diagram and data flow diagrams for computer systems, blueprints and engineering diagrams for construction, storyboards for movies, and so forth, should also be defined and tracked.
- Feel free to modify document names or add or change documents to suit the needs of your project and your company. This list was designed to be both comprehensive and generic. You can use it as a checklist to make sure that you have not left out any crucial documents. You can also make a checklist appropriate to your own projects at your company.
- Document status and ownership should be tracked, either in a project tracking tool or in some other form. Based on Table 8-1, you can create a document completion tracking checklist.

Key Concepts for the Development Stage

Here is how we address issues from each of the nine project management areas of knowledge during the development stage:

- We make sure that our project management efforts support, rather than interfere with, the work of the project.
- The primary activity from scope management is written change control.
- For time management, we perform *action control*, ensuring timely completion of tasks, through the weekly status meeting, and adjust the project schedule as necessary.
- For cost management, we prepare budget vs. actual cost reports, perform per-task earned value analysis, and produce variance reports and cost reports related to change control as needed.
- For quality management, we oversee and improve the project process with quality control and validate the testing through quality assurance.

- Human resources management includes whatever we do to keep the team going and also any work needed to replace staff.
- Communications management includes our status reports to the sponsor, customers, and stakeholders. It also includes escalation of issues as needed and effective management of the team's communications with stakeholders.
- Risk management is mostly a combination of risk reduction and mitigation, also with ongoing risk assessment and revisions of the plan. We should be sure to revise the risk plan for transition and deployment.
- Procurement management, as we discussed above, varies greatly depending on the degree to which the project depends on external resources.

For definitions of the terms above, and for tools to assist with the process, see Part Three. These activities seem routine when we read them, but, if the project is not going smoothly, then they are not routine at all. If we are close to our team, but objective, we will sense when something is wrong. But we cannot always do that. What are the first clear signs of something going wrong?

- Tasks not being delivered on time.
- Tasks not actually being completed, so that the deliverable is not really a complete, working, independent deliverable.
- Excessive failures in testing.
- Risk events requiring extra effort and resources.
- Earned value analysis showing that we will not finish within our budget.
- Discovery of a major error in scope definition or requirements definition.
- A change external to the project that alters scope or requirements.
- A change external to the project that prevents on-time, on-budget completion.
- The discovery of a major technical problem.
- Loss of key team members.
- Severe problems managing procurement or contracted services.

It is important to spot these signs early. The sooner we see that we are off course, the less it costs to get back on track. The first two items should be identified in the weekly status meetings. Others we identify by comparing what is actually happening to the project plan. Once we see a problem, we should work with our team to respond immediately and effectively.

GREEN, YELLOW, RED ALERT SYSTEM

We can set up a very simple, clear system for escalating issues. This solves several common management misunderstandings:

- Executives do not like to be blindsided, that is, hit with a problem when they thought nothing was wrong.
- Executives often misread manager's status reports, either jumping in when they are not wanted, or not addressing issues where their help is needed.
- Executives like to hear problems and solutions.

Our solution is built on the model of traffic lights: Green means everything is okay, the project should come in with quality, on time, and on budget. Yellow means: alert, caution, there may be trouble ahead. We are giving the project sponsor a heads-up, so he will not be blindsided later. With yellow alert, we are also telling the sponsor that we do not need any help right now. Red alert means we need help: a meeting, ideas, approvals, money, or a change of schedule, right now.

If it appears that a problem may be impossible to resolve with existing resources, we escalate it early, going to yellow alert.

It is better to go to yellow alert several times, and return to green each time, than it is to not be forthcoming about problems, and then jump to red alert, confronting the project sponsor with a problem he or she did not even know was coming. At least, that is true in a well-managed company. Sometimes, unfortunately, we have to choose a different approach to work with a difficult project sponsor. Some executives do not keep in touch with the project, and others have a tendency to jump in and micromanage at the first sign of trouble. We can educate executives by simply telling them what green, yellow, and red status mean. And, in our emails, we say exactly what we want, when we want it.

- In a yellow alert, identify the problem and the solution you are working on. Say that, if this solution doesn't work by a particular date, you will be asking for help.
- In a red alert, describe the problem and the proposed solution. Get help from your team to brainstorm solutions. Also ask the manager for exactly what you will need: Ideas, approval or whatever else.

We should also watch out for the situation where a number of medium-sized problems crop up all at once. We and our team may have the resources to handle each of them, but do we have the resources to handle all of them? Several yellow alerts internal to the project may add up to a red alert for the project as a whole.

Case Studies: Management Matters

When I think of how to show the value of good management during the development phase, two projects I managed come to mind. In one case, we followed the plan and it worked. In the other, we could not follow the plan, but we were successful anyway.

CREATING A NETWORK WITH NOBODY HOME

I live in Texas. My technical assistant lives in New Jersey. And the consultant I use for computer security lives in Florida. So, when a new client in Tucson, Arizona, called up and asked me to create a secure network connection between Tucson and Phoenix, I knew I had an interesting management challenge. The client had no in-house computer expertise, and could not afford to pay for travel for my team.

I used the project management tools in this book, plus a web site where we could share files. I specified requirements and designed the solution by holding phone meetings, writing up the ideas, and having the stakeholder, my technical experts, and pre-sales consultants from the vendor review them. When everyone was on the same page, Anna, my assistant in New Jersey, ordered the equipment, received it, set up the initial configuration, and tested it. She shipped the components to Tucson and Phoenix, where a network technician I never spoke to followed the instructions and plugged in the equipment. Then it was time for Mark, the computer security expert in Florida, to pitch in. He dialed into the equipment and set up the security system so that the two offices could share data securely over an internet connection.

When people are in remote locations, we have less room for error. Careful management makes all the difference. In this case, prior solutions had failed. All recommendations other than the one from my company were too expensive. Our solution worked as planned, and the system worked without failure for over a year, until a network component (not one of ours) failed and brought the system down for a couple of days. The documentation we kept on the project helped the customer restore the system quickly once the other problem was fixed.

SEVEN WEEKS LATE AND STILL ON SCHEDULE

For another client, I planned and implemented the translation of data from an old database running on a failing computer to a new, reliable system. The technical challenges of specifying the job were large, but familiar to me and my team. The client wanted the work completed as quickly as possible, and, at the end of design, I presented a ten-week schedule.

Almost all of the schedule was under my own control. However, the very first step was not. We needed an outside expert to get the data off the old computer hard drive and provide a description of the data structure. Unfortunately, we had to rely for the solution on the person who caused the problem. The only person who knew the data structure was the technician who installed and maintained the system. He had never documented it. He had also failed to maintain it, and that was why the computer was unreliable and the data largely unreadable. The operating system was in German, not English, just to make life more interesting.

I wrote up my requirements and sat down with the technician. We went over them together and he said that he could get me the data plus the information about the data structure in two weeks. That is when I calculated eight weeks for the rest of the job and told the client it would take ten weeks.

We got started. I ordered and installed equipment. The technician delivered files I could not use. I returned them with requested changes. The technician failed to deliver a second time. I saw clearly that the technician would not deliver on time. But there was no one else who could do the job at all. So I began to work around his delays. I got the whole new computer network up and running, and tested it with dummy data. I worked with my programmer, making best guesses about the data we would get by looking at printed reports, and defining the output exactly. The programmer began coding, so that the day we got the data from the technician we could start to translate it.

The technician finally delivered at the end of week nine. But everything else was ready. The programmer and I worked for two solid weeks, and we delivered in eleven weeks. We had only a one-week delay in delivery, in spite of a seven-week delay in receiving what we needed to start the development stage.

Flexibility and commitment to making the project work, plus effective use of planning tools, made it possible to adjust the schedule and work around a major problem. The client understood the situation, and was thrilled with the results.

Conclusion

The end of the development stage marks the second major shift in the project process. The first three stages, concept, analysis, and design, were planning activities. They represented the "1" of the 1:10:100 rule. Development was the build phase, the "10." Now, we are shifting into the final phase, where changes can cost 100 times as much as they would have cost if they had been included in the original plan. During transition to production, errors not discovered earlier start to become much more costly. Resolving the errors in transition to production is difficult because it requires rework plus extensive retesting on a very short schedule. To make it even harder, the customer is with us, watching everything that goes wrong.

There is also another major shift at this point. During concept and analysis, we focused on listening to the customer. During design and development, we focused on managing the team designing and building the system to specification. Technically, this is called the unfolding of a tautology. All the features of the final system were already defined by the customer's requirements specification, and we were creating it from that pattern. Our system was growing according to a fixed plan, the way a high school student learns by following a fixed curriculum. The unfolding of a tautology is a relatively linear, predictable type of growth.

As we enter transition to production, we face a new challenge, a new kind of growth. If development is like high school and college, then our product or service has been learning how to do a lot of things and taking a lot of tests. Transition to production is like leaving college and getting our first job: After final exams (the final system tests), the product or service faces the real world for the first time. The meeting between our new product or service and the real world is very different from linear growth; it is a kind of explosion of possibilities. As project managers, it is our job to make sure that, when the project and the real world meet one another, they get along well.

No matter how well we have built our system, designed our documentation and training, and prepared our plans, unexpected things will come up. One major company calls transition to production the "storm period," and it is a good name. Managing the launch of a product or service through a storm is an exciting challenge for project managers. We take a look at that in the next chapter.

Our Case Study: Negotiating and Closing the Deal

Our home theater project has an unusually short development stage. All of the research before buying fell into the design stage. Once the items are shipped to our house, we will be installing them and learning to use them, so that is transition to production. As a result, development is just negotiating the price, buying, and ensuring delivery.

The store that had given us excellent technical advice had good prices. Even better, they had a guarantee to match the best price from any certified dealer. So I got their list of certified dealers and spent a few hours hunting on the web. The time paid off in savings of about $200 when I asked them to match the prices I had found for the television and the receiver. We found some additional cost savings almost by accident. I had been visiting my mother for a few weeks while I did all the research. So, I bought from a store near her, and had the equipment shipped to my home. That sounds expensive, but, actually, the goods would have been shipped from a central warehouse no matter where I bought it. And, by buying out of state, I eliminated sales tax.

It is a good thing we lowered the price a bit, because, when it came to cables, there was something of a shock. These new high-resolution video and fiber-optic audio cables cost a lot more than conventional cables. And we had to buy longer cables because, as we remembered at the last minute, we had to roll the television away from the stereo cabinet when we wanted to watch it. Longer cables cost a lot more than shorter ones.

But, with the ups and downs of discounts and cables, the price came in just about where we had planned. I made the purchases, and I was the proud owner of the pieces of a half new, half old home theater system.

There was one more step in the development process: scheduling delivery. We gave very precise instructions on when we wanted delivery, because we would be in and out of town around the holidays. Well, the message did not cross state lines, and the shipper arrived on the one day we were not there. A frustrating half-hour and a few telephones straightened that out, and the system was due to be redelivered.

Your Project for Learning

Now the time has come for you to do your project. Depending on what you chose, it may be just a few hours of work, or it may be many hours over days or weeks. See the project as your chance to learn the tracking tools for time, cost, quality, risk, and the other five areas of project management knowledge that are covered in Part Three. Practice honest assessment and status reports. If you are working with others, ask them what you can do that would encourage them to be clear and honest about the status of their tasks.

As you do this, ask yourself: "What am I learning about how to keep a project on track?" Then take some time, write it down, and explain it to someone else. Or, if you can, arrange an opportunity to present what you are learning.

Questions for Learning

- Can you think of a project where testing was too little and too late? Take a moment and outline a good test plan for that project. How would you have done it?
- Think of a product or service that you like. You might think of a piece of consumer electronics or a web site. Consider its documentation or help function or customer service. Do you like that? If you do, think what it took to prepare that material or train the help desk staff during the project that created the system. Could you do the same on your next project?
- What do you do to keep track of a project, formally or informally? Have you ever been part of a good status meeting? What made it work right? Or, if the meetings have not been so good, how would you run a status meeting?
- What would you do if a project team member came to you with a problem? How would you handle it?
- Imagine that you have to tell the project sponsor that you need more money. A design error was made, and it turns out that you need a much larger, more expensive component than you thought. How would you prepare for that meeting? How would you escalate the problem?
- Think of a project that ended in success. List as many things as you can that were done right during the development stage.

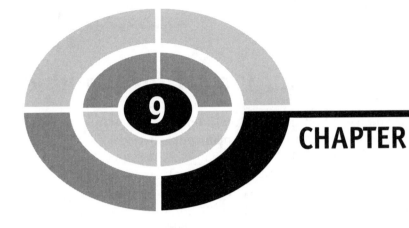

Transition to Production: The Storm Period

Transition to production is the last stage before delivering the product or service to the customer. Your new system has grown up, and soon it will not need its parents any more. The product you have created needs to succeed in the world (the production environment) without you, being supported by others and working with and for others. The product, in a very real sense, is passing tests, graduating, and getting its first job. And the project team will have to let go of taking care of the product, of answering every call for help. A successful new product or service runs on its own, without the support of the project team (its parents). The team, or its members, move on to other things.

The transition stage is the key to ensuring customer acceptance of the product or service. If customers have expectations that exceed what we deliver, they will be disappointed, and they may reject the product or not take the time to learn to use it well. On the other hand, if the product meets or exceeds customer expectations, and training and transition of support to the groups that will provide support from now on are successful, then the product or service is much more likely to be accepted and used by the customer. And the value of the project is only realized if the customers use the product or service.

A well-managed transition to production stage will have customers using and getting value from the product or service faster and also reduce support costs over the long term. Greater value at lower cost equals increased net value for the life of the product or service.

In This Chapter

- Key points of the transition stage
- Resources assigned to the transition stage
- Roles in the transition stage
- Inputs of the transition stage
- Process of the transition stage
- Outputs of the transition stage
- Tools for the transition stage
- Key concepts for the transition stage
- Conclusion: Completing the circle
- Our case study: No, no, that cable goes there!
- Your project for learning
- Questions for learning

Key Points of the Transition Stage

Some project management methodologies say the project ends at the end of development, when the product or service has passed testing and is ready for installation. This usually leads to dissatisfied customers who cannot use or support the system for which they paid. Several of these methods were developed for, or by, computer consulting firms that do software or system development. A common refrain from their customers is: "They left us a system, but they never taught us how to support it." The transition to production stage closes this gap. It includes:

- *Testing the product or service* to ensure that it meets all specified requirements, both in a pilot test and in full production.
- *Completing and testing all documentation*, including the help system and user instructions, user and technical training material, and technical reference material.
- *Ensuring that the help desk and the production operations group can support the users and the new system* without calling on the project team.
- *Implementing the production version* of the product or service through rollout or deployment.
- *Training of users coordinated with implementation.*
- *Project close.* The process of ensuring completion for the project.

Although I developed the details of this stage specifically for computer and telecommunications projects, the issues are worth considering for every project. If you can say, for certain, that no user training is required, then you can skip those steps. Sometimes we need to be sure to use a certain process, but it is a small job to do so. For example, if we are delivering a document by e-mail to complete a research project, testing may simply come down to a final review of the document before we attach the e-mail and send it. Doing that one little step, however, is crucial to delivering quality. Each point of a good transition should be considered for every project, and used if it is needed. Let us take a look at each of these in more detail.

TESTING

The complete system test series occurs at the end of the development stage. This paves the way for the tests of the transition stage: the pilot tests, final documentation tests, pre-acceptance tests, acceptance tests, and deployment tests. Also, if there are specialized tests, such as integration tests, stress tests, or disaster recovery tests, they will also be included in this stage. Everything possible should be done in testing to ensure that the product will work and be well used once it is fully implemented for all users. We must also do our best to deliver on time, as our delivery date is probably set (both in the schedule and, more importantly, in the customers' minds), even when the tests find unexpected problems we must resolve.

DOCUMENTATION

We must deliver complete documentation in draft form early in the transition to production stage. The customers, help desk, and operations support staff will review it and request revisions. Unfortunately, most project teams tend to delay the work of writing documentation, and then leave it out altogether or rush it at the end. Product quality and ease of support are much greater if documentation is created along with the product as an integral aspect of development, and if many of the project team members read and edit the documentation and test the system against it.

When our project is delivering a system that will be supported by others, a key element of the method is that the documentation is tested in use during the pilot test by support staff, and used to train support staff before the production implementation. Technical support staff will use, test, and request changes in installation and maintenance guides. End-user support staff will use, test, and request changes in the support plan and end-user documentation. This ensures that everyone who will support and use the final system has seen and approved the documents we deliver. Remember, we may write it in a few weeks, but they will need to live with it for many years.

TRANSITION TO PRODUCTION SUPPORT

Some products and services need little or no support after the project is over. This is the case when your team completes a statistical research study and delivers a report. In other cases the support may be thoroughly routine. For example, if you finish making a Hollywood movie, and the film reels go to the movie theaters, you do not have to tell the theaters how to show the movie or take care of the film. They do that all the time.

However, we often do projects that deliver production systems to businesses, or deliver products to consumers, where the businesses or consumers will receive support via a phone number or on the internet. In these cases, our project is not over until the product or service is fully supported by those who will continue support for the lifetime of the product or service. In this section, we will refer to those who support the product or service—the people who keep it working—as operations support, and we will call the people who help users the help desk. Your organization may have different terms for these functions, and they may be part of your company, part of your customer's company, or provided by a different company altogether. That last option is often called outsourcing.

By the end of the transition stage, operations support will support the product as part of the production environment. The help desk will handle end-user calls about the product. Ideally, there will be very few calls to the project team, and each of those will be resolved by giving training and documentation to production operations and the help desk so that they will be able to handle the problem on their own in the future.

Knowledge transfer is essential for the transition to production support. *Knowledge transfer* is the process of passing along information and understanding. It allows the receiving group to support the system independently, without relying on the project team. If this result is achieved, it lowers both maintenance cost and corporate risk. Maintenance cost is lowered for two reasons. First, the salary of support personnel is lower than the salary of people with development skills for projects. Second, once support is performed by the support staff, then production management methods can be brought to bear to make the support process more efficient. Corporate risk is also reduced in two ways. First, we avoid the situation where only one or two people (members of the original project team) know how to support the system. That knowledge moves from being an asset of the individuals who may leave to a documented asset of the corporation that can be implemented by any appropriately trained and skilled employee. Second, if a skilled project person is the only source of support for a particular system, then it is likely that that person will not be readily available to complete other projects on time. The particular technical skill of someone who can do unique work on a project is an asset that is difficult to replace. If the person is on call to maintain a production system, then that will interfere with those future projects that rely on his or her expertise, throwing the projects off schedule and reducing our project success rate.

IMPLEMENTATION IN THE PRODUCTION ENVIRONMENT

There is no one standard language for parts of the implementation process. To be clear in this book, we offer the definitions given below for terms related to the implementation process. However, we note that, in common use, many of the terms are used interchangeably or given different meanings.

- *An implementation* is an installation of a system fulfilling functional requirements. As a verb, implementation is the set of actions that result in an implementation.
- *Delivery* is the fulfillment process by which the customer receives the product or service. The term delivery sometimes is used to include both delivery and installation.
- *The work of installation* is the process of integrating a new product or service into the production environment.

- *Deployment* is the process of assigning resources for a particular purpose to particular locations. In military operations, we might deploy a single special operations force on a single mission, or deploy thousands of troops to many locations in a region. Similarly, we might deploy one team to install a server, or we might deploy dozens of technicians to deliver and install equipment at user locations. However, developers of computer systems tend to use the term deployment primarily in relations to large implementations at many locations.
- *Rollout* is the distribution of a system, or access to a system, to target users.

A successful implementation is the result of the coordinated management of delivery, installation, deployment, and rollout.

The *implementation phase* begins when the system is ready for users with acceptance tests passed, and ends when all users have it and are using it in the production environment. In our methodology, we include implementation as the second part of transition to production. These terms are generally used for products and services being implemented internally, or for just one customer. When we are preparing a product or service for sale, either as a fixed product or service line or as a set of customizable products or services, our implementation ends with production and delivery to the point of sale. If the product or service is customizable, then the customization team or teams also need to be ready.

You may notice that the terms deployment and rollout come from the military. The army deploys troops, and does it by rolling out in tanks and armored personnel carriers. Historically, many project methods were developed by the military or for military contracts. We can learn good logistics from the military and employ it to succeed on our projects. Surveying the territory and gaining cooperation from the civilian (end-user) population are essential to project success.

Nonetheless, if you are managing your project well, the users will not be hostile, and you will not need to send your staff out in armored personnel carriers. That is not to say that you should expect an entirely smooth ride. Testing the product in a real-world setting almost inevitably brings surprises. The goal is to make sure that they are manageable, and to know how to handle them. Also, in this phase, the project team, and the product itself, meet many more users and stakeholders, who may have different agendas from the ones who were involved in the project during design and development. Another source of tension is that the corporate and IT environments may have changed since the project was designed.

It would probably be better to think of this part of our work as the *implementation and training phase*. On a systems level, implementation ensures that the new product or service is reliable and works well at every interface with each non-human component of the larger system of which it is a part. Training ensures that the new product or service works well with the human components of the larger system. The two need to be coordinated closely.

TRAINING

The value of a project ultimately is the value gained by the use of the product or service that the project creates. No matter how good our work is, if people do not use what we give them, no value is realized. For internal projects, or projects for a single customer, success is determined by the degree to which the working staff of the organization (end-users) use the system in ways that benefit the organization. Training end-users is a key to a successful project. Depending on the nature of the interaction between the end-user and the new system, one or more of these types of training will be appropriate:

- Required hands-on training, either in a classroom, or with live teachers via distance learning, teleseminars, or internet-based webinars.
- Optional hands-on training either in a classroom, or with live teachers via distance learning, teleseminars, or internet-based webinars.
- Interactive help, *computer-based training (CBT)*, documentation, and videos.
- Training handled through help-desk calls.
- No training at all.

We can create a similar list for training for the products and services we sell to customers:

- Hands-on training either in a classroom, or with live teachers via distance learning, teleseminars, or internet-based webinars, included as part of the purchasing package.
- Hands-on training either in a classroom, or with live teachers via distance learning, teleseminars, or internet-based webinars, available separately.
- Interactive help, *computer-based training (CBT)*, documentation, and videos.

- Training handled through help-desk calls.
- No training at all.

The key to a successful project is to train people to do their work (using the new product or service), rather than training them to use the product or service. For systems delivered to businesses, our focus and the measure of our success is productivity. We need to choose the best training methods, implement them with quality, and evaluate the benefit to productivity. We also need to address the issue of providing incentives for learning the new system.

In the case of a consumer product, the goal may not be productivity. It may be enjoyment or some other value. The training should be oriented towards the customer realizing this value with the product, not towards the customer using the product. For example, if you buy a new digital camera, your goal is not to understand how the camera works. Ideally, you want to use the camera without thinking about it, to take the pictures you want to take.

PROJECT CLOSE

You might think that when we deliver, the project is finished. But that is not quite true. Every batter, golfer, and tennis player discovers that follow-through—the motion after the ball is hit—is crucial to the success of the swing. The same is true for the project manager. Project close is about the follow through after delivery that ensures success, not just for the project, but also for you as a professional project manager, for your team, and for other projects in your organization.

As an independent consultant, I have had to learn this lesson the hard way. Even if I deliver good results, a certain amount of confusion or ill feeling will keep a customer from coming back, or from giving me a referral. The same applies to project managers who work inside companies. Your customers may have to keep working with you, but if you want to grow with the organization and work to have new projects launched and good project management methods adopted, you will need to follow through on each project.

Closing a project successfully means dealing with these five areas of our responsibility as a project manager:

- Ensuring stakeholder satisfaction.
- Achieving legal and financial closure.
- Managing reassignment of the project team.

- Completing and sharing lessons learned from the project.
- Completing the post-project business review with the customer.

Let us look at each of these more closely.

Ensuring stakeholder satisfaction

Once we deliver the product or service, it just begins to show its value. It may be months—sometimes even years—before the value of the new product or service can be fully realized. Yet true success of the project is measured by that value being realized during those years in production. We should arrange for a post-project business review evaluating whether the value is being realized and the project is showing the expected return on investment.

In addition to this review, we can also do two other things. One is to ensure the satisfaction of peripheral stakeholders. The other is to ensure that the customer knows that value is being realized, and recognizes that value and gives credit to the project and the project team.

Achieving legal and financial closure

Achieving legal and financial closure is often—but not always—a simple matter. Were all payments delivered? Were they received and recorded? Is there a letter on file recognizing successful completion of each contract, not only for the project as a whole, but also with each vendor? For small projects, we may need to ask whether all warranty cards were sent to the manufacturers. Did everything get delivered, and was it received?

The best approach to ensuring that the paperwork file is complete is to make a checklist, and then make friendly contact with stakeholders to ensure that the paperwork is done.

Sometimes, however, difficulties, disagreements, procrastination, lost items, and forgetfulness get in the way. These problems do come up, and that is exactly why this work is important. If these issues are present, we find them. And, by taking a direct and cooperative approach, we can almost always resolve them before they expand out of control, using up time and money. In my experience, this is much easier to do while people still remember the project, rather than later, when they have put it out of their minds.

It is possible to come to good legal and financial closure even when a project fails or delivers only partial results. If we are able to maintain a no-blame environment throughout the project, even when parts of it are falling apart, then usually everyone will see it is in each person's best interest to bring things to closure in a fair way.

Managing reassignment of the project team

As the project finishes, team members will be leaving for other work, either within the company, or elsewhere. Some may need to leave earlier than we would like. Others may face a difficult time of inactivity before their next project. Either way, we need to take care of the project and the people during this transition.

Completing and sharing lessons learned from the project

Whether the project was a success or ran into big trouble—or more likely, had its mix of successes and failures—we can learn from what has happened. And what we learn should be in writing. A good review is an opportunity to improve, and we should share that opportunity with team members and with other project managers in our organization. This cycle of learning is one of the biggest benefits of the no-blame environment.

Completing the post-project business review with the customer

More and more, businesses want proof of value for completed projects. This is appropriate. Just as you want to know what money you are earning on your investments, so a company wants to know what it is getting for the effort and money invested in a project. But we may not be able to measure this until the system has been in production for a few months, at least. So we arrange a business review of the production system with the customer, which will take place some months after the product or service is stable and in use.

Resources Assigned to the Transition Stage

This section is written assuming your product or service is something that will need support. These days, information technology is the fastest growing branch of project management, so we use terms from that field. However, the issues are worth considering in any project.

The entire project team will be busy during transition to production. In addition, the help desk and the technical support teams will be heavily involved. We will create a transition team that has several functions:

- The help desk will evaluate and request improvements for user training materials.
- The technical support teams will assist in running the pilot test and installing or delivering the production system.
- The technical support team will use technical documentation and request improvements.
- The project team will revise all documents as needed to satisfy the stakeholders.
- The process of working together will support knowledge transfer to the production teams. *Knowledge transfer* is the process of passing along information and understanding. It allows the receiving group to support the system independently, without relying on the project team.

The customers will be learning the system and participating in the pilot test. They will also be involved in acceptance testing, which may be simultaneous with the pilot test. The peripheral stakeholders will each receive and review the component, interface, or reports that the product or service provides them, and may want changes.

The project sponsor should help ensure that the customer provides any resources needed for a successful transition, and also help resolve any schedule conflicts.

Roles in the Transition Stage

Here are the jobs done by people in each role during the transition to production stage:

- *The project manager* now tracks work, time, and cost daily, rather than weekly. The project manager manages quality and risk. The project manager focuses on meeting delivery schedules and assuring quality. The project manager coordinates the transition team's efforts and begins completion control tasks.
- *The transition team (TT)* will coordinate the project team with its key customers: the user groups, the help desk, and the production support staff; and will have representatives from each group on the team.
- *The transition team leader (TTL)* will coordinate the weekly transition team meeting and track all tasks and issues to appropriate resolution. Most of the time it is best if the project manager is the transition team leader. When a company has used transition teams for a period of time,

it is possible to delegate the TTL role to a senior member of the help desk or the production support staff.

- *The project sponsor* is available, and we need to keep him or her updated on progress. The sponsor is available to ensure sufficient customer resources for the transition stage and to resolve schedule conflicts.

- *Customer representatives and business analysts.* The customer representative has a major role in testing. He or she should review all interfaces prior to any tests by other users, and will probably coordinate user groups for the pilot and user acceptance tests. The customer representative or business analyst will probably also assist in preparing the rollout schedule.

- *Help desk and operations support staff* drive the efforts of the transition team. They are key customers in the transition process. The project team seeks to provide them with all they need to support users and maintain the system for the life of the project. Different organizations use different names for the groups that perform these functions, and may use multiple groups of either internal staff or outsourced consultants for these functions. Increasingly, automated assistants are also being used. From a systems perspective, the help desk function is the process of assisting users in doing production work using the product or service, or assisting customers in using the product or service and realizing value from it. Common terms are the help desk and customer service. The operations support function maintains the system in operating order in the production environment. It may also provide backup support for the help desk. Other terms are infrastructure, network support, and systems support.

- *The users* will perform the pilot and acceptance tests. They will provide feedback for our final changes to the product or service. Promotional effort for deployment should prepare the user for the day we go into production, aiming for them to have high hopes, but not excessive expectations.

- *Other stakeholders.* Each stakeholder will receive and test the component, interface, or reports about which he or she is concerned and we will provide necessary changes.

- *Technical and engineering staff.* The project team will shift focus from creating the product to responding to the transition team and customers. The focus is now on assuring quality in the final delivery and adding value through minor enhancements and smooth transition.

- *Vendors* will now be represented by consultants we have retained, technicians performing installations or service, or post-sales customer service representatives. These technicians may be performing installations, in which case we need to coordinate their work with the rollout schedule. They may be training help desk or providing customer service or support to production operations, and should be included in our transition team and support plan.

- *External resources.* Various groups, such as the audit department, the financial department, purchasing, or the legal department, may be involved in project closure. For example, there may be a quality audit, or the legal department may be involved in signing off on completed contracts.

Our work as project managers is to coordinate the activity of all of these resources daily with a focus on successful delivery.

Inputs of the Transition Stage

The outputs of the development stage are the inputs for transition to production. The team has prepared the following items:

- A product or service that has been tested and meets the requirements specification and design specification, as modified by change control.
- A nearly final user manual or help system.
- Technical engineering specifications such as software code documentation and hardware technical specifications designed to be used by future programmers and engineers who will support and modify the system.
- A proposed final support plan.
- A proposed final training plan.
- A complete high-level and low-level test plan.
- A test bed and test data files or test cases.
- Documentation of all test results.
- Documentation of any open issues.
- A draft training plan.

As project managers, we will deliver:

- A plan for transition to production and deployment, covering all steps to be taken and the management of issues from all nine areas of knowledge.

- A validated project overview, with any changes resulting from change control integrated.
- The business case, with the cost budget and delivery dates validated through PERT estimation.
- The project schedule, created by the WBS process and PERT, showing estimated vs. actual results and incorporating project change, probably maintained in a project management software tool.
- The project budget, in detail, with estimated vs. actual results to date.
- A risk plan for the remainder of the project.

We may have one other set of deliverables: presentations or demonstrations of the system for the sponsor and the customers. Since we have something to show for all of our work, we should show it!

Process of the Transition Stage

Transition to production is a complex process with many people and time-critical deadlines. During concept and analysis, we dealt with all stakeholders, but we had the time to get back to people if appointments were missed. Now, we need to coordinate the activities of all of these people towards our deployment dates. We will look at some key management actions that will help ensure a successful transition, then look at the three periods within the transition stage, and at a sample detailed transition schedule.

KEYS TO SUCCESSFUL TRANSITION

Here are the keys to a successful transition to production stage:

- *Begin early.* Start the transition stage well before the end of the development stage.
- *Include everyone.* Bring in people from operations support, the help desk, and end-user representatives right at the beginning.
- *Complete the documentation.* All documentation should be included in testing, and approved by those who will use it.
- *Do not skimp on testing.*
- *Plan carefully.* Use everyone's input in the plan—operations support, the help desk, end-users, production managers, and the project team.

- *Track everything daily.* Weekly meetings are no longer enough. Either speak to each team member on the phone every day, or have a five- to ten-minute stand-up meeting each day. Create and use a spreadsheet or similar tool to track open issues.

THE FOUR PERIODS OF THE TRANSITION STAGE

The best way to organize the transition stage is into four broad periods, each of which is divided into tasks.

- Prepare for and complete the pilot test
- Prepare to go live
- Implementation
- Project close

Figure 9-1 illustrates the first three of these periods, and their relationship to the rest of the project schedule. We begin transition to production near the end of the development stage. In the classic system development life cycle (SDLC), each phase must be complete before the next phase can start, because the milestone of one phase is the input for the next. However, through years of practice, we see that we can divide a milestone into multiple deliverables, allowing some things to get started before others are finished. This method is called *Fast Tracking*. We apply fast tracking here, allowing us to start some transition to production processes before we have completed all

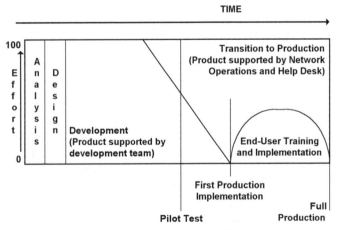

Fig. 9-1. The transition schedule.

the tasks in development. As a result, transition to production begins before development is complete.

Overlapping the two stages is beneficial to both the project schedule and project quality. It shortens project duration, allowing an earlier delivery date. It improves project quality because it gives us more time on transition to production tasks before that delivery date. If we manage the shift from one stage to another well, it can also help us manage project cost. Full-time team members can shift their workload from development to transition as they finish their tasks in development. For example, an engineer or programmer who has turned in components for testing can begin to work on technical documentation and still be available to respond to any problems found in his or her components during testing.

In Fig. 9-1, the diagonal line represents the shift in effort from development to transition to production. As development winds down, transition to production ramps up. In the first period of transition, the focus is on the pilot test as a milestone. The pilot test is often also the user acceptance test, or part of it. The second period of transition begins when we evaluate the pilot test results and ends with the first customers getting the production version of the product or service. This is called *first production implementation*, or, more informally, the *go-live date* or the *drop-dead date*. (It all depends on your view of life...) At that point the third period, implementation, begins, with simultaneous training. Sometimes, implementation is a single event. In other situations, implementation occurs over time as the product or service is rolled out to a number of locations. Implementation ends when all customers are using the production version and it is fully supported by the help desk and operations support. This also marks the end of the project. The horizontal time axis in Fig. 9-1 is generic; the actual duration of each stage may differ.

Project close begins at the end of transition to production, and is often a part-time process. Some of its activities are best done two to six months after the product has been in production. For example, a post-project business review includes an evaluation of the value received by the company from the new system. This is done through measuring the productivity of the new system after it is reliable and everyone knows how to use it.

Although the terms here come from information technology, the concepts apply to many kinds of projects. Here are some examples:

- In an audit, the meeting when the draft report is presented is equivalent to the pilot test. If communication has gone well up to that point, the audit is accepted by all parties. If not, there is still time for negotiation of the language so that the findings can be presented in a way that works for the department being audited, the recipient of the audit

report, and other stakeholders. By scheduling the meeting before the final due date, time is allowed for final modifications.

- Some theatrical plays and musicals go on tour before a scheduled Broadway opening. Often, they are too long, and cuts are made to the script based on audience feedback. Here, the tour is being used as a pilot test to find and make modifications before the more critical Broadway audience and before the Broadway critics have a chance to take a shot at the show.

On any project, we should plan the transition schedule to include as much real-world testing, and as much feedback from the customers, as possible.

EXERCISE

Create a Good Pilot Test
Think of a project where the customer was not satisfied with the result. Design some kind of pilot test or review meeting that would have detected the problems early enough so that the team would have had time to correct them. How would you plan the transition for that project, knowing what you know now?

THE TRANSITION SCHEDULE

Let us take a closer look at each of the three periods in the transition schedule. We will start by looking at the period from the beginning of transition to production through the go-live date, the first two periods.

Reaching the go-live date

In transition to production, we are focused on our go-live date, and so we need a more structured schedule for this stage than for other stages. A typical transition to production stage for a medium-sized computer software or hardware project might take nine weeks. Here is a summary of the most important events of those nine weeks:

- *Week one: Kickoff.* The project manager launches the transition team. Members from the help desk and production operations staff read project documentation and familiarize themselves with the project.

- *Weeks two and three: Prepare for pilot test.* All documentation is completed in draft form. The pilot test system is prepared.
- *Weeks four and five: Pilot test.* The pilot test is run, and results are gathered.
- *Weeks seven and eight: Prepare for go-live date.* All adjustments discovered in the pilot test are made, and the final system and installation method are prepared.
- *Week nine: Go live.* Installation begins.

During these nine weeks, transition team (TT) activities develop along these lines:

- The results of the weekly transition team meeting guides all work being done.
- The project team focuses on completion of the product or service and its documentation and preparation of the help desk and production operations TT members.
- The help desk TT member learns the system, provides help desk support during the pilot test, and teaches other help desk staff to support the system.
- The operations support TT member learns the system and how to install it, does this work during the pilot test, and trains the rest of operations support in how to maintain the system.

If the work of the transition team goes well, then the project team does not need to have any role in providing routine support as of the go-live date.

The benefit of a smooth transition period is that the system is supported by the production operations staff and help desk as soon as it is implemented. The users do not identify the project manager or project team as the source of system support. Instead, they call the same help desk that they call for all other systems. I have spoken to many project managers in organizations where this is not done. In those organizations, the project team members are permanently tied into a support role for the system they created. This is expensive, and it also slows down future project work.

Pilot test results

So far, we have assumed that everything is going to go well in the pilot test. But the pilot test is a test, and we have to be ready for failure as well as success. Here are the possible results of the pilot test:

- *Pilot test passed.* This does not mean that there were no problems. It means that the problems can be resolved before the go-live date, and there is no need to change the implementation schedule.
- *Too many problems found.* The pilot test ran to completion, but more problems were found than can be resolved before the go-live date. The best option is to delay the go-live date and resolve all issues before implementation. The second-best option is to enter a build–fix cycle during implementation, which we discuss below.
- *Pilot test failed.* In this case, there were so many problems that the pilot test could not be run all the way to completion. If we cannot arrange for a delayed deployment and a second pilot test, the project may be headed for failure.

Why is disaster looming if the pilot test fails? Because we have three sets of problems to resolve, and we only know what one set of the problems is:

- One set is the list of known problems, including the reason the pilot test failed and the other problems we have already discovered.
- The second set is the set of problems that we would have found had we completed the pilot test. But we did not discover them because we did not run those parts of the pilot test, or we did not give users enough time to find and report them.
- The third set of problems is the problems we will create while we are fixing the problems in set one. For example, in software development, research shows that one new bug is created for every five lines of code edited. Since we may have to edit more than one line of code to fix each problem we know about, we could be creating quite a number of new problems.

Since we have not found the problems in sets two and three, we cannot fix them until users discover them. This makes a second pilot test essential. If we attempt to go into production, even with a build–fix cycle, users are likely to be highly dissatisfied.

The pilot test results are reported in the pilot test lessons learned document, and tracked in the known problems and issues tracking document. We present these tools later in this chapter.

The implementation period

Many variables affect how we implement our system. Rather than providing a schedule for implementation, we can only offer a guide to planning the implementation where we define these variables and describe the best implementation methods in each case. The work of implementation planning is left to you and your team. And who could do it better? By the end of the project, you and your team are the experts on the product or service you have created, and you have a thorough understanding of its environment and your customers.

Implementation Plan Basics

The product or service we have created may have only one type of component, or have multiple types of components. Each component may need to be installed only once, or may need to be installed at or delivered to many locations. And the environments into which these components are being installed may all be similar, or they may not be standardized. These are the major variables we take into account in implementation planning. As a result, we can choose one of these types of implementation:

- *Single installation.* The product is installed at a single location.
- *Multiple installations.* The product is installed to a few sites.
- *Simple deployment.* A deployment to many locations, but all of those locations are functionally identical.
- *Complex deployment.* A deployment to many locations, with differences among the locations. For example, if we are putting in memory upgrades on all computers in a company, there may be many office locations, and many different types of computer at each location. We would need to give the installers the right memory chips and the right instructions for the types of computers they will encounter at each location.

These different possibilities should be analyzed when you prepare the implementation plan. Plan carefully for complex environments, particularly ones that are not standardized.

The implementation plan should consider more than just how to load the new product and get it running. Here are other issues:

- A backup and restore plan, so that if installation goes awry, the system receiving the installation can be restored to prior status. This is often called a *backout plan.*
- A schedule that minimizes down time of existing systems and interferes with work as little as possible.
- Time for pilot testing, evaluation, and revision before final deployment.

- Integration of the training of the permanent support staff into the deployment phase. They may have to reinstall the system, or install it to new or expanded sites, in the future.
- Coordination of the implementation schedule with the training schedule.

From Implementation Plan to Rollout Schedule

Once we have completed our implementation plan, we present it to the users, expecting them to make adjustments. We know the necessary steps, but we do not know the customer department's production schedules. We encourage the customer to adjust the schedule to reduce the interference that installation and training will create for production work. The result of this negotiation is the *rollout schedule*, the actual schedule we will follow when we deliver the new product or service to complete the project.

TRAINING

For our project to realize its full value, people need to make full use of the features of the product or service we create. Think for a moment. Do you use all the features of the software on your computer? How about your television and DVD player? Or even your refrigerator? I was at a friend's house recently, and I had to figure out some very obscure icons to see how to get water, chipped ice, or ice cubes from the door of the refrigerator without opening it.

For all the talk of intuitive user interfaces, people actually cannot use most of what we have these days. Training can close that gap—if our customers are willing to be trained.

So, design of training should go hand-in-hand with design of the product or service in terms of how it will be used. Training design is beyond the scope of this text, but we will raise a few issues here of which every project manager should be aware.

- *When should training be required?*
- *The cost of training includes the customer's time.*
- *Training should be focused on work productivity or consumer enjoyment.* People do not go to work to use computers, they go to work to get work done. Productivity (using the new system) should be the focus of training.
- *Training can be automated.*

- *Do not forget to train people who do not exist.* New employees will need to learn the system you give them when they are hired. New customers will need to learn the product you created when they buy it years from now. Make sure training will be available for the life of the product or service.

When the new product or service is tested, working, delivered, and installed, production is started, and the transition to production stage is completed.

PROJECT CLOSE

First, we will look at a standard project close, when everything has gone well. Then we will look at how to handle problems that might come up. Lastly, we will take a look at how to close a project that did not complete successfully.

Closing a successful, well-run project

We begin the process of project close by assessing what needs to be done. This work is not an organized stage but is a set of tasks with few dependencies. Once we know what all the tasks are, we can handle each one as opportunity arises. So, if we get to a meeting with the project sponsor, we might resolve several unrelated items such as: final signature on the contract closing letter; authorization for replacement of a lost check that a vendor never received; and a discussion of whether one of your team leaders is now ready to manage a project on his or her own. As we get in touch with each person, we walk through our checklist and take care of items. So, let us start by building the checklist.

Organizing the Work of Project Close

The best place to start is with the open issues document we created during the transition period. We can make a copy and delete all of the items that are marked done. Any that are not yet done stay on the list, and we have got a start on our checklist.

To expand the checklist and make sure it is as complete as possible, we review the following project documents, adding anything that might not be closed:

- *The project overview.* Review the goal and inclusions to be sure all was delivered. Make a note of the purpose in detail for planning the business review of the project.

- *The business case* is the primary starting point for the business review.
- *The work breakdown structure, task assignments, and work schedule.* Were all tasks completed? Are you sure that all deliverables were delivered?
- *The communications plan.* Make some kind of contact with each stakeholder. For the more central people, make a phone call or have a meeting. For the peripheral stakeholders, send an e-mail or a thank-you note. Be sure to ask them if they have any concerns, or if they are aware of anything left unfinished.
- *The budget.* Have a meeting with the accounting department to ensure all payments are completed and properly recorded.
- *The project work files.* Make a list of all contracts and agreements related to the project. For any items such as warranties on purchased equipment, which will be needed by the customer or support staff, make a copy for your files, and give the original to the customer manager. Confirm—in writing where appropriate—that all contracts and agreements are fulfilled. If any are not, complete them if possible. If not, delegate the remaining work to someone who will be able to complete it.

As you identify these items, add them to your open issues list. Then resolve them one by one. In general, they will fall into the five categories discussed below.

Ensuring Stakeholder Satisfaction

We know we are finished, but does the customer? The project has met its goal, but those of us with a technical focus tend not to look past the goal. And we need to, or the customer may not receive the value. We should review the project overview and ask if the purpose, as well as the goal, has been met. Then we should contact the customer at all levels, and also key stakeholders, and ask if they are satisfied, or if there is any more we should do. All other stakeholders should be sent an e-mail message, at a minimum.

WOWS AND WHOOPSES

The New Fax System With No Cost Savings

A few years ago, a company noticed that it had over 80 lines used for individual faxing from computers in the company. A decision was made to purchase and implement a new centralized faxing system that would take faxes from all corporate applications and send them out over a fax server using only one or two phone lines. This way, the old lines could be decommissioned, and a lot of money would be saved.

The package was selected, tested, configured, and modified to work with company software. It was deployed and put in place. Everyone was very happy with it.

And no money was saved, because no one ever went back and cancelled the 80 phone lines that were no longer being used.

A couple of months later, the financial department noticed that the phone bill had not gone down. Users were sent notices to make sure that they were not using the line, and the lines were decommissioned. But, the cost savings were delayed three months longer than necessary and the reputation of the computer services department suffered.

The lesson: A project is not over until the purpose is achieved.

WHAT THIS MEANS FOR YOU

Closing the Communications Loop
Sometimes, as in the above example, other people need to take action to achieve value from project results. We need to contact them and make sure they know they can do whatever they need to do. Other times, our contact is simply an opportunity to leave the customer with a clear memory of the smile they felt when the project finished. Either way, prompt closure leads to recognition and value.

Achieving Legal and Financial Closure
If you are a consultant, it is time to get the sign-off that the project is complete, deliver the final bill, and get paid. Do not forget to pay your sub-contractors. These procedures can be simple or complex, depending on the nature of the bureaucracy involved, the size of the project, and the quality of your financial record-keeping. But, obviously, they cannot be set aside for later or forgotten. If they are, final collections can take costly months.

In addition to the formal closure, informal closure is also important. Some executives have a hard time saying, "job well done," or "thanks." But, at least give them the chance to do it. If you are a working as a consulting firm, this is a good time to make sure that you have whatever references or recommendations you wanted to get out of the contract. If you work internally, corporate communications might announce the new product or service, or even include a short article from a satisfied customer in a corporate newsletter.

If you have done well, a little celebration is in order.

Managing Reassignment of the Project Team

At some point, perhaps as early as the beginning of the pilot test, some team members will be reassigned to other work. Of course, if the pilot test discovers problems, you may really wish you had their expertise. Keep this in mind. Perhaps you can retain the people most likely to be needed as others are reassigned. Perhaps you can arrange with their next project manager that they can be called back in an emergency. If neither of these is possible, hold a final meeting with each person a few days before he or she leaves. Make sure that their documentation is in your files. Ask them if there are any crucial components that they think require particular attention during final testing or deployment. Arrange for them to cross-train team members who are staying on, so their knowledge does not leave the project.

Of course, there is also an informal and personal side to the departure of team members. Pay attention to the morale and focus of those who are still with you. If they are consultants, or if they were hired only for the project, they may be job-hunting. Rather than just having a farewell lunch once or twice a week, organize time to appreciate the contributions of departing members, and let them express their appreciation to the team. Taking care of your team during the transition will help the smaller, remaining group do its job well. And, it will help you cope with the inevitable mixed feelings you will have when the project is over, the product is in the hands of other people, and the team is gone.

These days, many projects use temporary workers and consultants. Be sure to meet with each of these team members and ask them about their plans. If you are satisfied or pleased with their work, give them a written letter of reference. This is not only good for them, it is also good for you. You will be able to pull the letter out of your files if you get a call asking for a reference for this person many months later. If you can think of another project that might need this person's skills, be sure also to give a referral.

Completing and Sharing Lessons Learned from the Project

Whether we have done well or not, it is very valuable to review how well we did, and what we learned. The goal of creating a lessons learned document from the project is learning so that we and others can improve in the future. Although we may ask: "What would I have done differently?" We end up saying: "Here is what we can do differently next time."

There are three broad aspects of this review, which we can do shortly after the go-live date:

- *The project management review.* Did we do a good job managing the project? Were estimates accurate? How did we manage in applying each of the nine areas of knowledge? How well did we track work and manage each stage? At a larger level, would we design the project differently, knowing what we know now?

- *The technical review.* The technology used and our team's ability to work with that technology is also subject to review. What were the team's strengths and weaknesses? What are the implications of this for staffing future projects? Is this a technology we can use elsewhere at our company? What do you and your team recommend? We can also evaluate vendors and consultants.
- *Evaluation of the product or service.* Do the users like what they got? Is it working for them and helping them do their jobs? Or, is it selling well and satisfying customers? We should review individual features and functions, and include the help system and documentation. We should also contact the help desk, operations support, and peripheral stakeholders to find out their experience in the days or weeks after the product or service was delivered to them.

Here are some of the ways we can gather information and review the project:

- *Review the change control documents.* Could any of these added features been foreseen in the design stage? What could you do on your next project to reduce the need for changes during development?
- *Review cost and time variance reports.* What could you do to predict these costs and time changes, or make allowances for them, next time?
- *Review the risk plan.* Were any actual risk events not foreseen? Were risk events that did occur managed according to the plan? Did any risk events occur that could have been averted?
- *Review the test results.* If tests failed, what could be done to improve the quality of components or identify problems earlier next time?
- *Review your successes.* Compare this project to others you have done. What did you do better: less cost variance, fewer problems, or better on-time delivery? Whatever you did better, how did you do it?
- *Hold a brainstorming meeting with the whole team.* Let each person speak on what they learned during the project. Encourage each person to speak about improvements as a project-oriented team professional, and not just increased technical knowledge.
- *Ask for feedback for yourself as a project manager.* Either in a meeting, or privately, have an honest conversation with people with whom you worked on the team. If you are aware of any errors you made, like getting angry, or focusing only on cost, time, or quality, instead of on

balancing the three, acknowledge them, and then ask the person to share anything that they hope you will look at and learn to improve.

- *Help your team leaders improve.* Meet with them and offer negative feedback, that is, encouragement for improvement. Encourage them to ask the same questions of their team members and provide the same for their team.
- *Conduct post-project interviews with customers and stakeholders.* Using phone interviews or a web form, get feedback on the value of the product or service and suggestions for changes from the customer.

Some of the results of this should be written up in a lessons learned document for the project. Focus on those of greatest value for projects in your organization. Perhaps new forms and procedures were created or adapted that could simplify future projects. These can be added to a set of standard operating procedures and templates your company uses for projects. General lessons can also be distributed to other members of the team.

It may also be useful to share some of what you have learned more widely. Large companies that accept project management methods often have a project office or project management office that helps all project managers and teams improve their methods. If your organization has one, deliver your lessons learned so they can distribute it to others. You can choose whether to do this anonymously, or with an identification of the project. The goal is not to point fingers, or even to praise good work, but to learn and improve. However, the more specific you can be regarding how good results were achieved, the more useful your report will be. You might also consider writing an article, either for an in-house journal or for professional publication.

Do not confuse this project lessons learned document with the pilot test lessons learned document. This document helps us improve work on future projects. The pilot test lessons learned document lets us know what we need to do to finish the current project and deliver the product or service to the customer successfully.

Completing the Post-project Business Review With the Customer

At the beginning of the project, we defined the business value, calculated in either a cost/benefit analysis or a return on investment (ROI) calculation. In addition to measurable, hard-dollar value, we also anticipated some other benefits that were either harder to define or harder to measure, the soft-dollar value of the project.

Now it is time to find out if we have achieved those goals. The first step is to decide on the timing of the business review. If the product or service takes time to learn and use well, we cannot evaluate its benefits right away. If it is sold to customers, we need to see how soon it reaches the customers, what complaints come through, and how well it is selling. We should meet with the business analysts or customer representatives and set a time for the post-project review.

We can plan the review as a mini-project. The inputs are the planned value items from the business case, plus data we gather measuring each of these value items in actual practice. The business analysts or customer representatives can help us gather the data, and other departments, such as accounting or sales, may also be able to help. If support for the product or service was well designed, then these measurements should be available. If not, we work to get reasonable estimates of them.

When all the data are gathered, we hold a meeting to compare the expected results from the project's business case with the actual results shown in the data. We report the results for each value item as follows:

- If the value is being realized pretty much as planned, we report this to the project sponsor.
- If a greater value is being realized, we also report that.
- If the value item was originally in soft dollars, and we can now measure actual results, we report these.
- If value is not being realized for a given item, we report this. We also explain why, and make suggestions regarding changes in operating procedures or support practices that will allow the value to be realized.
- We also brainstorm how more value can be realized, even when goals are met.

All of this is written up in a report. If there are specific action items—such as improved training, or a change of procedures, or a stronger sales effort—they should be assigned to a production manager or to the project sponsor for follow-up. If value cannot be fully confirmed, then it might be appropriate to arrange for another review meeting. For example, if a new financial system is in place, some items can be reviewed after the first quarter of production operations, but other items might wait until after the end of the fiscal year.

Resolving problems during close

One of the major reasons we do the work of project close is that we might find problems that would otherwise have gone unnoticed. Usually, if we are prompt, it is fairly easy to take care of these items. A new check can be issued

to replace one that was lost. A copy of a contract closing letter can be sent a second time for signature, and so forth.

However, sometimes problems are more complicated. Perhaps a vendor was promised a bonus for early delivery, but, when the item was delivered, changes were required. As a result, the delivery date is in dispute, and it is not clear if the bonus should be delivered. Perhaps a requirement was not written down, and, although it is in the product, it is not in the documentation, and no one is using it. In these cases, some conflict resolution or extra work is needed to bring this item—and the project—to a close.

The good news is that you already have the tools to do this. The basic tools of same-side communication, including triangulation and the no-blame environment, work here, just as they worked at the beginning of the project. Speak to each party, and write up the perspectives of each party. These are your starting points. And a resolution satisfactory to all parties is on the other side of the gap. You have analyzed the gap, and now you can work to close it. As you cooperate with people, they will cooperate with you to come to good closure.

Creating good closure on a failed project

Not all projects succeed, and we now know many reasons for project failure. However, project failure does not need to be the end of the story. I used to think it did. I used to think that if things did not go right, people would never talk to me again. I have learned that I am wrong. Time does not heal all wounds, but it heals many of them. Here are two examples from earlier years of my consulting practice where things did not turn out well, and I was part of the problem, but I was able to come to good closure.

- *The unfinished installation tool.* I was asked to visit a company for a week and design an automated installation for Windows 95 to go out to hundreds of computers of 20 different types and brands. I put in some preparation time, but not enough. In addition, I asked the client to prepare one example of each kind of computer with complete system documentation, defining every hardware and software component. When I arrived, they had three machines waiting, but no documentation. I learned that they were very short staffed. I spent most of the week doing the work they did not do, and the rest working through some unexpected bugs in the installation program. When we were finished we had a way of installing Windows and some steps towards automatic installation of the programs, but we were far short of the complete installation package at which we were aiming. In retrospect, if I had prepared for about four hours more than I did, I could have completed the job. But I encountered the 1:10:100 rule, and needed an extra 40 hours I did not have to finish the job. When I reviewed this with senior management, they saw that they did get some value from the trip, and that the failure was due to errors on both sides. We agreed to a financial settlement of 50% of the project cost paid in return for the 50% delivered, and parted with respect for one another.

- *The strategic architecture plan that was not well received.* I had spent two years building a good working relationship with a major state police agency. I had trained most of their computer staff in project management, and also done some executive-level training. I was asked to come in and facilitate a meeting to define key points of their strategic architecture for new computer systems. We held the meeting. Everything seemed to go well, especially considering the challenge of helping four different bureaus with very different missions and perspectives work together. I asked in what format they wanted the report to be written, and the question was answered by the administrative assistant to the head of the division. She told me what she wanted, and I told her that would take some extra time. She accepted that. What I did not know is that her boss did not approve either the time or the format; they had not had time to talk. I delivered. The head of the division was, to put it mildly, upset. We negotiated partial payment, and I thought I was saying a permanent good-bye to one of my biggest clients. A year went by. I needed a reference for my training program for another state agency. I thought that the training work I had done for the first agency had gone well, even if the strategic planning had not. And it never hurts to ask. To my surprise, I was well received by the administrative assistant. She said that, looking back on it, everyone at the agency had been under a lot of stress, and there were a lot of reasons the plan did not work out. She gave me an excellent recommendation that got me a job with my new client in another state.

What have I learned from all of this? Quality work is rare. If we do our best to do good work and to maintain good professional relationships, we will make an impression that will outlast our failures. We will have a chance to try again.

That is far from a universal law. Some people will want to forget the whole mistake. Actually, though, you can leverage that, as well. If someone wants to put a quick end to a project review, tell them that you want to take as little of their time as possible. Reach them on a personal and professional level,

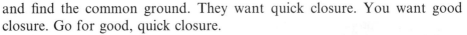

and find the common ground. They want quick closure. You want good closure. Go for good, quick closure.

If you get no response at all, then close the project noting that they did not respond to your efforts at communication. And keep in touch by sending an annual holiday card.

Ultimately, our own professionalism and thoroughness will allow us to recover from failure and give us an opportunity to make use of the lessons we have learned.

Outputs of the Transition Stage

The short version of the list of outputs is: It is done! (Dancing a jig is recommended.) A fuller list of outputs is:

- A product or service in production, generating value as it is used by customers and peripheral stakeholders.
- The product or service being maintained by operations staff, such as the help desk and operations support, with little or no reference to the project team. If a formal escalation procedure is in place, then members of the project team should be on the third or fourth tier, and should be called only rarely.
- Complete documentation satisfactory for all purposes, including future system upgrade or redesign.
- Satisfied customers who know they are satisfied. Where appropriate, letters of commendation and letters of referral.
- Confirmation of complete closure on all contracts, agreements, and payments. Where necessary, negotiated settlements.
- All work done by team members before they leave, team members appropriately reassigned, letters of reference and referrals delivered and on file.
- Project lessons documents learned, distributed to anyone who can learn from them.
- Post-project business review or reviews completed, with action items passed on to the project sponsor or others responsible for seeing them through.
- A file of all project notes appropriately archived, probably in the hands of the customer manager or sponsor, and proper disposal of other documents.

Tools for the Transition Stage

In this section, we offer three tools that were mentioned above: the known problems and issues tracking document; the pilot test lessons learned document; and a method for creating an accurate test schedule.

KNOWN PROBLEMS AND ISSUES

The known problems and issues tracking document is an excellent tool for any project in transition to production and also for any time when there is a crisis or a lot is happening all at once and we are not sure what is going on. I created it during one project's transition stage. I already had a to-do list, but it just was not working: I was not keeping up with all that was going on. I evaluated the to-do list and I realized that it did not work because it did not reflect the different types of tasks of which I needed to keep track. So I created a separate category for each type of task, and a different table to track the information needed to manage that type of task. You can build your own open issues tracking document using a word processor or spreadsheet. For each item, include an initial entry date, a deliverable, the person who will do the work, and a delivery date. You can set up six sections, one to track each of the following types of items:

- *Decisions still to be made.* Track what the question is, who should decide, and what should be delivered with the answer.
- *Recently resolved decisions.* Track who should be informed and what actions should be taken.
- *Work that needs to be done.* Track the deliverable. This is for items where the job is defined and you can estimate how long the work will take.
- *Problems that need to be solved.* This is for items where you need to do diagnosis, and you do not know exactly what work will be done or how long it will take.
- *Documentation that needs to be changed.* Track the document, the part that needs changing, and what the change is.
- *Information that needs to be gathered.* Sometimes, work gets stopped because information is missing. Identify the missing item, and to whom the information should be delivered.

One excellent way to maintain the known problems and issues document is in a spreadsheet program. We can sort the rows as needed and mark items done as we go.

If we have daily ten-minute project team meetings to coordinate the transition stage, we can use this form as our agenda. If we are managing people by phone, we can walk through this list as we talk to them. And we can build the agenda for the weekly transition team and project team meetings from this document.

PILOT TEST LESSONS LEARNED

This document is prepared in the week after the pilot test. It is a status report delivered to all stakeholders. The best format is a short memo with an updated copy of the known problems and issues tracking list attached. The memo should identify the good or bad news from the pilot test, whether it passed, identified excessive problems, or failed altogether. It should also confirm the original go-live date, revise it, or say that a change of date is being considered, and inform the reader when the decision will be made.

In cases where a delay seems appropriate, it may be useful to write a longer explanation of the situation.

ACCURATE ESTIMATION FOR THE TEST SCHEDULE

There is a fundamental uncertainty in testing that makes preparing a test schedule difficult. When you are preparing to run tests, you know that some will fail, but you do not know which ones. However, you probably do have a good sense of how reliable your product is as it enters testing. The solution, called a Monte Carlo simulation, is a statistical technique. Instead of just estimating how long successful passage of the tests will take, we estimate a variety of scenarios, based on the likelihood of failure of some tests. Monte Carlo simulations use sophisticated computer programs that are usually industry-specific. The result is a more accurate test schedule.

THE BUILD–FIX CYCLE

There is an approach to implementation that is not ideal, but is sometimes the best option when we face a difficult situation. What do we do when the product or service is not finished, or is not working properly, in time for our go-live date? In terms of delivering a quality system, the best choice is to delay the beginning of implementation. But this is not always possible. Sometimes, for financial, contractual, political, or practical reasons, it is better to deliver something on time than to delay delivery.

If we do this, we can plan implementation with a build–fix schedule. The first step should be to define the features that will be available in each version as we install the system. The second should be to work with our team to disable features that do not work, so that the users will not encounter errors or system failures. Instead, users will either be unable to access the feature (for example, because the menu item is removed) or they will receive a message saying that the feature is not yet operational.

We then plan a deployment schedule that includes delivering the best available version to each user group on each install date and also upgrading user groups with earlier versions to the final version when it becomes available.

Let us say, for example, that we will release three versions, 1.0, 1.1, and 1.2. Version 1.2 is the full production version as specified in the project plan with change control items included, but it is not ready for our go-live date. Let us also say that, in this example, we are installing to ten regional offices, named A through J. When we start, only version 1.0 is ready, and offices A, B, and C receive version 1.0. We continue to build forward. By the date set for deployment to office D, version 1.1 and its installation process are tested and ready. We install version 1.1 to offices D and E.

As we prepare for installation to regional office F, the team finishes the final version 1.2 of the product or service and its installation process, all tested and ready to go. Regional offices F, G, H, I, and J get version 1.2 as their first installed version. We build the system forward to those offices. During those installations, the project team develops two upgrade processes, one from version 1.0 to version 1.2, and the other from version 1.1 to version 1.2. When each upgrade process is fully tested, and we confirm that the upgrade to 1.2 is fully functional, we install it where it is needed. The 1.0 to 1.2 upgrade is installed at offices A through C, and the 1.1 to 1.2 upgrade is installed at offices D and E. We build forward, but we go back and fix the product or service at locations that did not receive the final version.

The build–fix cycle comes as close as we can to meeting our original commitment to our customer under the circumstances, and also allows the customer to begin to receive value earlier than they could if we delayed deployment. It is also a challenging process to manage and coordinate the upgrades, tests, and installations. Clearly, it requires extra effort by the project team, and that effort has an additional cost. If at all possible, we should try to arrange for automated or user-triggered upgrades that do not require a second visit by an installation technician.

Key Concepts for the Transition Stage

Let us take a look at the work we do during transition to production in each of the nine areas of project management.

INTEGRATION

This is the stage where our work of integration is tested. If all of our plans hold the project together, we will have a successful delivery.

SCOPE

The most important issue is the customer's acceptance that product and project scope requirements have been met. The system, each feature and component, and each document should be tested by users, improved to meet their requirements, and both formally and informally accepted by users and stakeholders. Be sure to remember that acceptance and testing are processes. Allow time for customer review, and be ready to revise as needed to satisfy the customer. Resolve all change management issues. If there will be one or more future releases, discuss which features and enhancements will be delivered on what dates.

TIME

The key time element is, of course, the deployment schedule. Here, you must ensure that you meet your go-live date. However, you must also be sure you are delivering a living, breathing system on those dates. It is better to be late than to deliver a system that does not work.

COST

Resolve the project budget and actual figures, and, in the completion control process, resolve all contracts and payments.

QUALITY

Project quality management becomes a daily activity in this stage. Maintain a list of all known problems and issues, and carry every one to complete resolution. As the time of the go-live date presses close, it becomes difficult to focus on quality, but it is essential to success. If we do not manage, assure, and deliver quality, then the product will have a decreased value over its production life. Whenever you forget this, remember the Hubble Space Telescope. It would have been better to catch the error in the mirror and delay the launch than do what happened. NASA put the telescope into space. It had reduced value for the first two years of operation. And, at a cost of several hundred million dollars, a replacement part was installed later.

True, your project is probably not being delivered all the way into orbit. But, these days, the world is so busy that few people take the time to fix what is broken. Instead, we live with bugs and flaws. As a result, there is a real, long-term cost to missing quality steps at the end of a project. Even if we could fix it later, we may never get the chance.

HUMAN RESOURCES

Help the team focus on the customer and delivering customer satisfaction. The goal is to turn an excellent system into a smile on the customer's face. Help each team member see how his or her work is connected to customer satisfaction.

COMMUNICATION

Daily meetings, careful listening, documentation changes as needed, and prompt resolution of all issues are all essential to managing customer expectations and getting support for the product.

Remember that your attitude will shape the customer's attitude. And the customer's attitude is ultimately the single most important variable in determining project success. Excellent systems have failed because users rejected them. Poor systems have succeeded because customers liked them. Focus on communication to obtain the crucial support and feedback you need for success.

RISK

All risk issues should be reviewed daily, managed as soon as they arise, and resolved as promptly as possible. You and your team will probably feel pressured by this, but that is our job. In this stage, we act as shock absorbers so the users have a comfortable ride on the new system.

PROCUREMENT

Procurement closes with customer acceptance and the follow-through of ensuring that all contracts and payments are complete.

Conclusion: Completing the Circle

We have viewed the stages of the project as linear, beginning with a concept and ending with production implementation. But we can also see that a cycle has been completed, as well. The project began with an idea meeting the customer in the concept stage. In that meeting, we discovered we had a good idea, so we moved ahead. In analysis, we turned the idea into a requirements specification, defining the features, functions, and qualities optimal for the customer and the operating environment. In the design stage, we moved away from the customer and on to the technical plan. Then, in development, we moved into the realm of building the product or service, which the customer does not understand and will never need to. Now, in transition to production, we bring the idea back to the customer in a very new form. It is no longer just an idea; it is a working reality.

If we look at the whole project from just one perspective, scope and requirements, we can see that we have done a lot of work to reach this point.

- A shared vision of the system makes it more likely that the system will meet user expectations.
- Detailed, traceable requirements help ensure that the system is that for which the customer asked.
- Thorough internal testing, plus testing the system as close to the real-world situation prior to the pilot test in this stage, has increased the likelihood of being able to deliver the system gracefully.
- Good customer communications will, we hope, have the customer eager to receive the system's benefits, and ready and willing to tell you about the problems so that you can fix them.

If the project cycle is successful in returning a useful product or service of high value with low cost of maintenance and a long potential life, then the continuing life cycle of the product or service in use or in the marketplace is likely to be long and bring a lot of value to the company.

Our Case Study: No, No, That Cable Goes There!

So, what does it take to install a home theater? My experience in transition to production makes me an unusual consumer. For one thing, I read the manuals. I even fill out warranty cards and check off those packing checklists that come inside each box. And I suppose that installation will take a while, that testing will be frustrating, and that it will take a while to learn how to use everything. In fact, I figure the more user-friendly and intuitive it is supposed to be, the longer it will take for me to figure it out.

The unpacking and reading of the manuals went well. Then we started plugging things in. Our first discovery was that the grounded outlet near the stereo cabinet was not grounded. It would still work, but the warranty against electrical damage would not be valid until the landlord called an electrician in to take care of it.

The data cables were clearly marked, and it was pretty easy to connect everything. The next big challenge came when we needed to figure out how to tell the television and the receiver whether to pay attention to the video recorder or to the DVD player. The codes on the remote did not quite match the codes on the ports for the cables. After a little while, though, we had good pictures and good sound. Now, it was time to begin enjoying the home theater—and learning how to use it.

A day later, music and adventure movies were doing just fine. But tender moments of dialog tended not to come out clearly. With 27 different options for sound quality, it was hard to find the right one for quiet voices, or for female vocalists. Adjusting the options while playing with the volume controls gave us what we needed within a week.

A successful project ended with a successful transition. The main reason it worked is that we did not expect too much. We did not think, "Oh, we'll just plug it in, turn it on, and it will be fine." After all, there is a reason why professional installation costs over $1,000. We spent our time saving our money. But, since we planned for it, we were happy with what we got.

A few weeks later, we added a new shelf to hold the DVD player. When we did, I unplugged the cable to the television, and accidentally plugged it back in to a different port. When I tested everything, the picture was much better! And, all of a sudden, those instructions where the remote control buttons did not match the input ports on the television all made sense. Lesson learned: Just because it is working does not mean it is right.

Your Project for Learning

Even if your project for learning is small, and only for yourself, take the time to plan a good transition. Define a pilot test or review. Create a schedule for transition to production and follow it. Review your project in all nine areas of management, and make sure that you are delivering quality.

Questions for Learning

Evaluating things we use all the time can give us insight into what makes for a successful transition to production.

- Think of a product or service you use at home or at work that is highly reliable. Try to find out what kind of testing made that possible, or draft your own outline of a test plan that would do the job. For example, if you were given a new cellular telephone to test, what tests would you perform?
- Think of a product or service that is easy to learn to use. It requires no, or almost no, instructions. What design approach and features made that possible? Can you adopt that approach or those features in a project on which you are working? How would you confirm customer acceptance of your approach?
- Think of a product or service that has excellent documentation or an excellent help system. What makes it excellent? How much work do you think it took to create it? What can you learn from it for creating documentation on your next project?
- Think of a product or service that has a great help desk and technical support. How would you set that up for your next product or service?
- Think of an excellent training program you have attended. What ideas or methods could you apply from that program to the training you will provide to users, help desk staff, or support technicians on your next project?
- Think of a product or service that was delivered easily to all its users. How would you do the same to finish your project?

PART THREE

Skills and Tools

In Part Three of *Project Management Demystified* we turn our attention to the specific skills and tools project managers use to plan, track, and control projects. Building and using your own tools and templates from this book, the support at *www.qualitytechnology.com*, and other sources will save you hundreds of hours of work per year, and ensure higher quality project results. Tools and templates are not just conveniences: they are essential parts of the best practices of project management. Using them, we remember and practice managing like a professional.

We need to choose our tools intelligently. If we try to use every tool on a small project, we will over-manage it and bury ourselves in forms. If we skip a crucial tool for a large or risky project, it may well go out of control before we know what is wrong. Nothing replaces an intelligent assessment at the beginning of the project. Review a checklist of all your tools. Ask: "Is this necessary? How will I use it?"

We can ask the same question of project management software such as Microsoft Project®. In choosing whether or not to use a software program, there are two key things to remember. First, they are tools, nothing more. They do not manage a project for you. Second, they are not really project management tools at all. They will not help you with defining the project, creating a scope statement, building a team, or resolving quality issues. They are really project tracking, not project management, tools. After you create a project plan with a work breakdown structure, a schedule, and a budget, they will help you track the schedule and budget and present status reports and projections. Other software will help you track risks. But the work of management is done by people with people, and not by computers.

We open Part Three with Chapter 10. First we look at early estimation tools that can tell us about how big a project will be before we have a detailed plan. Then we learn work breakdown structuring, which is probably the most important skill for planning a project. From the work breakdown structure we build our detailed schedule and budget. In Chapter 11 we learn simple, straightforward methods for managing what might go wrong, and managing changes that happen on a project. In Chapter 12 we learn effective ways of creating a team and leading it to success. We finish by turning to my favorite topic, quality, in Chapter 13 where we learn the five steps to managing quality, defining value, and delivering customer satisfaction.

Planning and Estimation Tools

In this chapter we will begin by looking at early planning and estimation tools that help you define a project during the concept, analysis, and early design stages. Then you will learn an excellent step-by-step method for creating a work breakdown structure (WBS), planning the project in detail by listing all of the project tasks. Lastly, we will turn to detailed estimation techniques that allow you to create a schedule and budget from the WBS.

Tools for Defining Value

This section provides a tool for defining the seven sources of *hard-dollar value* and *soft-dollar value* of a product or service, as defined in the explanation of the project overview template in Chapter 5. It then provides a tool for comparing value to cost.

THE SEVEN TYPES OF VALUE

Table 10-1 lists the seven types of value.

Below are the steps to defining value and documenting it in the project overview:

- Create a blank table similar to Table 10-1, but with three columns instead of two. Each row of your table should list one of the seven types of value. The left-hand column names the type of value, the same as in Table 10-1. In the middle column you will enter hard-dollar value with specific figures, and place soft-dollar value information related to the particular type of value in the right-hand column. Using that table, you can define all the hard- and soft-value items for your project.
- Summarize it in the purpose section of the project overview.
- List the one or two most important types of value added in the short purpose field of the project overview, and include the total hard-dollar value.
- Make reference to this table as a supporting document in the project overview.
- In this table, make reference to any additional supporting documents used to estimate value, including process analysis documents and marketing studies.

Below are some guidelines about how a business will respond to a statement of value for a project:

- In general, a project is approved primarily on its hard-dollar value.
- Soft-dollar value enhances the likelihood of project acceptance, and may encourage commitment from various stakeholders. But soft-dollar value alone is not generally enough to justify a project.
- Soft-dollar value should be couched in the business terms of your organization, for example its vision, mission, and values, and also match the concepts in the table on defining value.
- Technical items, such as increased reliability, are not value in themselves, but may be translated into either hard-dollar or soft-dollar value.

A clearly written value statement enhances the chances of project acceptance.

Table 10-1   The seven types of value.

Type of organizational change that results in added value	Definition
Cost reduction and cost avoidance	Cost reduction: allows you to maintain current production levels at lower cost Cost avoidance: allows you to prevent a foreseeable future cost
Increased production	The ability to produce more of what you produce in a given period of time. Only of value if you can sell the increased quantity of product

Faster cycle time	Speeding up any business process, including:
	    Delivery of products and services to customer
	    Problem resolution
	    Delivery of new services and products to the market
	    Faster cycle time increases organizational flexibility

Increased market share	Serving more of the existing customer base than you currently serve
New marketing methods	New ways of reaching current potential customers that increase the likelihood that they will use your services, or use them more often, resulting in increased sales
New markets and customers	The opportunity to serve customer groups that you have not been able to serve before. This includes operating in new regions or locations, and reaching new customer groups, such as different age groups or cultural groups. This is also called market development and market penetration

Protection or enhancement of staff, assets, shareholder value, the ability to do business, and customers	Any activity that protects or increases the value of anything that benefits the company. This includes:
	    Anything that assists with staff retention
	    Security of all types
	    Reduction of legal liability, which protects financial assets
	    Regulatory compliance, which protects financial assets and the ability to operate as a business or organization
	    Increase of customer satisfaction and customer retention
	    Improving or maintaining the perceived value of the organization, retention and development of shareholder value and good will
	    Anything necessary to continue business operations

A BENEFIT/COST MODEL USING RETURN ON INVESTMENT (ROI) AND TOTAL COST OF OWNERSHIP (TCO)

Once we have defined the value, or benefit of a project, we have to compare that value with the cost of doing the project. There are many ways of doing this. The approach we give here uses two of the newest models: return on investment (ROI) and total cost of ownership (TCO).

The annual *net value* of a project is the value realized in one year of operation minus the cost of that year of operation. Let us say that, in creating our value statement, we realize that, after the annual cost of supporting the new system, each year the product is in operation it will save the company $1,000,000. This means that the annual net value of the project is $1,000,000.

To consider TCO, we have to take into account annual operating costs (as we did above), plus the cost of the project and the cost of decommissioning (although some models do not include the last).

To understand ROI, we need to add only one more idea. That idea is the time value of money. To put it simply, if I offered you either one hundred dollars today, or one hundred dollars next year, which would you take? Most people agree that money today is worth more than money next year. If I give you one hundred dollars today, you can put it in an interest-bearing savings account, and have more than one hundred dollars next year. Financial managers define the rate of decrease of value of money over time, and redefine money into the value the money has in the present. The *net present value* (NPV) of a project is the net value of the project, with the time value of the money taken into account.

A given amount of money today, if held at 8% interest in the bank, will be worth more in the future. Similarly, we can use the NPV of the net profit for each year of operation in our equation. Using the 8% annual interest rate, the current value of $1,000,000 for each succeeding year is lower than it was for the previous year. The present value (PV) of $1,000,000 per year over ten years at 8% is $6,710,081.40, not $10,000,000. (Spreadsheet programs such as Microsoft Excel® calculate NPV for us.) Our figures and results are shown in Equations 16.1 and 16.2.

Equation 16-1: ROI example using NPV

$$\text{ROI} = \frac{\text{PV (annual net revenue over production life at interest percent)}}{\text{(Cost of project)} \ + \ \text{PV (Cost of decommissioning)}}$$

Equation 16-2: ROI example modified with PV

$$\text{RPI} = \frac{\text{PV (\$1,000,000/year for 10 years at 8\%)}}{(\$1,950,000) + \text{PV (\$50,000 at 10 years)}} = \frac{\$6,710,081.40}{\$1,973,159.67} = 3.4$$

When calculating ROI with NPV, the result is a straight ratio between earned value over spent cost. In this case, the project is worth 3.4 times more (or 340% of) its cost. The project costs will be recovered in about three years, and the remaining seven years of use will generate the value above cost.

USING ROI TO DECIDE ON WHETHER TO GO AHEAD WITH A PROJECT

The executive sponsor for the project benefits from a consistent method for ROI calculation across all projects. It allows him or her to do several things:

- Justify projects to the chief financial officer and others concerned with cost.
- Defend the project budget in times of budgetary cutbacks.
- Compare the relative value of several projects to determine which one has the greatest value, and therefore, arguably, the highest priority.

Of course, ROI considers only hard-dollar value, and we need to do more. Soft-dollar value is a key consideration in deciding whether to go ahead with a project. Generally, a project will be approved even if it has a lower ROI if it has high soft-dollar value, such as support for overall organizational initiatives, or if it increases internal talent, which will reduce future costs for similar projects. Some organizations will weigh soft-dollar value more heavily in their decisions than others.

What is a good ROI in general? That is hard to define. Clearly, if the project is due to last ten years, and it recovers costs in three years or less, that is good. On the other hand, an ROI of only 10% per year is a good commercial bank investment. Ultimately, decisions based on ROI at any organization should be used to compare against realistic alternative uses of the money that will be spent on the project. Economists call this the opportunity cost. The *opportunity cost* of a project is the value of what we are not doing because we are doing this project. If we calculate ROI by the same method for all projects, the one with the highest ROI has the shortest payback period, and is the best investment. And good business choices are those that find the best way to use money.

Principles of Estimation

There are many methods of estimation, and they can each be valuable if certain key principles are followed in preparing the estimate. Estimation is an engineering art, not a precise science. It seeks to answer the questions: How long will this project take? What will it cost? The most important errors to avoid are those that introduce bias, that is, push the result in a particular direction—but away from reality.

- *Wishful thinking*, where you try to make an estimate fit into an imposed deadline or budget.
- *Resentful thinking*, where you set out to prove that the imposed deadline or budget is impossible.
- *Estimating the entire project as a unit* without thinking out the details.
- *Simply copying the estimate* from a past, similar project.

These errors most often arise out of frustration, when we do not know how to—or are not given the time to—prepare a high-quality estimate.

We can avoid most errors through these simple steps:

- Receive the customer's required or desired time and budget statements. Note them as imposed figures, and then completely set them aside. Do not start asking the wrong question: Can we deliver by this date?
- Estimate the project time and cost using the methods described below. We can focus on making an accurate estimate, because we know that, if it does not match the imposed requirements, we resolve that in the next step, not while we are estimating.
- If there is a gap between the estimate and the imposed dates, negotiate the gap. We offer several cooperative approaches for doing this.
- If the gap cannot be negotiated, recommend canceling the project.
- If the gap is negotiated, update the project overview and other project documents, and proceed to the approval process.

Early Time Estimation

We need several different methods of time estimation to use at different stages of the project. The most accurate methods, PERT and CPM, are described at the end of this chapter because they only work after we have completed the work breakdown structure. Earlier, in the concept and analysis stages, we can use informal methods based on experience, a modification of the Wide-Band Delphi method, or estimation from requirements.

ESTIMATION TECHNIQUES BASED ON EXPERIENCE

Each of us probably already has some more-or-less conscious method of quick estimation. I tend to create a quick work breakdown structure, a simple to-do list, and estimate by adding up times from the detailed items. Someone else might do a quick estimation of units of work multiplied by effort. Someone else might list the stages, and compare to time and cost of similar past projects. All of these quick techniques have their flaws. The more thoroughly developed methods presented below are better. But we can use these methods when we need them, and there are some ways of getting better results.

One key to success of any of these methods is to cross-check against one or more other methods. Did you include all major components? All stages? The cost of changes? The rework necessary during testing?

Another key is simply to write down your thoughts, set them aside, then read them again later, or show them to someone else if you can. Revise before doing your calculations.

If your organization tracks effort on past projects, you can estimate phases or milestones in comparison to similar past projects. It is better to do this by stage or by deliverable, and to draw from several different projects if you can. Be sure to use actual results, and not estimates from past projects. Also, when looking at a set of past projects, make adjustments based on intelligent questions, such as:

- Is the deliverable exactly the same, simpler, or more complicated?
- Is the customer more or less demanding than the customer on the past project?
- Are there any costly errors we will avoid this time?
- What are the important differences between the initial situation this time and the initial situation last time?
- Does the person doing the work now have more or less experience?

Any estimation method that avoids bias and asks these intelligent questions is a good start. If you review your assumptions and use two such methods, you are likely to get even better results. Now, let us take a look two more sophisticated methods of early time estimation.

USING A MODIFICATION OF THE WIDE-BAND DELPHI METHOD FOR TIME AND COST ESTIMATION

One of the methods, a modification of the Wide-Band Delphi technique, can be used to create a quick scope statement and estimate of value. It works for time, cost, risk, and other areas of concern on our project. Delphi sessions are expensive, as they require a team of experts. Table 10-2 gives a procedure for this modification of the Delphi approach.

Table 10-2   Time and cost estimation using modification of the Wide-Band Delphi method.

Schedule or trigger event:
A need to create an approximate cost estimate quickly in the early stages of a project.

Brief description:
This method is a structured brainstorming approach using a team of subject-matter experts guided by a Delphi facilitator.

Inputs:
A scope statement, or a rough scope statement with a range of possibilities.

Outputs:
A range of estimated duration for the project.
A range of estimated effort for the project.
A range of estimated cost for the project.
Notes on actions to refine the estimates and address risk.

Tools:
A meeting room with appropriate facilities for facilitation, taking of meeting notes, and interactive brainstorming.

Verification (QC):
Verification within the project can be first against other estimation methods through time gap management. On project completion, the Delphi results should be compared to actual project duration, effort, and cost. Any discrepancies should contribute to future improvement of the Delphi method.

Process:
Unless otherwise stated, all actions are taken by the Delphi facilitator.
1. *Organize meeting.* The project manager creates a Delphi meeting including every expert you can get on the technical and project management aspects of the project you want to estimate. It is possible to use the same Delphi team as used for scope estimation, though you may want to make some changes to the team based on availability and skill. Deliver the scope statement in writing (in advance, if possible).

Table 10-2   Time and cost estimation using modification of the Wide-Band Delphi method (*Continued*).

2. *Presentation of scope.* Present the scope of the project; if there are any uncertain elements, present a range of scopes, minimum, plus possible requirements, up to the maximum scope. Answer any questions that any expert in the room can answer definitively. (In this process, we assume our experts are the best we can get during the session. We trust what they say.) Everyone takes notes, and one or two people with laptops do nothing but take notes. Their notes are distributed to the Delphi team members.

3. *First round of estimation.* Each member of the Delphi team works separately from the scope plan plus his or her notes to build time and cost estimates. They use their own methods and forms. Each one prepares a presentation of their time and cost estimates to the group as a whole. The estimates will be ranges. The time estimate will include both effort and duration. The team members will prepare estimates for both the minimum and the maximum scope if the scope is uncertain.

4. *First presentations.* Each Delphi team member presents his or her estimates to the team. Everyone takes notes, using the presenter's expertise to modify his or her own plan. Questions are asked for clarification or expansion, but there is no effort to improve the presenter's own plan. Instead, each presenter improves his or her own plan through listening to other presenters and noting their comments.

5. *Second round of planning.* Everyone takes the notes from all the other presentations, and comments on his or her own presentation, and improves his or her own presentation.

6. *Second presentations.* Each person presents his or her revised estimates. You work with an assistant to build a wall-sized comparison chart of all estimates. (Giant Post-It notes are good tools, or you can work with a diagramming tool and a data projector.) At the end of each presentation, questions are asked for clarification. You verify your comparison chart with each presenter.

7. *Evaluation.* It is highly likely that all estimates are already within 5% of one another. If so, you have good enough estimates for now. If you are close to 5%, you can lead a team brainstorming session to resolve differences, focusing on contributions from the Delphi team members who proposed the highest and lowest estimates.

8. *Iteration.* If the estimates are not yet close to a 5% variance, have a brainstorming session identifying remaining issues, but not trying to resolve the differences. Then run a third round of planning and presentation, and re-evaluate. In the third-round evaluation, have those who differ on key points work them out with each other with the help of the Delphi team.

9. *Wrap-up.* Identify constraints used and assumptions made by most or all team members. Identify different approaches or assumptions regarding drivers, constraints, and degrees of freedom. Verify the estimates with the team.

10. *Results.* The Delphi team has provided a set of estimates, or two (one for the minimum scope and the other for the maximum scope). Each set of estimates contains a range for duration, a range for effort, and a range for cost.

11. *Additional brainstorming (optional).* While the team is together, you can run a brainstorming session, or an additional Delphi series, to get a risk plan.

ESTIMATION FROM REQUIREMENTS

This method cannot be used until the analysis stage is nearly complete. The primary input is the requirements document, either complete and approved, or nearly so. It is also essential that the architecture be defined. However, it has some advantages over Delphi-based methods. It does not require high-level experts; the project team who will do the work of design and development does it best. For projects where the team has experience in the development tools, it is likely to be more accurate than Delphi-based methods. The result of this process is only an estimated range of effort. However, at this point in the project, the project manager can use this estimated range of effort with other inputs and tools to produce duration and cost estimates. To estimate from requirements, follow the procedure given in Table 10-3.

Table 10-3 Procedure for effort estimation from requirements.

Schedule or trigger event: A need to create an approximate cost estimate quickly before a work breakdown structure is available.
Brief description: This method calculates estimated effort project tasks need to create product or service components of similar type and size.
Inputs: All project documents near or at the end of analysis, especially requirements statements or architecture specification. Actual results that track effort per component of past similar projects, if available. An engineering or programming team experienced with the type(s) of development that will be used on the project.
Outputs: A range of estimated effort that the project manager can use, along with other tools, to produce an estimate and a budget.
Tools: A spreadsheet program.
Verification (QC): Verification within the project can be first against other estimation methods through time gap management. On project completion, estimate based on requirement results should be compared to actual project duration, effort, and cost. Any discrepancies should contribute to future improvement of this method.

Table 10-3   Procedure for effort estimation from requirements (*Continued*).

Process:
Unless otherwise stated, all actions are performed by the project team members who will do the work of design and development, working together or separately. 1. The project manager calls a meeting and introduces the method. The team brainstorms to decide what the basic unit of measure will be for each part of the project. For hardware devices, it will be physical or logical components; for interfaces, it might be application windows or use cases; for a database, it might be tables and queries. The team also agrees on a unit of measure, such as person-hours or person-days. 2. Project team members read the requirements and create a list of unit items for each of the categories above. 3. For each unit item (a window, a use case, an electronic component), the team members rate it as small, medium, or large, and as simple, average, or complex. This defines each unit item into one of nine categories, from small and simple to large and complex. 4. For each unit, the team makes a list of the steps necessary to complete one unit. Be sure to include design, design validation, development, test planning, low-level and high-level module testing, and documentation. 5. The team estimates the effort required to complete one item in each of the nine categories, including low-level and high-level component tests with necessary rework so that the unit item will pass all component QA tests. 6. The team enters the total number of items in each category into a spreadsheet. They also enter the effort for each of the nine categories. The number of items times the effort per item yields nine totals, which are summed to produce an estimate of total effort. 7. If step 1 resulted in two or more types of basic unit (hardware and software, for instance), then steps 2 through 6 are repeated, creating a nine-cell spreadsheet for each type of basic unit. The totals from each spreadsheet are summed.

The result of this process is estimated effort for the creation of all components. The project manager can use records from past projects or industry standards to identify a ratio of this effort to total project work effort and project management effort. He or she can also use other estimation methods for estimating project management effort, and combine the methods. In addition, the method for adding contingencies from Chapter 11 can be used.

Work Breakdown Structuring

The lowest level of detail in project scope specification is obtained through a process called work breakdown structuring (WBS). The goal is to define every deliverable in the project precisely. When we do this well, we also build a list of tasks. A task, also called a step or an action, is a single piece of work done by one person or one small group of people resulting in a deliverable. A deliverable is the result of a task that can be given to another person so that person can use the result without needing to refer back to the person who did the first task.

The method offered here is a step-by-step method that will allow anyone—even someone who is not good at writing a to-do list—to make an excellent WBS and validate it against the project and product plans.

For our example, we will use a simple corporate web site. The components of a web site are familiar to everyone. This allows you to focus on the process of creating a WBS, rather than on the technical content of the work being organized.

THE WBS AS A TEAM EFFORT

Working in pairs makes the best WBS. The person who will do the work pictures the work to be done and answers guiding questions from the project manager or a team leader. This allows the worker to focus on the work to be done and the work results, while having someone else focus on the process of creating the WBS and checking it against other documents. It is genuinely best if we actually visualize ourselves doing the steps. If you think that this is too "new age," the method was first promoted about 100 years ago by Andrew Carnegie, and included in the business bestseller *Think and Grow Rich* by Napoleon Hill in 1926.

People visualize most effectively when they do not have to look at or read anything, and are not interrupted. The time taken to create a good WBS as a team is well worth it: the results will ensure more accurate time and cost estimates, improve the risk and quality plan, and increase team motivation and focus. When team members sit down to do the work later, they will feel empowered because they are doing the work in the best way that they know, the way they determined themselves.

For the example below, we put you in the role of the worker, and have someone guide you through the process. As a project manager, you will need to learn to do the process well first, and then learn to guide others.

WBS PROCESS OVERVIEW

Here are the steps of making a WBS:

1. Make an incomplete list of tasks.
2. Complete the list through visualization and using experts. (Do not worry, we will show you how.)
3. Put the list in groups.
4. Put the groups in order.
5. Organize the list into a WBS.
6. Check the list: key questions.
7. Format the completed list.

Make an incomplete list of tasks

If you have already worked out the milestones for phases in the project overview, that is all you need. If you have not, you can write down just three or four things you know you need to do. They do not have to be in the right order. You do not have to know how you would do them. We are just getting a seed, and we will grow the list from that.

For example, suppose you are building a small web page for your own company. It will be a simple brochure with no shopping cart and no fancy database. Your first list might look like this:

- Learn Microsoft FrontPage® 2002.
- Get graphics.
- Find an internet service provider (ISP) to host the site.
- Get text from marketing and public affairs.

This list is not complete. It is not in any useful order. And it is all we need to get started.

Complete the list

Next, you want to make sure you have got all the steps. There are two things you should do: picture the steps and ask an expert.

Picture the Steps

First, picture doing the first step on the list. Imagine it clearly, fingers on the keyboard, launching FrontPage® 2002.

Have someone ask you: "Could you do this step right now, or is there something else you need to do first?"

Then you realize, "Learn it? I don't even own it. Besides, I always learn software from books. So I'd better buy some books."

From this, you add two tasks to your list:

- Buy FrontPage® 2002.
- Buy books about FrontPage® 2002.

Picturing the steps leads to results that seem obvious, even too simple to believe. But they are obvious only to you, in your situation. Another person, or a person in a different situation, would have a completely different list of obvious steps.

Someone else might say, "Learn it, are you kidding? I haven't had time to learn new software in ten years! And we don't even own it. Maybe we won't need to buy it." For this person, the list becomes:

- Hire a consultant who builds web pages in FrontPage® 2002.
- Ask the consultant if we are going to have to own our own copy.
- If we will, order it and decide which member of the team is going to learn to use it.

As you can see, this is a simple process, but also a creative one. As you do it, you may think, "This is obvious. Of course we have to do this." In a way, you are right. These steps are necessary. Or others like them are. But each project manager or worker would think about it slightly differently. A good project manager knows how his or her company works, and what resources are available. When we picture the process, we are planning a project in a way that will work.

The process is iterative. Now, we picture the new first step, buying FrontPage® 2002. When your co-worker asks, "Could you go do this right now?" you answer with a clear, definitive "yes." Note that if you are guiding this process, and the person is anything less than very definite, probe further, "What else would you want to do first?"

Once the guide hears a definitive "yes" that this is the first (or any subsequent) step, he or she asks "How would you do that?" If the answer is "I would just do it, it's easy," then that step is complete. If the answer includes more separate steps, then the guide creates an indented list underneath the point, and makes a list of sub-items.

Picture every step this way, and watch your list grow. Then, go back and picture all the steps again, until you see yourself doing one and then another, and you cannot think of any more. If you want a fancy term for that, call it *iterative project design.*

Do not be fooled by the simplicity of this process of picturing what you will do. Do not think, "Oh, this is so obvious, I won't bother to write it down." It is obvious to you because you are thinking about it now. If you do not write it down, no one else will think of it later, steps will be missed, and the project will run awry. Remember that every hour you spend in this stage saves ten hours worth of problems down the road. And the more detailed your plan is, the more accurate your time schedule will be.

Ask an Expert

If you are not an expert in a particular area of the project work, find someone who has done this kind of project before. Do the work yourself first, so that you take into account your own understanding of what the customer wants and how your organization works. Rely on the subject-matter expert only for expertise on the subject, and not for expertise on your customer or your company. It is actually very hard to revise a boilerplate WBS or a WBS from a prior project without missing any steps. Also, an expert is more willing to help if you respect his or her time by making your own best effort first, and then asking him or her to fill in the gaps.

Put the list in groups by milestone

Think about the major deliverables for the project and organize the tasks into groups of tasks that lead to each milestone. Continuing with our web page example, here are some of the groups and some of the steps in each group. Note that the list is not complete:

- Text steps
  - Prepare text
- Graphics steps
  - Get graphics from graphic artist
  - Prepare graphics for web
- Page assembly
  - Combine text and graphics
- Approval
  - Present to the president for approval
- Technical details
  - Arrange for web hosting
  - Post on the web

This is still not a good list. But that is the point of this exercise. I hope to show you that you can be poor at making to-do lists, and still make a great one. All you have to do is repeat the process of guiding the person who will do the work in picturing his or her own work, ask the questions above, and write down the answer. Following that process leads to a list like this one. Here is the higher level of the list, the groups of tasks:

- Initial planning
- Text preparation
- Graphics preparation
- Web page design
- Web site preparation
- Approval
- Posting
- Follow up

The detailed list of tasks with two levels from this project was over two pages long, so we will just show two representative sections here:

- Graphics preparation
    - Get graphics from graphic artist
    - Select graphics
    - Convert to JPG/GIF for web
    - Build automated GIF montage for home page
    - Build automated GIFs of corporate logo and motto
- Web page design
    - Lay out navigation
    - Lay out design elements
    - Add forms and searches
    - Integrate text and graphics
    - Review with customer
    - Make adjustments from review meeting

We now have a thorough, detailed list of tasks. We can do a walk-through with the customer, asking if there is anything else they want or need—and are willing to pay for.

Put the groups in order

Now it is time to think about what comes first. Within each group, it may be obvious that certain steps have to come first. Let us look at the steps within graphics preparation.

1. Get graphics from corporate graphic artist
2. Select graphics for web page

3. Convert to JPG/GIF for web
4. Build automated GIF montage for home page
5. Build automated GIFs of corporate logo and motto

You might switch steps 4 and 5, but the other steps will only work in this order, because the deliverable of each step is an input for the next step. When putting each group in order, do not worry about exact order or steps that perhaps can be done at any time. We will work that out later. Create a *loose order*, that is, just make sure that the steps that have to be done first are listed before the ones that depend on them and have to be done later.

Then look at the groups. Some can be done at the same time. But sometimes one whole group cannot start until another one finishes. Here are the groups of tasks in order:

1. Initial planning
2. Text preparation
3. Graphics preparation
4. Web page design
5. Web site preparation
6. Approval
7. Posting
8. Follow up

Here, you could switch tasks 2 and 3. Also, step 5 can be done any time, as long as it comes after step 1 and is ready before step 7. Those orders would be equally good for a WBS. What makes this a good loose order is that there is nothing out of order. Be sure to list reviews, tests, decisions, approvals, and rework related to all of these as steps. It is also important to link the WBS into the stages and gates listed in our project overview.

Organize the list into a WBS for big and complicated projects

Congratulations! You have created a simple WBS. For larger projects, of course, you may break the list down even further. The WBS for our simple web page has two levels. A typical medium-sized project will have three to five levels. You do not have to break every part of the project down to the same level of detail. In fact, you should not. Some parts of the project need just two or three levels. Others might need five or six. The largest high-technology project I have ever heard of, the ten-year reorganization of all the mainframe computers at the IRS, only needed seven levels of detail.

How much detail do you need? There is a precise answer to that question. Technically, you take your WBS down to the level of detail at which you plan to exercise control. What does that mean?

It is very simple. If you can look at a step, and say, "One person or team can do this, and he or she will know what to do, and it can be done in two weeks or less," then you are done. If you look at a step and see that it requires several people who are not on the same team, break it down into smaller steps until one person or one working team does each step. If you find a step is longer than two weeks, break it up into pieces so that they can report what has been done every two weeks (or less).

The level of control is an important concept. The *level of control* is the level at which the project manager, sub-project manager, or worker keeps track of the work being done. Remember that control here means to check task status and correct the course of the project. It does not mean micromanagement. On a large project, each manager and team lead will manage the project according to the list of tasks and deliverables from the WBS down to a certain level. The manager or team lead will manage at a lower level of detail. Finally, the worker is likely to make a list of self-managed steps to accomplish a task. That way, if he or she does not finish on Friday, there is a list reminding him or her of the next step on Monday morning.

Should that self-management list be included in the WBS? Classic project management methods would say no, that is too detailed. I would propose a different approach for projects that are very technical. I think that there are several advantages to including the expert worker's self-managed task list:

- We will get a better time estimate.
- We reduce project risk related to loss of key staff. If an expert prepares the list, but is unavailable when work needs to be done, we have detailed steps to guide a less experienced person in doing the work. The self-management list is knowledge transfer from a given expert into the project management system.
- We increase team motivation. As mentioned earlier, if a worker prepares his or her schedule early, and comes back to it later, it increases focus, motivation, and a sense of being respected as someone making a unique contribution to the project.
- We increase project quality and reduce risk. When the worker takes time to think things through, it is natural to come up with better ways of doing things and ways to prevent problems.

Check the list: key questions

You have written and organized the list. How do you know you did not miss anything? How do we verify that a WBS is complete and correct? Here are the most important questions, from the bottom up.

Key Questions About Each Step: Verifying Each Step is Clear

Each step of a project does something and delivers something. Can you read each step and say what will be done, and what will be delivered? Each step should contain a verb describing what will be done, and a noun describing what will be delivered.

For example, here are several badly written steps (and what is wrong with them):

- Security plan (no verb)
- Plan security (verb and noun both too vague)
- Design security plan (verb and noun do not match)

If you see an item like any of the above, change it to: "Write security plan." Here, the step is clear. Writing is the action. A security plan, a document, is the deliverable. Every step should be written with a verb describing the action of the task followed by a noun defining the deliverable.

A very interesting thing will happen when we make these changes. I have seen many WBSs that were hard to read or even impossible to understand. I have seen more that seemed acceptable, but were somewhat vague, so that, as I read them, my mind started wandering. When I edited them, ensuring a clear noun and verb on each line, everything clicked into place. The whole project becomes crystal clear, and it is easy to visualize the work being done, and to picture each deliverable. That is shared vision.

Key Questions About Each Group of Steps

Go to the lowest level in your WBS. For each group of steps, ask: "If I do these steps, will I go from the starting point to the finishing point of this larger step, and get it all done without missing anything?"

Do a walk-through: Picture going through the steps and see if anything is missing. Is there a step that requires something that you did not get from an earlier step? Remember to ask experts if you need to.

For each group, also ask: "What is the deliverable?"

When you know each lowest-level group is going to work, then do the same at the next level up, using the groups as your steps of the larger groups.

Key Questions About the Whole List

Finally, look at the whole list of steps. Go back to your project overview. Will these steps take you from the project's initial situation to the project's goal? If so, the list is complete. If you missed something that is not ready at the starting point, add it to the beginning. If you missed something needed to complete the goal to the customer's satisfaction, add it at the end. Also, make sure you will have everything you need to start each group of steps.

When you have come this far, you have the WBS for the whole project. And you know that the project will take you all the way to a finished product.

Feeling uncertain is fine. In fact, this list is not perfect. Missing steps will be found: just not too many of them, we hope.

There are two final processes we can use to check the WBS before we take the last step. First, if you wrote it, have someone else read it and ask them if they understand each step. In writing, you always know what you meant. In good writing, everyone else also knows what you mean. Second, everyone on a project should read the WBS and understand what kind of work will be done and what will be delivered on every step. If some team members cannot follow it, then the WBS is too vague, or the language is too technical, or your sub-teams do not understand each other's jobs well enough.

Format the complete list

In a WBS document, the steps are ordered and numbered. There are applications that can help you write a WBS. But it is often good enough to use MS Word or WordPerfect with a hierarchical numbering scheme, often called a legal format, where items are numbered 1, 1.1, 1.2, 1.2.1, 1.2.2, and so forth. MS Word calls this an outline numbered format.

Now that the WBS is complete, we are ready to move from scope definition to detailed time estimation and the other areas of project planning. The most important input to all remaining planning work is the WBS. The time and effort taken to make a good WBS will pay for itself over and over through the 1:10:100 rule, as it increases the accuracy of our estimates, works as a tool for tracking and control, and makes it easier to prepare risk and quality plans.

If you use project tracking software, such as Microsoft Project, then putting the WBS into the tracking tool is your next step.

Detailed Time and Cost Estimation

In this section we first look at the technique for building a project schedule. Then we derive a budget from the schedule.

BUILDING A PROJECT SCHEDULE

We build a detailed schedule for the project based on the WBS. The methods for building a schedule from a WBS are called the critical path method (CPM) and the project evaluation and review technique (PERT). Full instructions on CPM and PERT are widely available. In addition, project management software packages, including Microsoft Project, allow you to enter data and get CPM calculations, PERT charts, Gantt charts, calendars, and a variety of other displays of the project schedule.

KEY POINT

A Gap in Time Management Practices
Most experienced project managers have learned PERT and CPM. Even so, they rarely use them. PERT and CPM are generally only implemented on projects where a fixed-price contract is written before work starts, and that is done to ensure that the consulting firm makes money on the contract. It should not be that way. Good time management is crucial on all projects because it allows us to deliver the highest possible quality. That is what really matters.

Rather than reproduce what is easily available elsewhere, we will discuss the key issues in the sequence of steps that create a schedule.

WHAT THIS MEANS FOR YOU

A Solid Schedule
Project management software programs are dangerous. You can create a full-color schedule that looks beautiful and convinces everyone, but will not work at all. Or you can create a schedule that works, but, as soon as one thing changes, you have to re-do the whole thing. However, if you follow the steps listed here, and address the issues we raise, you can create realistic schedules that can be adjusted as the project moves forward. At that point, the schedule in your project management software program becomes a real tool that helps the project.

Here are the issues we address in building a schedule, in order.

- *Assigning tasks to workers.* As soon as possible, we should name the worker or team responsible for each task. Our best estimates come from the person who is going to do the work. If we are estimating without knowing the worker, we will have to make guesses about the skill and speed of that worker.
- *Estimating effort for each task.* We start at the lowest level of the WBS, the task. For each task, we ask: "How long will it take one person to do this job?" That is the *per-task effort*. We should ask the person who is doing the work to make his or her own estimates.
- *Using history for estimates.* If we have accurate actual results from past projects, we can refer to them in making current estimates. But we must work at a low level of detail, ask intelligent questions, and adjust for changes in the task definition and the abilities of the worker or team.
- *Estimating accurately using PERT weighted averages.* It is not enough just to ask: How long will it take? We should actually ask four questions: How long will it usually take? What is the least amount of time it might take? If things do not go well, how long will it take? Then we show those answers to the worker, and ask them, given these, for their input. We record all these numbers. Then we create a weighted average: (minimum plus maximum plus (likely times four)) ÷ 6. That is the PERT estimate. Then we make an intelligent guess between the PERT estimate and the instinctive feeling, and use that figure as our per-task effort. We calculate this for each task.
- *Calculating task duration.* If more than one person is working on a task, then we divide effort by number of people to get duration. If one person can dig a hole in an hour, then two people can dig the same hole in half an hour. But could sixty people dig the hole in one minute? Probably not. We have to figure out if the job can really be divided, and what the ideal team size is. We also need to allow time for the team to communicate and coordinate work. With that done, we can calculate or estimate *per-task duration*, the length of time between the beginning of a task and when the results will be done and delivered with quality.
- *Entering dependencies or links.* Often, the output or deliverable of one task is the input for another task. If so, the second task can only start after the first task finishes. We say that these two tasks are linked by a finish-to-start dependency. Most links on a project schedule are finish-to-start. We can also use other links, such as start-to-start, finish-to-finish, and, rarely, start-to-finish.

- *Considering lag or lead time.* If I am baking cookies, I have a task called "start oven," and another one called "put cookies in hot oven." There is a finish-to-start dependency between them, but it is not immediate. I need to allow the oven to warm up after I turn it on and before the cookies go in. That is the lag time between the end of one task, and the beginning of another; the time we just have to wait while ovens warm up and paint dries. What is lead time? The opposite. Suppose we are baking together, but you are mixing the ingredients at your house, and you live 20 minutes away. We are on a tight schedule, so we want the oven to be just ready when you walk in the door. When you call to say you are leaving your house, I have 20 minutes to get the oven ready. That is 20 minutes of lead time on that task. If the oven takes 12 minutes to warm up, I can calculate that I need to turn on the oven 8 minutes after you call.
- *Putting together a theoretical schedule.* At this point, we have all the ingredients of a theoretical schedule. We link all of the tasks, and we can see when we can do each task, and how long the project will take.

The theoretical schedule is not a real-world calendar yet, but it is close. We can use it to calculate the total project effort, and get a sense of the total length of time the project will take. By adding more information, such as individual work calendars, we can finish building our real-world schedule. One calculation we can perform both on the theoretical calendar and the real-world calendar is the CPM. This looks at all of the linked tasks, and finds the chain of tasks that must be done in order, start to finish, that will take the longest. Tasks on this chain are on the *critical path*, and a delay in any one task pushes the next task, which pushes the delivery date back later. Tasks on the critical path have no float; that is, they must start and end on time. Other tasks have *float*; that is, we can start them early (as soon as deliverables are available) and so finish early, or we can wait and start them later, and still finish them in time to start other tasks that depend on them.

TERM

Effort   The number of person-hours it takes to do a task, or the total number of person-hours it takes to do a set of tasks or an entire project.

Duration   The time a task or a project will take from beginning to end, considering that more than one person might be working on a task, and that people will not be working all the time. The basic calculation is duration = effort divided by the number of workers, but this needs to be adjusted to practical circumstances.

PERT weighted average   A calculation of the most likely time a task will take. We consider minimum, likely, and maximum times, but give four times more weight to the likely time than to the minimum or maximum. The formula is PERT average = (minimum + maximum + (4 × likely))/6. We divide by six because we have a total of six data points (one minimum, four likelies, and one maximum) in our average.

Dependency   A relationship between two tasks, where one task's start or finish time is linked to another. The most common is a finish-to-start dependency, where, in finishing task A, we complete a deliverable that is a necessary input for task B. *Link* is a synonym for dependency.

Theoretical schedule   A schedule that shows project tasks, links, and duration, but does not yet include real-world calendars.

Work calendars   Calendars that bring in real-world information such as work schedules, holidays, and vacations.

Project schedule   A real-world schedule of project work, with start date, delivery date, and scheduled time and effort for each task. This is the schedule if all goes well. It does not take specific risks into account. It is also called the *baseline schedule*.

Let us take a look at the steps for turning a theoretical calendar into a real-world calendar.

- *Calculating total project effort.* If we add up all the time spent on doing tasks, we will have the total task effort on the project. But that is, literally, only half the story. We also need to allow time for work management, that is, meetings, thinking things through, getting started, working out small problems, and so forth. We can try to add those into the schedule. Or, we can apply a rule of thumb. Several good studies showed that, on a typical project, management time is just about equal to work effort. So we can apply this rule of thumb: Determine how much time the work will take, then double it. This is the original, and accurate, application of that rule of thumb.

- *Allowing for unknowns.* The best way to allow for unknowns is to do thorough risk management, as described in Chapter 11. If we have not done that yet, we can use our general sense of how new and different the project work is for us and for our team. If this project is similar to ones we have done many times before, then our estimate is probably good as is. But if we are trying something new, or using new tools, we need to allow for a learning curve, and also for making mistakes and fixing them.

- *Adding work calendars.* A work calendar is a schedule of when a given person or team is working. It includes the exact days of the week and hours of the day a person will work. It also makes allowances for breaks, meals, holidays, and vacations. In a project management software program, we can apply the theoretical schedule to the work calendars for our team.

We now have an accurate, real-world calendar. We know who will do what on each day of the project. We know when we will start, and when we will finish. Well, keep your fingers crossed. We have been realistic, and we have taken into account our team's ability to do work and our management time, but there is one big factor we have not taken a look at yet: What if things go wrong? We will take a look at that in Chapter 11.

COST ESTIMATION

The project estimate and budget are built from the schedule we created above and the purchasing or procurement plan we will create later in this chapter. We can then adjust it by adding contingencies that we will add from our work in Chapter 11. The estimate is a single figure or range representing what we think the total cost will be. The budget shows how we will need to spend that money over time, including when we will need to buy each item, when we will need to pay for work done, and how much each stage of the project will cost.

The total cost of a project is what we will spend on labor, plus what we will spend on purchasing. Labor cost should be calculated separately for internal staff and for external consulting services. Purchasing cost should consider both that which we buy for the process of the project, and that which we buy to include in the product or service we are delivering to the customer. The final element is the addition of a range of possible costs. We bring this in through the use of contingencies from the risk planning process. Table 10-4 gives a procedure for creating a detailed cost estimate and budget.

COST PER TIME UNIT FOR TEAM MEMBERS

The cost per time unit items in steps 3 and 4 of the detailed cost estimate and budget preparation procedure in Table 10-4 might warrant further explanation. We need to choose a cost per hour that meets two requirements. First, it must be the same one used by accounting, so that our budget matches corporate accounting procedures. Second, in most firms, we need to maintain salary privacy for individuals. It is easy to turn an hourly cost rate into an annual salary, and many people will see the budget. In most cases, human resources or accounting will have a solution for this. Solutions include using an average salary for a department or a job title, or using a formula, such as

Table 10-4   Detailed cost estimate and budget preparation procedure.

Trigger event:
In the design stage, when the project schedule, procurement plan, and risk plan are prepared. There should be agreement that these items are close to final, or they should have received final approval.
Brief description: Combining all sources of expense, we create an estimate of total project expense and a budget, that is, a schedule for spending money.
Inputs: • The detailed project schedule, complete and approved or expected to have little change. • The procurement plan, complete and approved or expected to have little change. • The risk plan, complete and approved or expected to have little change. • Cost per time unit figures for internal staff resources. • Cost per time unit or fixed-price contract figures for external staff resources and consulting services. • Cost per unit for items to be procured. • The project overview, and any other documents that specify constraints.
Outputs: • A detailed cost estimate presented as a range from the expected minimum to the expected maximum cost of the project. • A budget showing how that money will be spent over time. • A list of budgetary assumptions.
Tools: This is most easily done with a project tracking tool, but it can be done in a spreadsheet.
Verification (QC): A second person should review the estimate, the budget, and assumptions, checking for errors and risks. This estimate and budget should be compared to earlier estimates and issues should be resolved through gap reconciliation. At the end of the project, the estimate and budget should be compared to actual results, and the discrepancies used towards improving estimation methods.

Table 10-4   Detailed cost estimate and budget preparation procedure (*Continued*).

Process:

1. Review the schedule, procurement plan, and risk plan for clarity and understanding.
2. Insert the procurement plan into the project schedule, assigning purchasing dates for all items and creating procurement tasks for all procurement, if this has not already been done.
3. Validate the cost per time unit for internal resources with accounting or human resources, or with formal corporate policies. Do this for all internal staff assigned to the project.
4. Validate the cost per time unit or fixed-contract cost commitments for external staff resources and consulting services with the vendor or vendors.
5. Validate the cost per unit item to be procured with the vendor or vendors.
6. Validate all inputs against project constraints and assumptions and other relevant parts of the project overview. If necessary, change the plans and get them re-approved before proceeding.
7. Assign cost per time unit to all staffing resources, internal and external.
8. Make any adjustment for future salary increases or rate changes.
9. Enter cost per unit figures for each procurement task in the schedule. If only one item is being purchased, then the cost per unit equals the total cost for that item. If multiple items are being purchased, then the item line cost is the per-item cost times the number of items. Consider date of purchase and possible price changes when entering cost figures, and adjust if appropriate.
10. If the project tracking tool or spreadsheet does not automatically update its figures, then trigger a recalculation. Save the file.
11. Evaluate the results, viewing each item in detail, and viewing summaries and reports. Make any adjustments.
12. Create the budgetary assumptions document.
13. Review the risk plan, and add appropriate contingencies. Most likely, these will not appear in the project tracking tool. The project tracking tool holds the schedule and budget based on work that is definitely planned. The contingencies cover work that may need to be done to respond to risks and changing conditions, not the core plan.
14. Have someone review your work. Make any appropriate changes, recalculate, review, save the file, and print.
15. Initiate overall change management linking any change to the schedule, procurement plan, or risk plan to the project budget and detailed estimate.
16. Your final estimated minimum cost is the cost of the core plan in the project tracking tool. Your final estimated maximum cost is the minimum cost plus contingencies from the risk plan.

total cost of ownership (TCO), which includes the costs of acquiring, training, and retaining staff, plus the rental space for an office cubicle. This number is a useful accounting figure that has no simple correlation to salary. So, use the solution already in place in your company.

PROCUREMENT COSTS

We build the procurement plan from the WBS. Each task on the WBS has inputs and tools. Inputs become part of the final output, the product or service delivered to the customer. Tools are used for the project, but not delivered to the customer. We examine each task on the WBS, and identify if these items might need to be included in the project procurement plan and budget:

- Items that are part of the final product or service delivered to the customer.
- Items that are not part of the product or service, but are needed for the project to be done. Test machines and programming tools are examples.
- Input from consultants. They may think you are buying equipment that you think is included in their price.
- Input from vendors. They may be aware of components you must get or pricing you should know about.

If an item is going to be purchased early in the project, use a current cost from a current vendor for the estimate. If it will be purchased later, check back and see if the cost for this item has been going up or down. (Yes, one advantage of working in the computer field is that some costs do go down. Think about memory chips, down from $60 per megabyte to below $1.) Of course, prices do fluctuate, and you may be caught by surprise. But, if your budget is based on small enough tasks and items, then the total estimate will probably be very close to the actual cost.

There is one other cost category, but it is not usually included in the project budget. In addition to inputs and tools, we have resources that are used up, such as copier paper and printer toner. These expense items are usually budgeted to departmental overheads, rather than to individual projects. For example a project might have a travel budget well above the accepted corporate norm, and therefore we would need to allocate project money for travel.

Managing Risk and Change

Things do not always go according to plan. As project managers, we have two ways of handling this: risk management and change management. In risk management, we define what might create problems for the project—making it late, going over the budget, or reducing its value—and plan ways of preventing or handling those events. Change management is a process that defines all possible changes to the plan, structures a method for deciding if the change is good for the project, and ensures effective communication and action to ensure that the project, with all approved changes, is completed properly.

Risk Management

The steps of risk management are:

- *Risk identification and assessment*, where we find risks and decide how important they are.

- *Risk planning*, where we decide how we will manage each risk on the project.
- *Risk control*, the process of tracking risks and taking care of them throughout the project.

KEY POINT

What Did You Plan To Do About It?

A colleague of mine is a professional project manager for a small consulting firm that installs computer systems. Whenever something goes wrong, he asks his team, "Did you expect that to happen?"

Most of the time, they say yes. Then he asks, "Well, what did you plan to do about it?"

They answer, "Nothing. We just expected it to happen."

They were good at risk assessment—thinking about what might go wrong. But they ignored risk planning. We will plan for things going wrong, and do what we need to do to keep things from going wrong.

RISK IDENTIFICATION AND ASSESSMENT

The first step in risk planning is risk assessment, which is a matter of turning uncertainty into risk. Uncertainty is undefined, but risk is defined. We turn uncertainty into risk by naming each risk item, and assigning a likelihood and a consequence to each item. For example, if I say, "Let's have a picnic on Saturday," and you say, "Something could ruin the day," that is uncertainty.

I begin risk identification by saying, "What could go wrong?" If you say, "It might rain" we have identified a risk. However, to assess it, we have to go further. If we consult a weather forecast and find out there will be a 60% chance of rain on Saturday, and we agree that if it rains there will be no picnic, then we have defined and assessed rain as a risk for our picnic.

There is an important difference between probability and likelihood. Probability is measured in percent, with 0% meaning it cannot happen, and 100% meaning it is certain to happen. However, we can only truly create a probability if we have a scientific theory and a large body of data for comparison, the way weather forecasters do. In project risk management, we usually do not have that kind of theory or that much data. So, we replace risk with likelihood. In doing so, we work with *qualitative risk analysis*, using identification and ranking, rather than *quantitative risk analysis*, which applies statistical tools.

Risk identification: From uncertainty to a list of risks

The first step is to produce a list of risks. We sit down with our team, put the plan in front of ourselves, and say, "This is a great plan. What could go wrong?" And we make a list of items. We can also use our team's experience of problems on past projects and written documents, such as lessons learned from past projects.

SOMETHING EXTRA

Proactive Pessimism

We want to look at what might go wrong, but we do not want to fall into doom and gloom. I suggest we take an attitude of proactive pessimism: What could go wrong, and what are we going to do about it? We can make this a fun brainstorming session with our team, and then expand the risk planning process to include key stakeholders and others.

The simplest approach is to look at each plan, particularly the project overview and the work breakdown structure (WBS), in detail, and ask about each item: What could go wrong?

Here are some guidelines for a team meeting to identify risks:

- *Work with all plans and project documents.* Each document tells you about a different part of the project. Review each one, and ask what could keep this plan from going smoothly.
- *Work at a detailed level.* For example, when looking at the WBS, ask what could keep each task from being delivered on time with quality.
- *Pay more attention to what is outside your control.* If we are relying on anything from outside the team, whether it is from a customer, from a vendor, from a consultant, or from some other source, we have less information about whether it will come on time and be of good quality. Items coming from outside the team are called *external dependencies*, because we are depending on something outside our core team. In some risk management models, every external dependency is automatically a risk. Certainly, we should look at each one and decide what communications, contingency plans, or other actions might be appropriate.
- *The newer or more innovative a task is, the greater the risk.* Is the team using any tools they have not used before? Or even new versions of

tools? Experience and expertise reduce risk. And the converse is true: the more we are entering unfamiliar territory, or working with less experienced personnel, the greater the risk.

- *Conflict is a sign of risk.* Review your experience of every stakeholder. Are there signs that anyone might not be available, or might not cooperate? If so, add that to your risk list and plan what to do about it.
- *Every gap is a risk.* Every gap you need to close might not close. That makes it a risk.
- *Get everyone involved.* You can include customers, stakeholders, and outside experts in your composition of a good risk list.

Risk assessment: Likelihood and consequence

Moving into the details, we define each risk on two independent scales: likelihood and consequence. *Likelihood* is a measure of the chance that an event will happen. The simplest scale is a three-point scale, very likely, might happen, and unlikely. The *consequence* of a risk action is unrelated to likelihood. To define the consequence, we consider that if this risk event does take place then what happens to the project. At the high end, we have a project-killer, such as rain on our picnic. In the middle, we have significant increases to time and cost, or reductions of scope or quality. At the low end, we have events that will have only a minor effect on the project.

Table 11-1 is a sample risk assessment using a five-point scale for likelihood, and a 0.0 to 1.0 scale for consequence.

For a consequence rating, QTI uses a scale from 1.0 down to 0.0, with 1.0 being a project-killer. For example in the second row of Table 11-1, if the whole company runs into a budget "crunch," and the project is canceled, that gives a consequence rating of 1.0.

Consequences between 0.0 and 1.0 are measured by cost, time or quality, whichever is most relevant to the project.

For items that will add to the cost of the project, the number used is the ratio of the additional cost to the total plan cost of the project. For example, in the fourth row of Table 11-1, if capacity is misestimated, then an additional server will need to be purchased and installed at a cost of $20,000. The project was expected to cost $100,000. So, the increase in project cost is a factor of 0.2 (20,000/100,000 = 0.2).

For items that have a major impact on schedule, we use the added time to determine the consequence factor. For example, in the third row of Table 11-1,

Table 11-1   A sample risk assessment.

Risk item	Likelihood	Consequence	Risk factor
Project canceled, lack of funds	1	1.0	1.0
Loss of key staff	3	0.3	0.9
Capacity estimation error	4	0.2	0.8
Failure of shopping cart	1	0.3	0.3
Equipment failure	2	0.1	0.2
QTI uses this likelihood scale:			
	5	likely to happen	
	4	might well happen	
	3	could happen	
	2	unlikely to happen	
	1	probably will not happen	

loss of key staff will delay the project by three weeks. The project was originally planned to take ten weeks. This is an increase of duration of 0.3.

For items that have a major impact on quality, we use the loss of quality as the consequence measure. For example, in the fifth row of Table 11-1, if the shopping cart program does not work, then direct sales will not be a feature of the new web page. Say that this is one of three major features. A loss of one out of three features is a one-third, or 0.3 consequence in reduced project quality.

Creating a *risk factor* by multiplying likelihood times consequence is optional. If you trust your numbers, go ahead and do it. Then sort the list with the highest risk factor at the top, as you see in the example. If you do not multiply likelihood by consequence, then make two copies of the list. Sort it highest to lowest by likelihood once, and highest to lowest by consequence the second time. Preparation of this list with appropriate descriptions of each risk completes risk assessment, delivering a prioritized risk list for the project.

RISK PLANNING

Now we need to decide what we are going to do about each risk, and add our decision to the risk plan. These choices are not exclusive; that is, we can choose to take several of these actions in relation to any one risk. And we must choose at least one for each risk. Here are the choices:

- *Risk avoidance.* We change the project plan to avoid the risk altogether. For example, we move the picnic to southern California because, after all, it never rains in southern California.
- *Risk reduction.* We reduce the likelihood that a risk event will happen by taking action before it does. For example, if we see that a vendor might deliver a key component late, we offer a bonus as an incentive for on-time delivery.
- *Risk mitigation.* We take action to reduce the consequence of a risk event in case it does happen. For example, if we see that a key staff person might be pulled away to another, higher-profile project, we have that staff member write a detailed plan with instructions. That way, if the staff member has to go, we can continue the work, though perhaps at a slower pace.
- *Risk transference.* This is more of an administrative solution than a real help to the project. Buying insurance is one kind of risk transference. Or we might include a clause in an equipment purchase that, if the project does not go through, we can return the equipment, so that the cost is not the project's responsibility. But, for the most part, if we own the project and our focus is on making it succeed, we do not try to transfer risk to others.
- *Risk acceptance.* To accept a risk means to realize that it might happen, and to choose not to take any action about it before it does. This is especially appropriate for items with a low likelihood. Not taking action, however, is different from doing nothing. When we accept a risk, we keep it in the risk plan, and track the project, so we are ready to handle the risk even if it happens.

When we have created a risk assessment and defined the actions we will take in relation to each risk, we have our initial risk plan. If we take actions to avoid risk, reduce the likelihood of a risk event, or mitigate the consequences of a risk event, we should update the likelihood, consequence, and risk factor for that item. This document is reviewed and approved at the end of the design stage.

Low-cost Risk Mitigation
Good communication, building teamwork and commitment, is low-cost risk mitigation. Suppose we know a vendor might deliver a product late, but we do not have the authority to create a bonus or a penalty as an incentive. We can simply talk to the vendor, explain the time-critical nature of the project, and ask the representative to do his or her best. We can ask probing questions to see if the vendor has the authority to make sure the order gets priority. Explaining our situation and building cooperation is an excellent way to reduce project risk.

Contingency planning

Contingency planning is one type of risk mitigation. A contingency plan is a statement: "If this risk event happens, here is what we will do." The contingency plan can be short and simple, or it can be very detailed. An example of a detailed plan would be a full WBS for handling the risk event, with a budget. If the risk event occurs, we insert the WBS into the main plan.

Contingency plans are useful for individual risk events. We can create one for each risk in our plan, and we should create one for any risk that is likely and that will be difficult to manage if it happens.

Note that a contingency plan for a single risk is very different from our *contingencies* for risk, which are allocations of time and money related to risk for the whole project.

Adding contingencies to our schedule and budget

We face a basic problem when we try to incorporate the risk plan into the project plan. We are planning for what might not happen. Any given risk event might not happen. But, life being what it is, some of the risk events are almost certain to occur. We just do not know which ones.

The solution is a contingency. A *contingency* is an amount of time or money set aside to be used if and when risk events occur. For example, we might say to the customer: "If our project goes exactly as planned, it will cost $100,000 and take ten weeks. But we've made a list of what might cause trouble, and we'd like to ask for an additional $20,000 and one extra week to use if we need them. We will only spend the extra money and take the extra time if something goes wrong, if one of the risk events occurs." In this

example, we have asked for a 20% contingency fund for money, but only a 10% contingency for our time schedule.

Some companies track two separate contingency funds for each project. One is for risk and the other is for change requests that come from the customer. If a risk event occurs, and it will increase cost or delay our schedule as we work to deliver on the original plan, we draw from the contingency for risk.

On the other hand, if the customer makes change requests, not to fix errors, but to add new features, we draw from the contingency for change requests. Basically, we are saying, "If you want this, we'll do it. But you'll have to pay for it, and you'll have to give us time to do it right."

Scope creep is a big risk for a project. If we allow too much change, the whole project can go over budget or simply fall apart under its own weight. We can avoid this by adding a contingency fund and time budget for customer change requests. To do this, we explain change control from the start. Then we tell the customers that, if they request a change later on, the money will be drawn from their contingency fund, and they may need to allow for later delivery.

If this is done well, it helps customers take responsibility for the changes they request. It gives incentive for them to make an accurate assessment of the value of the change, and decide if they want to incur the costs of adding work to the project so that they can get the extra feature added to the product or service.

However, we need to be careful. It would not be fair to use the contingency for customer change requests for fixing a problem the customer finds in our work, or for solving a problem outside their control. For that, we use the contingency for risk events.

How big should our contingencies be? There is no easy answer to this question. Major corporations that use quantitative risk analysis can adapt statistical formulas to determine the size of contingencies. However, most of the time, we have to evaluate the project, the risk plan, and the customer.

- Evaluating the project means asking how routine vs. how unique the work and the tools are for the team.
- We evaluate the risk plan by reading it through and thinking about what contingencies we will need to cover the amount of risk that is likely to occur overall, plus a bit more for bad luck.
- We evaluate the customer, based on past experience if we have any, on how quickly and clearly they respond to information we give them, on the degree to which they understand the 1:10:100 rule and the importance of stages, gates, and project management, on the

priority they give to this project, and on their willingness to let us manage the project well. Based on this assessment, we can determine the size of our contingency for change requests and the contingency for risk.

RISK CONTROL

There was an episode of a television hospital drama in which the hospital emergency room was contaminated with toxic chemicals and needed to be evacuated. In the rush, no one could find the evacuation plan. We cannot let the same happen to us. After the risk plan is approved at the end of the design stage, we cannot throw it into the drawer and hope everything goes well. We continue the work of risk management by incorporating the risk plan into the project plan as a whole, by tracking risk in our weekly status meetings, and by managing both risk events and the project when a risk event occurs.

Tracking risk

We can track risk at the weekly status meeting. After we check the time and cost status of each item, we ask about risk events. If a work task is completed, and it had a risk event associated with it, we can cross that risk off our list. We are out of danger. We note whether the event did not happen, or we managed it well. If we managed the event, we calculate the actual cost, effort, and effect on project duration, and update the schedule and budget accordingly.

We ask the team to review the risk plan items that are related to work happening now or coming up in the next two to three weeks. Have any of the events become more or less likely? Do we need to initiate some risk reduction work or some extra contingency planning? Train your team to alert you at the first sign of possible danger by letting them know you want to know, but you will not interfere if they say they can handle it.

Lastly, if a risk event does occur, it is time to swing into emergency action.

Emergency action: Managing the risk event and the project

Risk events will happen. If we have planned and tracked well, we will be ready when they do. Still, running a project while taking care of a risk event is a challenge. I call it *emergency action*, and it can be exciting. The challenge is

to manage the risk, and also to keep the project moving ahead at the same time.

How we do that depends on the nature of the risk, and also on how prepared we are. If we prepared a contingency plan for this event, then we integrate that into the main project plan and move ahead. If we did not have a contingency plan, we will have to plan as we go. That may mean some difficult work.

There is a tendency to just jump into action. A few times, I have managed a risk event, and then only later remembered that I had a contingency plan. It is better to review our risk plan and communications plan, and then decide what action to take.

If handling the risk event is going to take more than two or three days, we should delegate some management responsibility. Here are some ways of doing this.

- If the risk event is technical, we turn management of it over to the technical person. We continue to manage the project and integrate the changes related to the risk into the overall schedule and plan.
- If the risk event is major, or it involves personnel issues, we should probably handle it ourselves. If so, we can deputize a member of our team to handle some of the more routine tasks of managing the whole project.
- If we have a well-organized team with team leaders under us, we can ask each team leader to do slightly more of the project management work so that we can spend more time managing the risk event.

When we have successfully navigated a major risk event, we will need to jump back onto the helm of the project and evaluate status and make changes to the plan as needed.

Change Management

As was discussed in prior chapters, due to the 1:10:100 rule, change adds a lot of expense—and a lot of risk—to a project. Two of the biggest risks are changes of which we lose track, and scope creep—the expansion of a project through too many changes. We avoid these by using a written system of change management, and by educating our customers about the costs of change.

THE CHANGE REQUEST FORM

The change request form shown in Table 11-2 defines the requested change, links it to other project documents, shows the status of the change in the process of change control, and shows the ultimate disposition of the change.

THE STEPS OF CHANGE CONTROL

Table 11-3 provides the steps of change control. After writing this, I thought, "No wonder its good to get it right the first time." Some changes are small, and many of the 19 steps can be skipped, but only if we know that they can be skipped. If any step is skipped when it really needs to be done, then the project is at greater risk, and time, cost, and quality may all be affected. This is why the cost of including a requirement or specification after approval is ten times higher than it is if the requirement or specification is defined during the appropriate stage. In reality, our choice is either to do all the work of change control or have the problem cost even more because it is poorly managed.

CRITERIA FOR DECIDING WHETHER TO ACCEPT A CHANGE

Because changes to the plan create so many risks of increased cost, delayed delivery, and poor quality, it is best to be as strict as we can regarding accepting a change. The strictest possible rule is to ask: "Will the project meet its goal and purpose without this change?" If the answer is yes, we can do without the change, then we leave the change out.

A gentler approach is to say: "Will the value of the project be much greater if we include the change, great enough to justify not only the cost and extra work, but also the risk that this change will create other problems?" To do this, we need to evaluate the consequences of the change to the project in terms of time, cost, reduced quality, and increased risk. Once we are already entering the testing process near the end of the production stage, then the risk of missing a problem created by the change is very high, and we should plan on refusing all but the most essential changes.

The ideal solution is to use the double waterfall introduced in Chapter 6 so that we can preserve the reliability of the original project plan and also give the customer all desired changes at a later date.

Table 11-2 Change request form with field definitions.

Section A: Initial change request	
Project name	Name of project (add sub-projects affected, if appropriate)
Request submitted by	Name of person making request
Request submitted by	Department, user group, or team, and contact information
Purpose of change	Simple statement of why the change is either necessary or valuable
Brief description of change	What change will be made
List of documents and components for which change is requested	What existing documents, such as specifications, or components, such as prototype screens, or reports given to the user for review need to be changed? Include all items. Be as specific as possible The project team will verify, and possibly add to, this section

Value of change: Does requester think it is essential? If not, what value is assigned?	Pick one:
	    Essential (core): product or service will fail in production, or project will not be delivered at all, if change is not made
	    Not essential: define the value of the change, so it can be compared to cost and risk factors. This could be measured on a simple high/medium/low scale, or it could be a dollar value calculated as change in ROI
	    If the value of the change is not yet agreed upon, state the disagreement and identify the issues

Cause or source of the change	What happened that makes this change desirable? Select from the list of sources of change below. Customer/team/event outside the project Missed item/unclear item/new idea/responding to change in work purpose or objectives/responding to change in system or work environment (box on context diagram)/responding to change of available components
Full, detailed description of change	Identify each item in each source document or component that needs to be changed. For each item, use one row. There may be multiple items per document. For each one, define the desired result of the change. This section may have some items added at the time of the initial request. It will be completed by the project team if the change request is approved. It functions as a design statement for the change
Item to be changed	Required change

Table 11-2   Change request form with field definitions (*Continued*).

Section B: Status and issues	
Project manager	Name of project manager responsible for change control process
Others required for decision	Names of all stakeholders and team members who need to approve the change
Others who have input in decision	Names of anyone who should review the decision or provide technical work in its evaluation

Status	Select one:
	  Pending: decision process not yet started
	  Under review: owned by project manager, review happening soon, note expected completion date
	  Constrained: awaiting information or task completion. Highlight the active task constraining the decision process below
	  Decided: decision made, follow-up action in progress
	  Complete: change and its consequences fully integrated into project and product plans and deliverables

Time impact assessment	Effect on delivery date (duration) for any milestones. Effect on effort
Cost impact assessment	Effect on project cost. If this change is in excess of available funds, possible sources of funds
Risk assessment	High level: does introducing this change put the project as a whole at higher risk, for either management or technical reasons? Low level: what new risk events should be added to the risk plan if this change is adopted? If it is not?
Quality impact assessment	Effect on quality and test plans. If modules that have already been tested will need to be modified, note this and estimate additional effort and risk
Other assessments	Review all other areas of project management, and note any additional items. For example, if success for this change requires any particular people, or consulting services or purchases, note them here
Action items required for decision	
Owner	**Task, deliverable, due date**
Person who will perform the task	A task necessary to make the change decision. What will be delivered, when, and to whom?

Table 11-2   Change request form with field definitions (*Continued*).

	This includes technical research within the project, and also external items such as stakeholder evaluation of the change or sponsor's determination if funds are available
	When a task is complete, add DONE
Section C: Disposition and follow-up	
Decision	Choose one: accepted, accepted with modifications; rejected

Reason	Reason for decision. Choose one or more:
	    For acceptance: essential item or value exceeded cost; risk acceptable
	    For acceptance with modifications: note reason for modification after reason for acceptance
	    For rejection: change not needed, desired result already obtained by project; risk too high (specify undesirable consequences); cost exceeded value; delay to project unacceptable; change not possible due to staffing or technical reasons; change would create quality problems (due to incompatibility); change required modification of modules past testing

Documents or components changed to implement change	All specific items in all documents or components that need to be changed to implement the change itself
Documents or components reviewed and modified (if needed) to integrate change into project	List of all documents or components reviewed. (Should include entire project plan, and any relevant product documents or components.)
Quality control steps to ensure change is properly managed	Application of quality control for change control
Person who requested change	Sign and date
Project manager	Sign and date
Other approvals	Sign and date

Table 11-3   Change control process.

Activity triggered by: Verbal or written request for change
Brief description: Carries the change request form through the process of change control to resolution and integration of results into the project
Inputs: Informal change request (verbal or written) plus blank change control form, or formal change request (prepared on form) from any source of change from any stakeholder on the project
Outputs: Decision regarding change. Description of change (including any modifications). Description of actions to be taken to accomplish and verify change, and integrate change into project. Description of quality control steps taken to ensure change is appropriately completed and integrated
Tools: Change request form
Verification (QC): Status review of all change requests weekly by project manager. End-of-stage review of all change requests. Review of change request integration into test plan before testing begins
Process: Actions to be performed by project manager unless otherwise specified. The form refers to the change request form unless otherwise specified. 1. Review initial change request. 2. Create or complete first version of change request form with customer, including as much of sections A and B as possible. 3. Receive customer agreement that the change request form adequately describes the request. Reach agreement on whether the change is essential to project success, or merely beneficial, and the degree of benefit. 4. Identify technical issues to be addressed in evaluating the change, assign tasks, and list them on the form. 5. Identify stakeholders who need to review or approve the change, contact them, and identify them on the form.

Table 11-3   Change control process (*Continued*).

6. Identify vendor or external issues requiring research, assign tasks, and list them on the form.
7. Receive results of above action items, generated in steps 4–6.
8. Modify and expand the change request to include items received in step 7.
9. Determine if the change is actually unneeded, that is, if the result the customer desires is already in the product or service. If it is, confirm this with customer and close the change request.
10. Determine if the change needs further definition or modification, and if so, iterate steps 4–8, as needed.
11. Evaluate time and cost considerations related to change. Note them on the form.
12. Evaluate risk and quality considerations related to change. Note them on the form.
13. Determine if the project sponsor needs to be included in the decision process for this change. Reasons to include the sponsor are: approval of delay in delivery; approval of additional funds; approval of high risk to project; significant change in overall scope of project; conflict regarding whether the change is essential that calls for escalation; opposition to the change that calls for escalation.
14. Arrange for a decision process (with meeting if necessary) regarding the change. Schedule all decision process events.
15. Complete decision process and update change request form.
16. Inform person who made the initial request, other stakeholders, and the team.
17. Modify all project plans: work plan, schedule, budget, risk plan, quality plan, and test schedule to perform the work of the change, quality assurance to changed requirements, and the work of integrating the change into the project.
18. Have the project team modify all product or service plans and components as needed to implement the change, ensure quality of the changed system, and integrate the change into the product or service plan and the product or service as a whole.
19. Include this change request in quality control for change control.

Managing Your Team

Ultimately, projects succeed if people understand their roles and do good work.

The Only Thing We Can Manage Is People

A friend of mine named Gary was once asked to teach a class on time management. Gary said he could not, because no one could manage time. The customer asked him what he meant. Gary told the customer to look at his watch for 30 seconds, and the customer did. Then Gary asked, "Could you make that 30 seconds go any faster or slower? Could you manage time, making it do something different? No. On the other hand, if you want me to teach a class on how to help them manage what they do with their time, I'd be happy to."

The lesson: We manage people and work, but not anything else.

In this chapter we will look at how to lead a team to success, and how to manage project communications to keep everyone on the same page and focused towards our goal.

The Foundation of Team Success

I have taught thousands of project managers, and I always ask for success stories. Then I ask, "What made that project work?" Most of the time it boils down to this: the right people doing the right job. That makes project human resource management—in a word, teamwork—central to project success. How do we get there?

The good news is we are almost already there. If we have done the work of the concept and analysis stage, we have defined the right job. If we have created a good work breakdown structure (WBS), we have defined that job precisely. Our next step is to apply techniques from Chapter 2 to the job of creating our team and leading to success. Simply by working with the team and putting the focus on a clearly defined, written plan for the job, we are already doing several things right:

- *Triangulation.* We are putting the job in front of us, and putting everyone on the same side.
- *Supporting a no-blame environment.* By defining job roles, responsibilities, and resources, we are creating a balance of responsibility and authority.
- *Starting and teaching plan, do, follow through.* We lay the plan out, and help build a picture of the goal. This initiates a practical focus on getting the right work done.
- *Customer service within the team.* When the team sees how, in the WBS, one person's output is another person's input, they also see that doing their own work well is supporting the team.

Managing a team is a big job—probably the biggest job on any project. But, if we have done good work in all the other areas, we have cut the job down to size.

Getting the Right Team

Sometimes, as project managers, we get to choose who will work on the project team—or we may get to pick some of the people. We will be picking from a limited pool—perhaps just people at our company who are available, or perhaps candidates we can interview. In either case, we will need to look at both the person's technical skills for the job and also at their ability to work well on a goal-oriented project team.

Since we are unlikely to find the perfect blend of skills and personality, we will need to evaluate each person in both areas, and then decide who is best for the job. In some projects and roles, such as those that require specific engineering, programming, or other professional skills, the technical qualifications are most important. In other projects or roles, the teamwork skills are most important, and a willing person can pick up the knowledge to do the job.

TECHNICAL SKILLS

Technical skills can be derived from the WBS. If we—or experts in the appropriate fields—look at the WBS, we will be able to say what professional skills, and what level of skill, are required for each job. If you are managing a technical project in an area outside your expertise, be careful. It can be more complicated than you might think. For example, setting up a web page can require any of these skills: computer graphics design; ability to use a web tool such as Microsoft FrontPage® or Macromedia DreamWeaver®; ability to write HTML code; ability to write scripts in a programming language such as JavaScript® or PHP; and the ability to put all of this together, send it to a web site, and make it work. One person is unlikely to have all of these skills. Exactly which ones does your project need?

To find out, get expert help defining the tasks in the WBS. Then write a job description, and look for people with many of the skills you need. When you do, you will also need to be concerned with the level of skill. Is the person trained in school? Certified? How many months or years of experience does the applicant have using skills relevant to this job? Can you take a look at samples of work done? In looking at a person's skill level, we will need to assess: appropriateness of skill to the project; ability to deliver quality work; and speed or productivity in a limited time. Which of these is most important for your current project?

PROJECT AND TEAM SKILLS

A project is a team effort on a tight deadline. This defines the key skills required for people on projects and teams. Key skills for people on projects include:

- Ability to get work done and delivered on time.
- A start-driven focus. We want people who will start a job as soon as they can, not ones who will wait until a deadline is pressing.
- Self-responsibility.

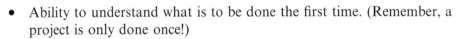

- Ability to understand what is to be done the first time. (Remember, a project is only done once!)
- Flexibility to handle changing circumstances. Some people work better at stable, routine jobs. Others are more stimulated by a job where they need to change plans as circumstances constantly change around them.

We also need to assess the key skills for people on teams:

- The ability to listen.
- The ability to express themselves clearly.
- Patience.
- Flexibility.
- A sense of humor.

If you meet people with all these skills, grab them! Realistically, everyone will have strengths and weaknesses. As you build the team, identify those and balance them. For example, if you are filling one position on a team that already has technical excellence, find a good communicator who is willing to learn, and he or she might just pull everyone together. If resources allow time for training, you might give the more technical people training in teamwork or communications, and the more people-oriented team members technical training. Team members—and project managers—become more productive by strengthening our weaknesses than we do by focusing on our strengths and avoiding our weaknesses.

A Makeover for the Team You Have

When we have some, or all, of our team assigned to us, that is called an *imposed team*. This is not a bad situation; it is simply a reality, given organizational work rules or project cost constraints. Whether we put the team together ourselves, or we work with a team we are given, our job as a project manager is straightforward: focus the team on the job, solve problems without blame by finding gaps and resolving them; and get roadblocks out of the way so the team can progress the goal.

We focus the team on the job by assigning tasks out of the WBS or the project schedule. We can do this inside a project management software tool, or using a paper system called a responsibility/activity matrix. Simply put, each task is given to a team member, and that team member is responsible for delivering the result on time with quality. In larger projects, we may also want to set up teams within the project, with team leaders coordinating the work of three to five people and helping us track work status.

Gap Analysis for Team Management

Problems will come up. Our main job is to see them coming. The sooner we see a potential problem, the less effort it will take to get back on course. It is just like making a wrong turn while driving. If we have good maps and know we are coming to a complicated intersection, we slow down, make the right choice, and lose only a little time. If we miss that, then we try to catch the fact that we are on the wrong road quickly, and plot a new course. We only get into real trouble if we ignore—or are oblivious to—a problem and keep driving down the wrong road for hours.

That need to catch problems early is what makes the weekly status meeting—with accurate status reports—so essential. As project managers, we turn status reports—where we are today—into performance reports and forecasts. Project performance reports show how far we have come, and forecasts show how we are doing in relation to the project plan and goal of delivering a quality result on time and under budget.

When a deliverable is delayed, or of poor quality, or costs more to produce than expected, we evaluate why that happened. When we understand why it happened, we look at it as one of these situations:

- *A one-time event.* For example, a team member was out sick. The team works to catch up, and no more action is needed.
- *A problem that might, or will, happen again.* For example, a piece of equipment or a software programming language is proving unreliable. Or perhaps a team member does not have the skill for assigned work. We perform a gap analysis and look for solutions.
- *A weakness in the project plan.* We discover that the WBS does not have enough detail, or that time or cost estimates were too optimistic. We review the plan and make adjustments, instituting project change, and escalating if necessary.

None of these is a disaster if we are aware of it early. When we see a possible problem, we can watch it, make the team aware of it, and decide when and how to intervene.

KEY POINT

The More Problems, the Better

When a major US automobile manufacturer decided to take a radically new approach to project management, things looked bad at first. Instead of a few dozen technical problems, the planning team was reporting hundreds of them. One executive wanted to call a halt, but, instead, chose to wait it out. In the long run, he was glad he did. The new project management method, a teamwork approach called *concurrent project management*, was designed to find problems early. Later studies showed that there were no more problems than usual with the new Dodge/Plymouth Neon; it was just that the team found, and resolved, problems sooner. The result: a highly successful new car made it to market in 18 months, instead of the usual 5 years.

The lesson: Problems we see are not problems, they are challenges. The problems we do not see are the ones to worry about.

Leading a Goal-oriented Team

Our first goal, then, in team management is to keep the team focused on the job, and to keep a free flow of information coming to us about how the work is going. In the status meeting, each team member reports on the work of current and upcoming tasks listed in the WBS. Let us take a close look at how to work with the information we receive.

The single most important thing we want to hear is the truth. We do not want to hear everything is fine—unless it is. I have tried to teach project management in blame-oriented environments, and it just does not work. If people are afraid of harsh criticism, they will not tell you what is really going on until it is too late. And the same is true for overly bureaucratic environments where, when problems are reported, they disappear into a black hole and there is no effective response. We encourage people telling us the truth by:

- Asking for clear, accurate status reports, and demonstrating them by giving them ourselves.
- Thanking people for information, whether the news is good or bad.
- Not interfering—letting people manage their own work until they want help.
- Taking effective action—doing what we can do to prevent and solve problems.

When we receive a status report, we will hear one of five things. Here they are, ordered from best news to worst news, with how we should respond to each one. Note that our response always has two steps. First, we receive the news as it is and take it in well, with thanks. Only after we are sure the team member heard that do we move on to our response.

- *Everything is fine.* Offer thanks for both the news and the good work. Then help the team member look at the next step.
- *There was a problem, but we resolved it.* Appreciate their proactive self-management. Ask if they have any other concerns.
- *Here is a problem, and here is how I would like to solve it.* Thank them for approaching the problem directly and working on it. Work with them to ensure it is the best solution, or to improve it if necessary. Authorize the correct action. If their choice was correct, ask them, "In the future, what would you need to feel confident to go ahead and solve the problem before checking with me?"
- *I have got a problem.* Thank the team member for defining the problem clearly. Then ask: "How would you solve it?"
- *Help! I am completely lost.* Thank the team member for coming to you. Ask, "What's the problem?"

In each case, we are receiving the status report as it is, and appreciating it. Then we are taking team members up to the next level. From "help" we take them to problem definition. From a defined problem, we take them to thinking about solutions. From a proposed solution, we take them to greater independence in self-management. In this way, we cultivate better self-management and leadership on our team.

What do we do if we are told about a problem, but the person assures us that our help is not wanted? Yet, we know from our own experience that the person's approach will not work. How do we intervene without undercutting the person's authority or self-respect? It is simple: We ask the person for permission to help. We can say something like, "I know you want to take care of this yourself, and I respect that. And, also, I have a lot of experience here. I was wondering if I could come to you, not as your manager, but as an expert advisor, and share my thoughts so that you can make your plan better?" If we have established a history of not micromanaging, and we are genuine when we say this, most often the person will let us give them the guidance we want to offer. If not, we can say, "Could you talk to me about it so that I understand your plan? I'm concerned about the project, and I want to make sure I know how this will work." This puts the team member in the role of teacher, and makes it even easier for him or her to accept your support.

With this kind of support, team members will naturally plan, do, and follow through to success on each step. When something comes up that the team cannot handle, we will hear about it right away. Let us look at how to address that.

Gap Reconciliation for Team Management

What do we do when the team cannot do the job? The key is to solve the problem without introducing blame, and the best tool is gap analysis and gap reconciliation. If a team member lacks the skill to complete assigned work, we do not say he or she is a bad worker, we say that there is a mismatch of the skills and the job. How do we correct a mismatch? Perhaps through training, perhaps through reassignment, or perhaps through hiring a team member or consultant with the right expertise. But never through blame, because it does not solve the problem.

The same applies with more difficult personnel issues. We focus on what the project needs, and whether the team member can, and is willing to, do what the project requires. If they are willing to, but are not able to, then we assess the gap. Could the team member gain the skill and do the job within the time limits of the project? That might work—if the team member understands what is needed, and what is needed is not a major personality change. But it may be the case that a person's attitude or approach to work is just not a good match for the project deadline or the team. In that case, our first step is to own the problem. As project managers, it is our job to get the right team for the job, or, working with an imposed team, make sure that the project schedule is realistic with the people and resources we are given. We have now discovered that that is not so. There is no blame—but there is a situation to be managed.

Next, we need to decide if we have the authority to solve the problem, or if it needs escalation to the project sponsor. If escalation is required, then we define the problem without blame, propose one or more solutions, and bring the issue to the sponsor.

Stewardship Delegation

Stewardship delegation is an approach to team management that supports independence and self-management; it is the opposite of micromanagement.

A steward is someone who acts like an owner, even though he or she does not own the item. How does an owner act? By taking full responsibility for property. But a project is not property, it is a process. What does it mean to own a process? It means that we take full responsibility for success: If we do not have what we need, we will get it; if we run into a problem, we will solve it. And we will deliver success. As project managers, we are stewards to the project. The company owns the project, but we commit to making it succeed as if it is our own. And, as project managers, we ask the same from every team member for whatever tasks they are assigned.

A team member can own a task or a set of tasks if they are clearly defined. The WBS is a good start. But we should be sure that the team member has all that is needed. For that, we use the stewardship delegation tool in Table 12-1.

There is a side benefit to stewardship delegation, which many people find is the most important benefit of all. It says to each person, "We are each responsible for asking for what we need, committing to do what we will say we will do, and creatively finding ways to accomplish goals we have made our own." Stewardship delegation is a method that cultivates the highest levels of professionalism and professional responsibility.

EFFECTIVE MEETINGS

I once spoke to a project manager from a major maker of computers that was well known for creating excellent machines. They had been bought out by an even bigger company, and gone out of business within two years. I asked him what went wrong. He told me that the new parent company had eliminated their team meetings, and, without those meetings, they were not able to work together.

In contrast, everyone I have talked to who has worked in an environment where meeting methods improved found that good meetings make for good work. Many managers who have never been to an effective meeting find this hard to believe. But when a meeting covers the necessary communication effectively, the team gets work done. Meetings are worthwhile because they make the work effective.

Projects need three kinds of meetings: status meetings, which are discussed above, brainstorming sessions, and decision meetings. Brainstorming begins with a problem or issue that might not even be well defined, and ends with options for further research. After that research, we pick up with a decision meeting where the options are reviewed and one is chosen.

Table 12-1   The stewardship delegation tool.

The leader (who delegates) defines:

1. The starting point, both time and situation
2. The ending point, both delivery date and desired results
3. The working environment—situation, overall work rules, and policies
4. The resources available, including extra help and guidance
5. A date and time by which the worker should inform the leader if it is possible that the delivery date cannot be met or desired result cannot be delivered
6. The consequences of successful delivery
7. A summary of the consequences of unsuccessful delivery

Every time you pass a task on to someone, make sure you deliver these seven pieces of information. Also check to make sure that the steward understands and receives each one.

The steward, the worker or supervisor receiving the delegation:

1. Decides how the work will be done, and by whom under his or her supervision
2. Develops and implements a project plan for the work
3. Gathers the resources and takes responsibility for getting them and managing them
4. Does the work, supervises the work, and takes responsibility for the work being done on schedule
5. Reports on all interim report dates, saying "everything is fine," or "we may not be able to deliver on time/to specification because, and here is how I suggest we remedy the situation," or "I think we're okay, but here's something that concerns me," or "help!"
6. Delivers the result on time and to specification, and makes sure that the delivery is confirmed for everyone involved

Every time you receive a task from someone, picture yourself doing these steps, and make sure you have everything you need to be able to do them.

Notes:

An entire project can be seen as a stewardship delegation from the organization or customer to the project manager. Projects run this way work very well.

A good project manager is an effective steward for the entire project, and empowers the group or sub-team leaders to be effective stewards of their sub-projects. He or she also empowers individual team members to be self-managed, that is, to be effective stewards of their own work.

Table 12-1 The stewardship delegation tool (*Continued*).

It takes time to do this well. We recommend that you give this page to everyone on the project team. Each time a task is passed on, both people check this list to make sure that they are giving and receiving it well. If problems arise (miscommunications, missed deadlines, and so forth) come together to resolve the problem. Also take time to go back to this list and see what steps could be done more clearly next time to prevent this kind of problem in the future.

This method can be used between equals, as well. If you and I make an agreement or have a commitment, you can be the steward of your commitment, as I am the steward of mine. Then, in creating the agreement, we make sure we give ourselves and each other the things the leader offers, and we make sure we have received what we need to be effective stewards (worker or supervisor). Then, as we carry through on what we do, we operate according to the role of steward (worker or supervisor).

It can also work from a junior to his or her manager or supervisor. When a team member comes to us with a problem, and asks us to get authorization, or funding, or acceptance of a change of schedule from the sponsor or the customer, we are receiving a delegation upwards from a team member. And we respond by doing what the team member needs to succeed, and reporting back the results.

Brainstorming

When people come together on an issue, you will have either an argument or a brainstorming session. People bring energy to an issue: it is like two rivers running together. If there is a big rock where the rivers meet, there is a loud splash, a lot of noise, and all of the energy swirls off to the sides in muddy pools. Arguments are like that: a lot of noise, and no energy left afterwards. A good manager will learn the art of leading a brainstorming session. We do this by simply removing the rocks, and creating a clear channel for everyone's energy to flow into the problem and through it to a solution. To turn an argument into a brainstorming session, we need to remove the rocks by adding three ingredients: time, space, and focus.

- *Time.* People often say that they cannot waste time on meetings. But that is because most meetings are a waste of time. A well-organized brainstorming session with a clear problem, a good structure, and a goal gets results and saves time. Set up a meeting, or meetings, with enough time to define the issue and find solutions.
- *Space.* In the most obvious sense, a meeting room free of interruptions gives us space. We can also add space in other ways. Respect is a kind

of space: If we agree not to interrupt one another and give one another the space to think, then everyone can contribute his or her best.

- *Focus.* Bring people together and lay out the problem in front of them clearly. Place everyone on the same side of the table, facing the problem illustrated in front of us all. Then we are on the same side, tackling the problem. Do not allow other issues to enter the meeting. Like a swift-running stream, the meeting should have a starting place and move towards the best solution. It will not always move in a straight line—we need to explore side streams to find the best way—but we must always keep the goal in front of us.

With these ingredients, we can set up a brainstorming process. If the team is committed to a solution, this could be one meeting with breaks. The more conflict there is, and the less willingness to work together, the more we slow down the process. But we should always take breaks between the four steps outlined below, as they require very different types of thinking from the team:

- *Gathering ideas.* In this stage, we offer a question to the group, and get at least one answer from each person. The question could be: "What do you think our biggest problem is?" Or, "What is one factor we should consider in a solution?" Or, for a quality brainstorming session, "Fill in the blank: it's good if it _____." We ask people not to interrupt, and we gather ideas without evaluation or critique. We allow ideas to come up more than once. If possible, we should even hold off clarification until step two.
- *Clarifying and organizing ideas.* In this stage, we first check if every idea is clear to everyone. We ask the originator of the idea for clarification. Then we combine similar and identical ideas. Then, if the ideas seem to form groups, we put them together.
- *Evaluating ideas.* After a break, we look at the different ideas. We think about each group or set, and improve it. We decide which ideas are the most valuable to pursue.
- *Assigning ideas for further development.* Lastly, we define a reasonable number of possibilities with which to work, and then we assign each workable idea to a team member for further development. That team member will research the idea, make it as good as possible, and present it at a decision meeting.

It is good to note that not all problems need one solution. Sometimes, we just need to come up with a group of ideas and let people use any one that works. For an example of that, see the brainstorming example below, where a team creates its own ground rules for meetings or for working together.

Decision-making

It is important to separate decision-making from brainstorming. Decision-making begins with just a few options, and ends with the selection of a single course of action. This might be a go/no-go decision, such as whether to launch a project after the concept stage is complete, or whether to implement a particular product feature that is costing more than expected. The other type of decision is an option decision. With an option decision, we know we will go ahead, but the question is how to do it. Which vendor will we use? Which software programming language will we use? Will we do the work ourselves, or hire a consultant?

Ground rules created by the team

Teamwork and meetings operate best when people know the ground rules. And people understand and keep to ground rules if they own them. Here is an exercise for your team that will help them create ground rules for meetings, or for working together as a team.

EXERCISE

A Brainstorming Meeting About How to Have Meetings

Explain to the team that the purpose of this meeting is to come to agreement about how the team will work together and support one another, particularly around meetings. The results will be a written document, often called a *code of conduct* or *ground rules*.

Ask the team to take a moment and remember a time when they were treated well, or when they felt that they were respected, or appreciated, or what mattered to them was addressed at a meeting. Then go around the room and have the person say what it was that mattered. You will hear things like, "I was respected," or "everyone arrived on time." Write these down on a list. You can go around a second time, or just ask people if they have more ideas.

Then ask people to remember a time when they treated someone else in a way that seemed good. Add those items. And do it twice more, this time with experiences where people did not like the way they were treated, or did not like the results of what they did.

Organize the items. For example, some might be about time, and others about respect, and so forth. Phrase as many as you can in the positive.

Add the magic words, *We will* to the beginning of each phrase. "We will respect one another. We will arrive on time. We will listen without interrupting." Read the entire list, and see how everyone feels.

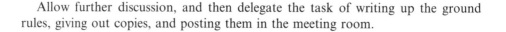
Allow further discussion, and then delegate the task of writing up the ground rules, giving out copies, and posting them in the meeting room.

We can do the same with ground rules for project work, as well as for meetings. Once the team has created this agreement, we each do our best to keep the rules, and to support one another—in a no-blame, friendly way—to keep them. It can help to agree on a friendly, humorous, perhaps non-verbal signal to act as a reminder. Some groups just allow anyone to say, "Ground rules," as a reminder. Others use a bell, or a particular hand sign, or a humorous picture that people hold up as a reminder.

A MANAGER'S COVENANT

Our goal as project managers is to support our team. Rather than seeing us as above them, we want to see ourselves beneath our team, assisting them, helping them to get the job done. Yet our society—and our authority to evaluate their work, and change the direction of their future career—puts us on top. One way to handle this is to develop a manager's covenant.

A covenant is an agreement from someone in a higher position to someone in a lower position. But it begins with what I will give, from a higher position. Only after I give am I entitled to say what I want to receive. So, a covenant begins with generosity and support.

As managers, we should each think deeply about our covenant. What do we most want from those in authority? What has been most difficult for us? We can allow our experience to guide our actions.

We should not adopt someone else's covenant. But we can think about a covenant we see, and decide if we want to make parts of it our own. In that spirit, here is a covenant from an excellent project manager. Years ago, I worked for Henry, and started with what he offered, and made just a few changes.

- I surround myself with people I respect and trust.
- Then act so that they will respect and trust me.
- I provide my team with the tools they need to be productive: hardware and software, policies and procedures, and a healthy work environment.
- I provide challenges, clearly defined work, and a clearly defined growth path.
- I listen closely and respond quickly.

- I get feedback constantly and project status regularly.
- I reward in public, but criticize work in private.

When you create your own covenant, first read it yourself daily, and check yourself against it. When you are confident that you live by it reasonably well, post it so everyone can see. Henry wrote his on the whiteboard in his office. And everyone knew that we could come in and bring him a problem at any time. He always knew the pulse of the project, and he kept it running well.

Communications Management

For the rest of the chapter we will look at how to communicate with customers, the sponsor, and other stakeholders who are not on our project team. This group is not close-knit, the way a project team should be. Their participation in the project will be intermittent, and we need to plan how to keep everyone informed and to keep the information flowing. The flow of information feeds the project, letting the team know what to do.

THE THREE LEVELS OF THE CUSTOMER AND THEIR CONCERNS

When our customer is a business group, such as a company or department, we need to be aware of three different levels of the customer, each of which has different legitimate concerns, as follows:

- *Executive.* This level is responsible for defining the mission and direction of the customer group, and includes the sponsor or customer executive who sees project success as contributing to the mission of the organization.
- *Managerial.* Managers are responsible for getting work done. If they see the value of the project in terms of productivity, they will support it. Even so, time taken by the customer department in analysis, and interruptions during transition to production, are difficult for managers. Projects bring in change, and even change for the better creates disruption and reduces productivity.
- *Worker.* Workers are rated by how much work they get done. We need to demonstrate that the new product or service will improve the way work is done, leading to greater effectiveness and efficiency, not just for

the department as a whole, but for the workers' specific jobs. It does not work to tell someone that we are making the work harder so it is easier for the department. In addition, workers know what is really going on in the department. Their knowledge of the initial situation and the real needs and problems is essential to project success. Their resistance to change is not something we need to overcome; it is something to which we need to listen. When we really understand the workers' issues, we can make a product or service that will really solve the department's problems.

In addition to legitimate issues about the project, people at each level may also have issues that are not legitimate. We may encounter prejudice for one method over another, or biased preferences. We may encounter people who think they are expert when they are not. This brings us into the realm of politics. We can minimize this by using the tools of the no-blame environment and triangulation for the same side approach. We keep bringing the focus back to the needs of the project—not our needs—the project's needs.

KEY COMMUNICATIONS CONCEPTS

There are three key ideas that lead to successful communications:

- *Closing the loop*. The only way we can know that communication has been successful is if we hear back from the person we are trying to reach. In our plan, we must ask and answer questions like: "How will we know if an e-mail was read? How will we know if someone understood what was said at a meeting?"
- *Defining the purpose of each communication and the desired response*. Sometimes, our goal is just to inform. Then we want to get a reply that says, "I hear and understand." Other times, we are asking for a decision, such as approval for a purchase. Then we want to receive the results of that decision. Other times, we are delegating work. In those cases, we want to know that the action item was understood, and we want to see the deliverables on time. In each project communication, we should make the desired response clear, and give a date when we want to receive that response. That increases the likelihood of effective action, and also gives us a reason to follow up if we do not hear anything.
- *Feedback*. As discussed in Chapter 3, communication is effective only if it leads to an effect—a change of plan, or work that actually gets done.

MANAGING ALL TYPES OF COMMUNICATIONS

In the communications plan, we should define how we will handle each of these types of communications:

- *Routine reports* that keep the sponsor, the customers, and other stakeholders informed of project status.
- *Deliverables at the gates*, which include both inputs to the review and approval process at the gate at the end of each stage, and also the outputs of the gate: requests for change or rework, project cancellation, or approval of the stage and authorization for the next stage.
- *Informal communications*, where project members talk to customers and stakeholders. Usually these take care of themselves, but there are some things of which to be aware.
- *Escalation of problems and changes*, which are the formal communications we use when we need to report on a risk event that is happening, request a change to the schedule, budget, or project scope, or get help.

Let us take a closer look at the two of these.

Informal communications

Informal communications include conversations, e-mails, and quick notes to explain things. They are the constant lifeblood of the project. (Formal communications are just a skeleton.) When these go well, everyone learns and grows and the project continues by itself. As project managers, we should always model and foster positive informal communication.

There are four dangers to watch for in informal communications:

- *Technical decisions not reaching the project plan.* Sometimes, technical people on a team will split up into small groups and brainstorm. Often, they will not participate in whole team meetings when you are updating the project plan. The result is that good ideas are changing the project in good ways, but the plan is not up to date. If you see this happening, do not stop it. But do get the changes into the plan. You can do it informally, by just asking people what ideas they are putting forward; or you can do it formally by opening the weekly meeting with at ten-minute update, letting the group split up into small teams for 30 minutes, and then bringing them back together at the end of each meeting for a ten-minute conclusion. During this conclusion, everyone hears the changes and you update the plan.

- *Negativity such as anger, blame, and criticism.* It will happen. You will probably find yourself doing it sometimes. But, if it happens regularly, then something is wrong. Perhaps a conflict has erupted between two people, or someone on the project is over-stressed. Private conferences, mediations, and meetings to clear the air are required.

- *Team members saying yes to project change.* The third danger of informal communication occurs between team members and customers or stakeholders. Many project professionals are friendly and supportive. That is good. Just make sure that they know that no one on the project ever commits to anything verbally. If anyone on the project is asked to do something, they have two choices: Look on the project schedule and tell the stakeholder if it will be done, and when; or offer to bring the request up at the next weekly meeting, or sooner, if appropriate. Once this is done, a change control process is started.

- *Chatting that interferes with work.* One sign of this is meetings that go on a long time, with people not wanting to get back to work. If people are getting work done on schedule, a lot of talk may be part of the process. If there is more talk and less work, then there is a morale problem. Address it, but not by telling people to stop chatting and get back to work. Find out why people are avoiding work: Do they think it is hopeless? Do they feel criticized? Correct the problem and support people in refocusing on delivering the deliverables.

Escalation of problems and changes

Sometimes, the solution to a problem requires authority that we, as project managers, do not have. For whatever reason, we may come to see that the best solution—or the only solution—requires more money, a delay in delivery, a change to project scope, or a change in the project team. It is good to know why this has happened, but it is not the central point. Our focus should be on the present and future—identifying the problem, proposing a solution, and getting the help we need. And we should not do this alone. It is easy to feel isolated when a big problem occurs, but this is an excellent time to brainstorm with our team.

If we need to escalate a problem to the sponsor, we should not see it as a failure. Rather, we should see it as part of our job. We track work against the plan, and close the gaps. This time, the best way to close the gap is to change the plan. It happens. On the other hand, no one likes to go to the boss and ask for help. We can ask for help well by following the Green–Yellow–Red traffic light escalation method described in Chapter 8.

13

Project Quality Management

It would be nearly true to say, "Quality is everything." If we include the due date and the project budget in our requirements specifications, then quality, which is conformance to specifications, is indeed everything—assuming, of course, that the specification actually describes what the customer wants.

Working with the customer to define quality in all its aspects, writing down what we learn, and delivering to that specification is, indeed, the heart of project management. First we will look at key quality concepts. Then we will learn a five-step process for defining, managing, and delivering quality on a project.

Key Quality Concepts

We introduced important ideas about quality in Chapter 3. Before we go further, let us bring in a few more.

QUALITY IS ESSENTIAL TO PURPOSE AND SCOPE

Quality is essential to our project because we need quality planning and quality work to meet the project's purpose and deliver the project's goal. In plain English, quality is what makes something good. In business, what is good is what adds value to the business. Deming, the creator of the field of total quality management (TQM), defined quality as "conformance to specifications." Deming, operating in a production manufacturing environment, figured the specifications were already correct, that the finished item, if made as specified, would satisfy the customer.

However, in project management, there is a fundamental connection from value, to purpose, to goal, to detailed requirements, to specifications, and from specifications to a working product and a successful project. Quality is what holds them all together. Because each project is unique, we must define quality differently for each project. And we must make sure that the definition of quality is the customer's, not just our own. When we have a picture and a set of requirements, we know what is really of value to the customer. If the requirements are right, then, we can build a good specification. Then, when we deliver a product or service conforming to that specification, we deliver quality and value. Following that formula is a recipe for success.

QUALITY AS AN INDIVIDUAL AND A TEAM EFFORT

For a team to deliver quality, each person on the team must do quality work, and, at the same time, the team must improve teamwork and communication, focusing on quality. Why are both necessary?

- *Nothing can replace good work*. If one person is not doing quality work, the best anyone else on the team can do is try to fix it. We do our best work by getting it right the first time.
- *We need someone else to check our assumptions*. Most errors that lead to poor quality are the result of assumptions. Two heads—or as many heads as we have on our team—are better than one.
- *Others can review our work better than we can*. When we look at what we have written, we tend to see what we thought we wrote. We remember our ideas. But if we put one word in place of another, we are not likely to notice that. And the same goes if we are building a physical object. We know what we wanted to do, and we expect to see it. It is much easier for anyone but us to catch our own errors.

For these reasons, a project manager does two things to deliver quality results: Encourage quality work from everyone on the team, and define work rules and procedures that ensure that everything is cross-checked.

Encouraging quality work on your team

People want to do good work. If you do not believe me, try this and see. Set up a project with clearly defined jobs, a no-blame environment, and a balance of responsibility with ability and resources, as described in Chapter 2. Encourage and praise good work. Correct errors in a supportive way, encouraging people to do better the next time. Believe in people and avoid personality and politics. See what happens.

We can add a focus on quality to make this even better. Live quality. Teach quality. Explain quality to your team. Focus on clear goals and achieving them, on making mistakes but doing better. Support people in defining quality for themselves and talking about it.

Procedures for cross-checking

The key principle here is that, to avoid making assumptions and missing errors, quality checking must be independent of work. Here are a number of ways to ensure we do this, starting with the simplest.

- *Everything is seen by two pairs of eyes before it leaves.* Make this a team rule. Include yourself—have someone check your own work. Let people know that this is simply because we do not see our own mistakes.
- *People always make mistakes, but, as a team, we do not make as many.* Given we make mistakes, we would much rather have them found by a team member than by our customer. And we would also like them found sooner, rather than later.
- *Buddy-checking.* Whenever possible, work in pairs or small teams. Each day, have each person work, and also check another person's work.
- *Checking inputs when we get them.* Almost every deliverable is an input for someone on the team for some step in the work breakdown structure (WBS). Ask team members to check their deliverables as soon as they arrive, even if they are not going to start the task yet.
- *Create test plans separately from work results.* Both are derived from the WBS. If only one person is doing both, have the person make the test plans first. Even better, have two different people or teams, one to create the test plans, another to create the product itself.

- *Use formal methods of review and testing.* Formal methods of review, such as software inspection, are beyond the scope of this book. These methods work. Although most software is loaded with bugs, we have been able to produce zero-defect computer programs. The same range of quality can be found in every field. Learn the best methods of quality in your industry, and make them work for your project.

THE NEED FOR INDEPENDENCE IN THE QUALITY MANAGEMENT PROCESS

One issue that pervades all of quality management is that good quality management requires independence from the work being done and from other management processes. There are three reasons for this:

- Even with the best of intentions, people will carry the same assumptions in their work and in the checking of their own work. It is very good to encourage people to check their own work. However, because of the possibility of assumptions not being tested, it is not sufficient.
- When we check up on ourselves, it creates two problems. The first is that it opens opportunities for us to succumb to pressure to do a poor job. If the boss just yelled at me for not being on time, I will find it hard to stop and fill out my quality control checklist. I know I did the job right, and I do not have time, and my boss just made it very clear that time, not checklists, are what really matter. I might succumb to that pressure, which could create problems later on. Perhaps, by skipping the checklist, I innocently omit one key step. That could force rework or create delays later on. The second problem created by self-checking is the appearance of impropriety. Everything may be just fine, but with no independent review of that fact, we are open to criticism anyway.
- In those rare cases where unethical behavior is occurring, we can catch it or prevent it through independent processes that check that we are working according to established methods and accepted principles.

The principle of independence in quality management does not mean that all quality management work should be done only by separate people or groups. Just the opposite is true. The more focus on quality each worker has, the better. And the more there is a focus on quality, the less work there is for the independent group to do. The point is that the independent reviews, checks, and tests add value to the quality process that cannot be gained through any other means.

REDUCING THE COST OF QUALITY

Creating quality results pays off in the long run, after the product is delivered to the customer. But doing quality work takes time and money—limited resources on any project—for quality planning, quality control, and quality assurance. How do we get the most for our money when it comes to quality? There are two things we can do: Focus our efforts, and work with prevention, checking, and testing.

Focusing our efforts

Let us be pessimistic for a moment and assume that some mistakes will be made, and that some of them will not be caught. We will have errors in our final product at the end of the project. A question: Where in the process of our work would those errors do the most harm? Wherever those areas are, we should focus most of our QA and QC effort there. Evaluate your project after reviewing these ideas:

- *The worst mistake is never being on the same page.* Project failure is often the result of never really knowing what the customer wanted. Or giving the customer what they asked for, without helping the customer determine what was really needed. We can avoid this by focusing on quality definition with words and pictures, and QA and QC for the planning documents.
- *Due to the 1:10:100 rule, early mistakes are more costly.* Quality efforts should be strong from the beginning. This also helps the team own the project and do what it takes to make it good.
- *Some components are more important—or more sensitive—than others.* Identify what matters most to the customer. Perform a technical evaluation of the product or service to determine what is most crucial. Focus more effort—but not all your effort—on those areas.
- *Do not leave anything out.* Occasionally, a peripheral stakeholder knows something or needs something absolutely key to success. While we must focus our efforts, we must not skip anyone or anything. In the real world, the smallest side piece can turn out to be crucial to operational success and value.

Prevention, checking, and testing

We can make quality management most efficient by focusing first on prevention, second on checking, and third on testing.

Prevention is any effort we make to get it right the first time. If we choose intelligently from best practices and follow those procedures carefully, we are preventing future problems. If we understand the project goals and include the right expertise on the team, we are doing good project human resources management, and the result is good-quality work. If we perform gap analysis and resolve problems early, we are preventing problems. Prevention of defects is achieved through the application of the 1:10:100 rule by doing quality work in every process.

Checking is a generic term for any process that reviews and validates our work other than testing. Choose from the formal and informal methods discussed above, and check project documents and product or service components as thoroughly as possible.

To *test* something means to actually use a component—in a simulation, or in the real world—and see if it works. The testing cycle is our last, and most expensive, chance to get it right. When errors are discovered in testing components, it is an indication that we did quite a lot of work before we knew something was wrong. We are far off course, and the effort in the wrong direction was expensive. The diagnosis to determine where we are and the rework to get us back on course adds more cost. We want to do good, thorough testing, but we want to have already done good enough prevention and checking that we find very few errors even with very thorough testing.

Now that we have looked at the key concepts of quality, let us get the tools we need for the five steps of quality management: defining, planning for, controlling, assuring, and delivering quality.

The Five Steps to Quality

The five steps to project quality are:

- *Defining quality*, where we write down what qualities add value to the product or service we are creating, and how to measure them.
- *Planning for quality*, where we add steps to the project process for controlling, assuring, and delivering quality.
- *Quality control* is the process of reviewing work processes and deliverables to ensure quality and gather information for process improvement.
- *Quality assurance* is the process for testing the product to ensure quality, and also the process of auditing results to ensure proper quality procedures.
- *Delivering quality* is the process of assuring customer satisfaction.

DEFINING QUALITY

There is a fundamental principle of management: to manage something, we must be able to measure it. And there is a principle of engineering: to measure something, we need to define it. So, to manage quality, we must first define it.

Why did this issue not arise for time and cost management? For a very simple reason. For time and money, society has already done this step for us. We all know what time is, and we have units of measure—hours and days. And we all know what money is, and we have units of measure—dollars and cents, for example. But what is the unit of measure for quality?

There is no unit of measure for quality because there is no single definition of quality. Quality has many aspects. And the definition of quality that matters most is our customer's definition of quality. A lot of companies have gone out of business building what they thought the customer would want. When we find out what really matters to the consumer—or what really helps the business customer—we are defining quality.

The tool we use to define quality is the quality definition table. We can create it near the beginning of analysis, as long as we have a draft statement of our purpose, our goal, and our list of stakeholders. We begin with two brainstorming sessions, one with the customer, and one with our team.

Here are the steps we recommend in building a quality definition table.

1. Brainstorm with customers and team members to identify quality items. Review the draft project overview. Then have each person give one or more suggestions to: "Fill in the blank. It will be good if it _____."
2. Brainstorm with each peripheral stakeholder regarding the component or feature that matters to him or her. Have each one complete the statement: "It will be good if it _____." Then say, "And what else?" Get as many thoughts as you can.
3. Do the same brainstorming session with the project team.
4. Write up a list of the results. Combine similar items.
5. Organize them into a draft quality definition table similar to the one in Table 13-1. Fill in the first column with the list of items.
6. Brainstorm with the team to define the measurable items, units of measure, and standards for each item.
7. Bring this list back to the customer and other stakeholders. Have them review it, understand it, and correct it. Ask them if, seeing this, they can think of any more items. Expand the list.
8. Bring this back to the customer for prioritization. Ask which items are essential. Essential items are those that if they are not good enough will lead to the customer rejecting the final product or service and declaring

the project a failure. If the customer insists that all items are essential, ask how much he or she would pay for each one.

9. Once essential items are defined, ask the customer, "If you could have just one more item, which would it be?" Use this to prioritize the rest of the list.

10. Bring the prioritized list to your team. Review and improve the measurable items, standards, and units of measure. If appropriate, check with standards agencies and other bodies that can provide tools and methods that support quality.

11. The quality definition table is complete. It is an input to quality planning.

If you look through Table 13-1, the sample quality definition table, you will see that many different computer software buzzwords are mixed in with a bunch of practical customer requirements, such as good end-user documentation. This is about what we would want in the middle of step six of the quality definition process.

EXERCISE

Have Fun Defining Quality

Get together with your family or some friends and pick something you all like to buy, or to do. It could be a dinner out or a toy for the children. Practice the brainstorming session: "It would be good if it _____." This can be a great way to select a restaurant or buy someone a present. It is also a fun way to get to know someone. Very quickly, you will see that quality means different things for different people. It is not just that we like different things. It is that the kind of things that matter to us are different. For example, one person might be most concerned about the ambiance of a restaurant, another about the taste of the food, and another that the kitchen can prepare meals avoiding foods to which that person is allergic. And each of those items really matters. That is why brainstorming—making quality a teamwork process—is so important.

Give it a try. Then write it up as an exercise, practicing making a quality definition table.

PLANNING FOR QUALITY

With the quality definition table in hand, you know what will make the product good. Creating the quality plan, you answer the question: How

Table 13-1 Sample quality definition table from a software development project.

Quality Definition Table		
Quality item	**Measurable item**	**Unit of measure and standard**
Reliability Zero defects Stable	Error reports Uptime Downtime	MTBF (mean time between failures) % uptime/% downtime (Be sure to define hours of availability needed)
Maintainable Well documented	Cost of support Documents tested and approved by those who use them	MTTR (mean time to repair) Documentation approval checklist
Meets stakeholder expectations/ specifications Does what the customer wants it to do, is usable Meets detailed requirements specification	Satisfaction survey Track help desk calls Use cases (a requirements, specification, and testing method) Feature verification	User acceptance test Each use case reviewed, tested, and approved by the team and the customer Feature test
Change control well managed Good analysis	Review change management	Number of changes per project created by poor communication/poor expectation management Number of changes per project that could have been prevented by better analysis
Performance Functional speed Appropriate appearance	Screen refresh, query speed, etc. Approval	Measure speed, in testing and in production

Table 13-1   Sample quality definition table from a software development project (*Continued*).

Easy to use	Fewer support calls	Number of calls to help desk
Intuitive/user friendly	Productivity	
Appropriate training		Measure actual productivity of users in their work before and after new system
Good end-user documentation		
Help desk can support		
On time	Number of calls after initial release	Final project review
On budget		
Works the first time		
Easy to modify	Quality control review	
Configurable		
Customizable		
Coded to standard		
Scalable		

will we get there? The plan describes three areas of work: quality control, quality assurance, and quality control for change control. The first two are discussed in detail in the following sections. We explain quality control for change control here.

Above, we said that certain parts of the product—and certain parts of the project—were crucial to success. One of those is written change control. If a step is missed in change control, there is a good chance that the project team will not be on the same page, and will end up making a product with the head of a horse and the tail of a donkey. And you will end up looking foolish. To avoid this, we need to plan and implement a process for making sure that change control is done right. That is quality control for change control.

Here is a sample quality plan from a project to build a small web site to give a company a presence on the internet. Some of the technical points, such as video resolution and download speed, are from the last millennium, as the project was completed in early 1999.

WOWS AND WHOOPSES

A Quality Plan for Creating a Corporate Web Page

This plan defines the application of quality control and quality assurance to this project.

Quality Control

Quality control will be applied at each step by the worker performing the step, and by the worker on the next step receiving the deliverable.

Gary is extremely experienced and professional. He checks his own work as he goes. Sid will confirm with him at the beginning of each step that he has what he needs, and that he understands what he is to deliver.

Sid is an experienced project manager as well as a web-page designer. He will check all the work he receives from Gary as it comes in, to make sure that there are no problems.

Sid will receive all materials from the client and check them for usability. If any problems arise, he will return them to the client for rework at the beginning of the step. This will minimize lost time due to client errors.

The client is responsible for dealing with issues related to web hosting and domain names. This is of some concern, as the client got them into the present unsatisfactory position. Sid will monitor the work done by the IT manager, who is a mainframe person unfamiliar with web technology. The internal network manager has worked with Sid for five years on past projects and can be relied on to do quality work on his part.

QTI has convinced the customer to use a high-quality web host provider that provides excellent hosting, technical support, and customer service. Quality is assured there. In addition, they are likely to guide the IT manager to do work in a high-quality manner.

If we work in this way, QTI is confident that it can deliver to the customer what they want.

Certain design decisions determine the usability of the web page. QTI will follow these industry standards in developing the page.

Quality Control Procedures:
1. File size and speed standards. Fast download is essential for an exciting, interesting page. Each graphic file will be no larger than 22 kilobytes. Each page will be under 100 kilobytes. Gary set these standards as follows: AT&T corporate standard (which he helped write) was 11 kilobytes maximum per graphic and 50 kilobytes maximum per page, but assumed the public had 28.8 kilobytes modems. Now that the modem standard has increased to a norm of 56 kilobytes, we can double these numbers to achieve the same download speed with higher-quality graphics. We reviewed this issue in the initial meeting. The target population that the customer is most concerned about (students in college) will

be seeing the page at school, receiving data over a shared T1 link. Given this, these size standards will ensure sufficient speed, while giving us more leeway in using high-quality graphics, which the customer wants. Gary will check each file and page size as he completes each page.

2. Resolution standard. Discussion with the customer has determined that we should optimize for 800 × 600, and that the page should appear attractive at higher resolutions as well. A resolution of 640 × 480 is out of date at the schools that are the primary target. The page should be usable, but does not need to be optimal, if this will reduce the quality of the page at higher resolutions.

3. Browser compatibility. Gary writes in standard HTML. Sid will load the page into FrontPage and test with Netscape 3.x and 4.x, and IE 3.x and 4.x. We will use only basic search and forms Bots in FrontPage, and not the advanced Bots, which are not compatible with all Netscape versions.

4. Frames compatibility. The design will use frames, and the customer has accepted that older browsers that do not use frames will not be able to see the site. They will see a message that says, "You must have a frame-capable browser to view this site."

Quality control for change control
   Note: Insert the change control process from *Chapter 11*

Quality Assurance
   There are no external or regulatory standards to be met in creating the corporate web page. However, there are industry best practices to be employed by QTI, and quality elements to be reviewed by the customer.
   Issues QTI will test:

1. Download speed. Sid will double-check file sizes to make sure that they meet the standard. If time allows, the site will be posted on a test location (unpublished URL) and viewed over standard modem connections. If time does not allow, this step can be skipped because we are confident of Gary's formula and the web hosting company's performance level.

2. Usability at standard resolution. The customer agreed to optimize for 800 × 600 resolution. QTI will develop and test the page at this resolution.

3. Compatibility with web browsers. QTI will test the page on IE 3.x and 4.x, and Netscape 3.x and 4.x, the current browsers. Sid will make sure that there are no advanced FrontPage Bots installed by accident.

4. Sid will test the "You need a frames-capable browser to view this site" message.

5. Navigation functionality. Sid will check all links. No external links are planned.

6. Forms functionality. QTI will test this prior to delivery at each client meeting. The client will also test it prior to final posting.

7. Search functionality. QTI will test this prior to delivery at each client meeting. The client will also test it prior to final posting.

8. Visual quality. QTI will check the page before client meetings, but this is primarily a client concern.

Issues the client will test:

1. Graphics quality. Do they like the look and feel?
2. Appearance. Does it match the corporate image?
3. URL functionality. The customer will provide a list of URLs they obtained, and then test the list to make sure all hit the home page.
4. E-mail delivery of forms. Client will enter forms and make sure that they arrive at the appropriate HR mailbox.
5. Forms content. HR will review what it receives from the forms, and make sure that information is usable.

On larger projects, and on projects that have to meet safety, regulatory, or legal requirements, the plan would be much longer. It would specify those outside standards and describe how the project team would ensure compliance with them. It would also document contact with standards bodies and internal and external audit agencies, and, where appropriate, include their official approval of the plan.

In addition, there is more work the team can do to ensure quality. Here are some steps to consider for larger projects:

- At the beginning of each stage, create a quality plan for that stage. Then, in design, create the quality plan for the rest of the project.
- Address how we will assure the quality of every deliverable component of the product or service, and also of every project management deliverable.
- Address how we will educate the team about quality and support a focus on quality within the team and in communication with our customers.
- Address how we will include quality review in our weekly status meetings.
- Address how we will apply fundamental principles of quality, such as the need for independent review and testing, on the project.
- Address the use of formal quality methodologies in the project.
- Address how we will align quality management within the project with quality management methods used by the organization as a whole.
- Implement the quality plan through team training and checklists.

On some projects, we will need to create another plan, in addition to the project quality plan. It is the test plan, which is discussed in Chapter 9. The test plan will need to meet industry-specific standards.

CONTROLLING QUALITY

Quality control involves defining desired results in detail, reviewing results, and improving processes so that each item is delivered with quality throughout the project. Successful quality control is a team effort, and so introducing QC to the team is the most important step. We can do this at a status meeting early in the development stage. These meetings are usually pretty dull. You ask each team member how he or she is progressing, and the answer is, "I've just got started, nothing is due yet." Do not stop there. Instead, introduce quality.

Let us say that there is a task on the WBS that is due next week. Juan will finish a piece of work, and deliver it to Sue. Juan says he is still working, which is just fine. Turn to Sue and ask, "When you get this, what do you expect it to look like? If it is as good as it can be, what will it have in it?"

Sue answers by describing the qualities of the deliverable, with a focus on what will make her work easy. Perhaps Juan is surprised. Sue's vision of what he is delivering might be very different from his. Or, more likely, Sue may just have a quick idea of how to make it a bit better, or a bit easier for her. Either way, she specifies her ideal input, and he gets the definition of quality for her output. You, as project manager, record these details in the project plan. (If you are using Microsoft Project®, you can put them in a comment on the task description.) Now, Juan knows what to do to make Sue's job easier. And, when Sue gets the item in the best possible form, she can focus on doing quality work on her job, rather than rushing to fix problems with her inputs.

We continue this process. We have each recipient of a deliverable describe, in advance, what he or she wants to receive from the team member delivering on the prior task. The worker for the prior task redefines his or her work to this standard of quality, and we track the changes.

What are the advantages of this team approach to quality?

- *Customer service within the team*. Anyone who receives your deliverable is your customer, even when we are all on the same team. We now have an attitude of customer service within the team. Each team member is doing his or her best for the other team members.
- *Team commitment to quality*. Each team member can see and understand how receiving good work makes another team member's job easier. Enthusiasm for working well together grows.
- *Proactivity*. Each team member has a well-defined job before the work is started. That helps with the proactive, no-blame environment.
- *Conflict prevention*. To put it simply, you must have this meeting. If you have it early, while there is still time for workers to redefine what

they are doing, it will be proactive, friendly, and supportive. If you wait until later, when the deliverables are due, it will be reactive, hostile, and blaming. Sue might say, "I can't do my job because Juan didn't give me what he was supposed to." And Juan replies, "I did exactly what the plan asked for. And Sue never told me she wanted anything else."

For the person having difficulty delivering quality, it is best to start by being inquisitive. Meet privately. Ask the team member if he or she is aware of any quality problems. Walk through one example of what happened. Ask if the person knows why. Your goal is to get a sense that the person understands the importance of quality, understands that there is a problem, and wants to do better. If you get there, ask, "How can I help you do better?" and arrange appropriate quality control checks. If the person does not understand it, and repeats the same type of error, then you will need to have a second talk. Be positive, especially if you see some improvement or effort. But also be clear that, on a project with a set schedule, something must change, or the project will be in trouble. Work with the person to remove any sense of blame or bad feeling, and also to diagnose the source of the difficulty.

How do we help a perfectionist deliver on time? We need to help that team member understand the difference between his or her own, higher standards, and the requirements of the project, which include on-time delivery. In my experience, people with doctoral degrees from good schools want to keep working until their work meets the standard that their dissertation committee would meet, which is far higher than what would be needed in most business situations. I often say something like, "Go for making it perfect. When you are 90% there, deliver the task. It will be good enough. And we'll only succeed if it is on time." Perfectionism is a habit we probably do not want to break. A self-aware perfectionist who understands that quality, not perfection, is the goal, is a great team player. These people can do good work and also help other team members improve.

ASSURING QUALITY

We add quality assurance to our project process at key points to have independent validation that our work is correct. Here are some key points where we can add QA activities:

- *QA for procurement.* Vendors and consultants will, in all likelihood, not know our quality standards. Therefore, we should set up a process

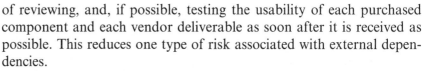

of reviewing, and, if possible, testing the usability of each purchased component and each vendor deliverable as soon after it is received as possible. This reduces one type of risk associated with external dependencies.

- *QA for milestones.* Remember that, in addition to milestones (major deliverables) at the end of each stage, we can also define smaller milestones within a stage. Creating several small milestones, with reviews and tests at each one, increases product quality. It also reduces the cost of quality, because we catch errors earlier.

- *QA at the end of each stage.* We need quality assurance at the end of each stage. For the customer to be satisfied with our work for the stage, they should find very few problems—or no problems—when the project is undergoing review and passing through the gate. How is this possible? It is simple: We define the requirements for each gate in the project plan, including all tests. Then we run those tests ourselves and fix any errors during the project work time, as QA just before the gate. That way, when we deliver the item to be reviewed and tested by the customer, they are repeating QA work we have already done, as much as possible. If we do good work and good testing, they will only have good things to say. Of course, there are some elements that we cannot test without help from the customer. But, if we have taken care of everything else, we can fix those as we move through the gate on schedule.

How do we ensure the independence of QA? There are several methods. Only the first two are essential. We can choose from the other items listed below, picking methods appropriate to the project goals and resources, and our company's way of working.

- *Establish independent review and test plans early.* That way, we do not have test plans that contain the same errors as our work plans.

- *Give the QA team all the authority necessary.* We need to support the QA team's findings. We cannot allow them to be set aside or ignored. As project managers, we are responsible for delivering a high-quality, working product or service, not just for meeting a deadline. So if a QA review or test demonstrates a need for rework or a change in work procedures, we should support that fully, allocate necessary resources, and do what it takes to make sure the job is done right. However, we can do this using a no-blame, gap reconciliation approach. And, if, in our own review, we find that QA is wandering off the mark or becoming too stringent—in excess of project requirements—then we make a decision of what is best for the project, and bring both the project team and the QA team in line with project goals.

- *Have an independent QA team within the project.* During the project, we can assign team members who do all the QA.
- *Use an independent QA team from outside the project team.* Some companies keep a permanent QA team. Others use outside consultants for QA.
- *Have a standards organization or internal audit group review your QA work.*

DELIVERING QUALITY

We discussed the importance of delivering quality in Chapter 3 and delivered a thorough method in Chapter 9. However, we may still face some resistance. Delivering quality and making sure the customer is satisfied is part of corporate culture in the best customer service organizations, but it is often a new idea to consulting firms and internal project development teams. Our team or our company may think the job is done when the product or service is delivered. My experience leads me to say that this attitude does not lead to success. As an independent consultant, I have learned that, if I deliver a good product or service, and leave it at that, the customer pays me (eventually), and leaves it at that. And a successful business is built on customers who keep coming back. If we want our customers to come back over and over, then the rule for quality should be: It (the project) is not over until the customer sings.

WHAT THIS MEANS FOR YOU

Customer Delight for Your Project
What can you do to achieve customer delight? Here are some key steps:

- Focus on ensuring that the product or service works, and is providing value. We do more than deliver. We ensure value.
- Make sure that we and our team are polite, courteous, respectful, and professional. Things do get tense. That is acceptable. Even so, respect is essential, and we should work to resolve difficulties.
- Extend the no-blame environment to the customer. The customer is not always right, but the customer always has a point. Work with triangulation to stay on the same side, and with gap analysis and reconciliation to deliver high value on the project.

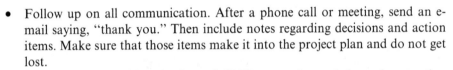

- Follow up on all communication. After a phone call or meeting, send an e-mail saying, "thank you." Then include notes regarding decisions and action items. Make sure that those items make it into the project plan and do not get lost.
- Ask, "Is there anything else I can do?" These magic words keep the attention on the customer. Of course, you may not be able to give them everything they want. But you can acknowledge the need, and suggest how they might be able to take care of it themselves.

I find that focusing on customer delight makes my own work delightful. When I enjoy my work and enjoy talking to my customers, that attitude spreads to my team and my customers. Then customer delight is easy, because we all appreciate doing good work and the results of good work together.

Glossary

Action	A synonym for *task*.
Architecture	The definition of a system's interfaces and its structure.
Assumption	Something thought, but not said, often leading to a misunderstanding. Also, a rule for a project created by the project manager, which can also be changed by the project manager.
Constraints	Rules, such as regulations, standards, and corporate procedures, imposed on the project by the organization or from outside the organization.
Contingency	An amount of time or money set aside to be used if and when risk events occur. Operates at the level of the whole project, unlike the *contingency plan*.
Contingency plan	A specific plan to be implemented in the situation where a particular risk event actually takes place.
Deliverable	The result of a task. It can be given from one person to another, or handed off, becoming an input for the next process without any need to

refer back to the process that created it. *Output* is a synonym.

Dependency	A relationship between two tasks, where one task's start or finish time is linked to another.
Driver	The aspect of the project, usually scope, time, cost, or quality, that matters most to the customer.
Duration	The time a task or a project will take from beginning to end, considering that more than one person might be working on a task, and that people will not be working all the time.
Effective	The delivery of useful results. Work is effective when it delivers the desired result. Communication is effective when a change of plan and action takes place as a result of the communication.
Effort	The number of person-hours it takes to do a task or the total number of person-hours it takes to do a set of tasks or an entire project.
Escalation	The communications process of going up to a higher level of authority to get help addressing a risk or problem.
Estimation	The engineering art of developing our best guess as to what the cost and delivery date will be, independent of what anyone wants.
Exclusion	Something we will be leaving out of the project.
Expectation	Something someone—most usually the customer—wants, which may not be clearly specified.
Feedback	Communications which, when received, change our course of action.
Gate	Another term for a milestone, with an emphasis on the process of approval to get through the gate.
Imposed	Set by the customer, whether or not it is possible in the project.
Inclusion	Something that will be part of the project.
Input	The information and things that we have at the start of the stage or task.
Iterate	To repeat over and over, usually to achieve greater accuracy, higher quality, or more detail.

Milestone	The end result of a stage; a large part of the project completed and delivered.
Output	A synonym for *deliverable*.
Phase	A synonym for *stage*.
Process	The steps of doing the work. The process is the work done on inputs to produce outputs.
Production	Regular, routine work that is repeated over and over, leading to the creation of the same products, services, or results time after time. For contrast, see *project*.
Project	A time-limited endeavor with a defined start and end date, undertaken with the purpose of delivering a unique product, service, or other result, and composed of interrelated and interdependent tasks.
Project management	The application of knowledge, skills, tools, and techniques to project activities to meet the project requirements. Particularly, planning and tracking of project tasks and leadership of the project team to deliver success and customer delight.
Project manager	The person who is assigned, and takes, responsibility for defining the purposes and goals of the project, building the team, defining the work to be done, tracking quality, time, cost, and other project elements, delivering success, and ensuring customer satisfaction.
Project plan	A set of documents evolved over the first three project stages, and completed by the end of design, which guide all the work of the project.
Project schedule	A real-world schedule of project work on a calendar, with start date, delivery date, and scheduled time and effort for each task, taking into account work periods, staff availability, holidays, and so forth.
Quality assurance	Refers to the actual testing of project deliverables, product components, and the entire product before and during delivery.
Quality control	Refers to ongoing quality management and review of the process of doing the work of the project.

Quality management	The processes required to ensure that a project will satisfy the needs for which it was undertaken.
Risk	Anything that decreases the chances of any aspect of project success.
Scope	A high-level description of what is included and excluded in the resulting product or system, and in the process of completing the project.
Scope creep	Occurs when additional features or customers are allowed to be included in the project in the middle. The scope grows, and then the delivery date creeps away down the calendar while the total cost creeps upwards.
Stage	A large set of related tasks leading to the completion of a major deliverable, or milestone. Also called a *phase*.
Step	A synonym for *task*.
Stewardship delegation	An approach to team management that supports independence and self-management; it is the opposite of micromanagement.
System development life cycle	A series of stages, based on the life cycle from biology, which are a template for planning a project and are used to increase the likelihood of project success.
Task	A small job done by one person or a small team at one time delivering a specific result.
Theoretical schedule	A schedule that shows project tasks, links, and duration, but does not yet include real-world calendars.
Track	To compare the actual situation to the plan we created, and note the difference.
Value	Anything that benefits the company or the person who receives it.
Winnowing	A process of sorting where what is good is retained, and what is bad is thrown away.
Work breakdown structure	A detailed work plan prepared during the *design stage*.
Work calendars	Calendars that bring in real-world information such as work schedules, holidays, and vacations.

Resources for Learning

Project management is a constantly growing and changing field. Rather than provide an extensive list of resources here, where it would quickly go out of date, the author's company, Quality Technology & Instruction (QTI), offers a web page of project management resources, which is kept up to date and is constantly growing. Please go to *www.qualitytechnology.com* and click on *Project Manager* and select *Project Management Demystified*, or go directly to *www.qualitytechnology.com/books/pmd.htm*. On this web page you will find many tools and templates from this book in electronic format that you can copy and use, as well as reports on advanced topics. Downloading these templates will speed you on your way to learning them, using them, and improving your skills as a project manager.

Those interested in project management certification should go to the Project Management Institute (PMI) web site at *www.PMI.org* to learn about the Project Management Professional (PMP) certification exam. If you plan to take the exam, membership is well worth it—the discount on the exam for members almost pays for the membership. The core text for the exam is *A Guide to the Project Management Body of Knowledge*, currently in its year 2000 edition, usually called PMBOK® 2000. At the time of writing it is available free for members to download. In addition, the PMI offers many books and other resources for PMP exam preparation, and the local chapters usually offer free training classes. Books that specifically focus on passing the PMP exam are available at the PMI bookstore at their site and at many other bookstores.

WORKS REFERRED TO IN THIS BOOK

A Guide to the Project Management Body of Knowledge (PMBOK® Guide), an American National Standard, ANSI-PMI 99-001-2000, 2000 Edition, Project Management Institute, Newtown Square, Pennsylvania, 2000.

"Richard P. Feynman's Minority Report to the Space Shuttle Challenger Inquiry," in *The Pleasure of Finding Things Out: The Best Short Works of Richard P. Feynman*, by Richard P. Feynman (Jeffrey Robbins, Ed.), pages 151–171, Perseus Publishing, 1999.

Software Inspection, by Tom Gilb and Dorothy Graham (Susannah Finzi, Ed.), Addison-Wesley, 1993.

INDEX

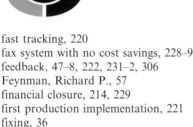